Chinese Women in a
Century of Revolution,
1850-1950

TRANSLATORS
Kathryn Bernhardt
Timothy Brook
Joshua A. Fogel
Jonathan Lipman
Susan Mann
Laurel Rhodes

Chinese Women in a Century of Revolution, 1850–1950

Ono Kazuko
edited by Joshua A. Fogel

 Stanford University Press
Stanford, California

Chinese Women in a Century of Revolution, 1850–1950
was originally published in Japanese under the title
Chūgoku Josei-shi, © 1978 by Ono Kazuko. First
published by Heibonsha Ltd., Publishers, Tokyo.
For the present edition, many new notes and a new
Preface and Introduction have been prepared and
Chapter 8 has been abridged.

Stanford University Press
Stanford, California
© 1989 by the Board of Trustees of the
Leland Stanford Junior University
Printed in the United States of America

CIP data appear at the end of the book

Editor's Note

This translation was a group effort. I first thought of preparing an English edition of Ono Kazuko's book several years ago, but I was not sufficiently confident in the area of Chinese women's history to go it alone. When I discussed the idea with Susan Mann in Tokyo in the summer of 1986, she was excited by the project and agreed to participate. From there I located a handful of others willing both to translate individual chapters dealing with topics on which they had some expertise and to supplement the notes with references and information useful to readers of the English edition. I translated the Prefaces, Chapters 2 and 4, the Chronology, and the Supplementary References. The remaining chapters were translated as follows: Chapter 1 by Kathryn Bernhardt; Chapter 5 by Susan Mann; Chapter 6 by Timothy Brook; Chapter 7 by Laurel Rhodes; and Chapter 8 by Jonathan Lipman. I then exercised an editor's prerogative in trying to render the entire translation as if it were the work of one hand. My model for this approach to a translation was the group effort of Marius Jansen and others in their translation of Irokawa Daikichi's *The Culture of the Meiji Period* (Princeton, N.J.: Princeton University Press, 1986).

We have chosen to use the *pinyin* transcription system with one exception: we use the Cantonese approximation for Sun Yat-sen, rather than Sun Zhongshan or Sun Yixian.

J.A.F.

Contents

Tables

Prefaces

Preface to the Japanese Edition

When was it that I decided to try to write a history of women in modern China?

I was the first woman student in East Asian studies at Kyoto University, and I had virtually no interest in women's history at the time of my graduation. Actually, it would probably be a truer representation of my feelings then to say that I avoided things specifically involving women or women's history. Given this background, it seems strange that I should come to write about women's history. I think my initial point of departure was at a gathering of the study group on the history of the Chinese Revolution held at Kyoto University, to which I presented a report on the woman revolutionary Qiu Jin. I had been working in Ming and Qing history and, since "modern history" was outside my specialty, had undertaken to do the report in a rather casual spirit.

While polishing the rougher edges of this paper and doing a bit more research, I also put together, at Professor Shimada Kenji's prodding, an essay entitled "Shinmatsu no fujin kaihō shisō" [Women's liberation thought at the end of the Qing dynasty]. This was published in the journal *Shisō* in March 1968 and so represented my first real foray into Chinese women's history.

Two or three years later, I was asked by Professor Ōshima Toshikazu of Nara Women's University to offer a course of lectures there over a two-year period on "The History of the Women's Movement in Modern China." Those lectures, following in outline fashion the periods in Chinese history from the Taiping Rebellion through the post-1949 years, proved to be unbelievably exhausting. Almost no research had been done on the subject, and for each lecture I had no choice but to start by collecting documentary materials myself. Even the day before their presentation, the lectures were still not finished, and often I would be making last-minute searches through detailed source materials from newspapers and magazines. To this day I retain the greatest sense of gratitude toward the students who had to listen to those wretched lectures. I still was not thinking of writing a survey of women's history, though.

As I began to work in the area of women's history, I found it an enormous pleasure; for my own accumulated experiences as a woman made it possible for me to bring a wide range of feelings to my work. So, I proceeded to do a bit more research in this area.

About this time, a number of women students from various places who wanted to write their theses on Chinese women's history came to visit me. There were no appropriate texts for them to work with, and inasmuch as it was uncharted territory, recommendations from an adviser would have been completely pointless. Some students had in fact been seriously advised that, if they really wanted to do women's history, then they ought to write "biographies of women." I regret that these students were unable to develop their interests in Chinese women's history fully.

Of course, not only students specializing in Chinese history were attracted to Chinese women's history. The women's liberation movement from the late 1960's raised penetrating questions about the earlier women's movement. It seemed to me that Chinese women's history had much that could help to answer these questions. I began to feel that I had to respond to these issues through my work in Chinese history. This, it seemed, was the minimum responsibility I had in pursuing the research itself.

Over the next few years, I gathered books and articles in the field and published several essays covering various periods in the modern era. The ten articles of mine listed in the Supplementary References at the end of this book are the results of that research. Of course I was unable to cover every aspect of the period, but ultimately this book emerged from those articles and my earlier lectures.

As will be apparent, this book is still incomplete as a history of women in modern China. I hope that young people who are growing up now will correct its deficiencies and make our history of Chinese women richer yet. I will be happy if this book can even to some small extent serve as a guide toward that end.

In addition, it is my aim that this book may serve women searching for their own independence and freedom by deepening their understanding of the history of women not only in Europe and the United States but in neighboring China as well—as one more source to be consulted in selecting their own path. It is my hope as well that it will help women in China and Japan, countries which have enjoyed unhappy relations, particularly over the past few decades, to deepen their mutual understanding and strengthen their solidarity.

In closing, I would like to acknowledge the gracious guidance of Professor Emeritus Tanaka Kenji of Kyoto University in translating some of the popular songs that appear in this volume. Furthermore, for helping me with source materials in the process of writing this book as well as the articles on which it is based, I want to thank the following people: Kojima Reiitsu of the Ajia keizai kenkyūjo, Hirai Keiko and Tamura Yōko of the Chūgoku kenkyūjo, Suganuma Hisayoshi, and Kojima Kotoko.

O.K.

1978

Preface to the English Edition

This book was first published in Japan more than ten years ago. Now, through the efforts of Joshua Fogel and his colleagues, an English translation is appearing in print. The publication of this book in the United States, a nation that experienced the tempestuous storms of the women's liberation movement of the 1960's and 1970's and that is now witnessing a resurgence of familism in the 1980's, is a truly joyous event for me.

Research into Chinese women's history has been extremely slow in getting off the ground. Since the publication in 1927 of Chen Dongyuan's *Zhongguo funü shenghuo shi* [A history of the life of Chinese women], scarcely a single comprehensive account has seen the light of day. If women "hold up half the sky," why has there been no comparable accumulation of studies in this area? For an answer to this question, one must recognize that the modern period in China differed from that of the capitalist countries in the West and took a semi-feudal, semi-colonial form.

It is well known that the Chinese Revolution of 1911 toppled the traditional imperial form of government that had reigned in China for the previous two thousand years. Despite the bourgeois-democratic nature of this revolution, imperialist aggression and warlord rule continued in its wake, even as democratic thought took firm root.

According to Mao Zedong's "Report on an Investigation of the Peasant Movement in Hunan," Chinese men were ordinarily dominated by three systems of authority: political, clan, and religious. For women, there was a fourth source of domination: the authority of the husband. On the basis of traditional Chinese clan control, men were shackled by the family, and it was extremely difficult for them to attain autonomy as individuals in the modern sense. It was utterly impossible for Chinese women to consider the level of independence of Chinese men as a goal they might wish to attain for themselves. "The Declaration of the Rights of Man," which European women took as the key to the formulation of a theory of women's liberation, had not yet emerged in China. Thus, Chinese women were not that deeply aware of contradictions between men and women. Rather, they remained bound by the same "thick ropes" (as Mao called them) of political, clan, and religious authority that bound men. A definite sense of solidarity was fostered between men and women as subjects of oppression. In other words, in early twentieth-century China, class and ethnic contradictions were more acute than the contradiction between the sexes.

Under these circumstances, Chinese women won their emancipation, not by participating in a women's rights movement to gain equal rights for their sex, but by participating in the New Democratic revolutionary movement. The establishment of the People's Republic of China in 1949 was epochal in the liberation of women as well. As a result, Chinese historians naturally considered women's history simply as one part of the larger history of the revolution. These circumstances are largely responsible for the fact that no comprehensive study of Chinese women's history has been produced in China since the work of Chen Dongyuan in 1927. Even if a women's history were to be written in China in the near future, it would probably still view women's history as a part of the revolution's history.

That being the case, how has research on Chinese women's history progressed outside China? In Japan the postwar period has seen considerable development of Chinese historical studies, but work on Chinese women has not kept pace. Perhaps one reason for this deficiency is the fact that most scholars are men. Under the sexual division of labor, men spend most of their time participating in the production of life's necessities and are socially detached from the reproduction of life itself. It is only natural that they try to reconstruct history along the lines of the production of "things" and that they pay scant attention to the history of women and the family, which are connected to basic reproduction. This perspective on "things" profoundly reflects the sense of value one finds in modern capitalist society.

Recent research on women and the family make the following points clear. Modern capitalist society preserves the established order by rendering the monogamous nuclear family an indispensable prop. And, in spite of this, it considers the area of the production of things as "public" and the family as "private," hiding in the shadow of the former. Women who take part in domestic labor form an invisible part of this shadow, and they support the arena of the production of things from without. Given that society operates in this way, historical research must sensitively reflect these conditions. Thus, not only do men form the majority of those who engage in research; the structure of society is such that it makes it difficult to establish a perspective or a field of women's history itself.

I began my studies with research on the political thought of the Ming and Qing periods (1368–1911). Later I came to work in parallel fashion on women's history as well, but people tended to regard Ming-Qing studies as my main area and women's history as a kind of hobby. Perhaps that was because family and women seemed to belong to the realm of the shadows. In our society, since studies of women's history have a kind of private quality about them, they had to be carried out as "private" matters.

This was the situation in which I found research on Chinese women's history. Thus, after collecting as much primary and secondary material in the field as I could, I wanted to write a general survey capturing the flow of modern Chinese women's history. Of course, inasmuch as this book is a first attempt, there are naturally many problems in it, and perhaps its shortcomings may serve as the points of departure for future research. I sincerely hope that new research will use this book as its springboard.

Finally, there is one item I must explain to the reader. In the Japanese edition of this book, the first part of Chapter 8, "The Impact of the New Marriage Law," was followed by two more sections, entitled "The New People's Communes" and "The Cultural Revolution and Two Views of Women." The latter two sections dealt with women's issues from the period of the Great Leap Forward through the Cultural Revolution. When I set out to write this book, I hoped to locate the possibility of the eradication of gender discrimination within the Cultural Revolution's drive to abolish the "three great distinctions" of industry versus agriculture, city versus countryside, and mental versus manual labor. Being overseas where information was incomplete, we tended to idealize the Cultural Revolution and to take its rhetoric at face value.

Now, as the actualities of the Cultural Revolution become clearer and large quantities of material have been published on the subject, it does not seem appropriate to translate these two sections in their original form. Joshua Fogel encouraged me to write a new supplementary chapter on the basis of the great changes in China over the past ten years. I set out to do this several times, but felt I was groping in the dark and was ultimately unable to complete a chapter. For a historian to recount in an objective manner the history of women in the postrevolutionary period (of course, this is true not only for women's history) will still perhaps require the passage of a certain amount of time. In the future I hope to rewrite this part of the book as the modernization program now in place in China moves forward.

I have heard that extremely ambitious efforts are under way in women's studies in the United States: efforts to transform the very structure of theory that encompasses the whole of society, by analyzing in particular the position of women in the labor process and in the family. How fortunate that in the midst of this new movement my book has been translated into English, thereby making it available to those undertaking this effort. I expect and indeed hope to receive merciless criticism.

Finally, let me once again express my deep gratitude to the translators.

O.K.
1987

Introduction

Joshua A. Fogel and Susan Mann

Ono Kazuko began this book in 1968, a year of global awakening for women historians. It was the eve of a new worldwide women's liberation movement that for the first time swept into the academy, carrying a few struggling members into a new era—among them, historians like Ono. Although the experience of these women scholars varied from country to country, they all faced similar obstacles: they had no materials, no guidelines, no institutional support, no mentors, no role models. In the United States, Gerda Lerner taught her first women's history class as a "somewhat superannuated undergraduate." She later described what happened when she designed "Great Women in American History," to be offered for the first time in 1962 at the New School for Social Research. That year the class was canceled; it enrolled less than the required minimum of ten students. For the next two years, when the course *was* given, it was, so far as Lerner knew, "the first class on the subject since a short-lived attempt had been made to teach such a class at Radcliffe in the 1930's."[1]

Nearly a decade later, in 1971, Renaissance historian Joan Kelly received a telephone call from Lerner. By that time Lerner had joined Kelly on the faculty of the history department at Sarah Lawrence College and was urging her colleagues to develop courses on the history of women. Some persuasion was necessary. Kelly later recalled her reaction to Lerner's overture: "I remember dropping

---

[1] Gerda Lerner, "Autobiographical Notes," in *The Majority Finds Its Past: Placing Women in History* (New York: Oxford University Press, 1979), p. xviii.

her a note, commending her for her interests but saying that since I was in Renaissance history, there was nothing much I could offer about women." Undeterred, Lerner then went to Kelly's office and regaled her for four hours on the "almost infinite possibilities" for doing women's history in the Renaissance. Kelly's own words capture the impact of her conversation with Lerner, as she spent the following weekend thinking about the Renaissance in relation to women:

> That turned out to be the most exciting intellectual adventure I can recall. It was like a very rapid repetition of the confusion into which I had been plunged in adolescence: the profoundly frightening feeling of all coherence gone, followed by restoration, if not of a new order, at least of a new direction. Suddenly, the entire world of learning was open to me. It had a new and compelling attraction and was utterly questionable at the same time. Most compelling, and most questionable, was everything I thought I had known about the Renaissance.
>
> The change I went through was kaleidoscopic. I had not read a new book. I did not stumble upon a new archive. No fresh piece of information was added to anything I knew. But I knew now that the entire picture I had held of the Renaissance was partial, distorted, limited, and deeply flawed by those limitations.[2]

In 1977 Kelly published the pathbreaking essay that grew out of that transformation in her thinking, "Did Women Have a Renaissance?"[3]

The titles of books and articles on women's history published in English during the mid-1970's echo the sense of awakening that Kelly described: "The Majority Finds Its Past"; *Becoming Visible*; *Clio's Consciousness Raised*; *Liberating Women's History*.[4] New feminist scholarly journals were founded, and their first issues reviewed the state of women's history and charted its future, in essays that spoke of "definitions and challenges," of "history in transition," of pro-

---

[2] Joan Kelly, "Author's Preface," in *Women, History, and Theory: The Essays of Joan Kelly* (Chicago: University of Chicago Press, 1984), pp. xii–xiii.

[3] In Renate Bridenthal and Claudia Koonz, eds., *Becoming Visible: Women in European History* (Boston: Houghton Mifflin, 1977), pp. 137–64.

[4] Respectively: *Current History* 70: 416 (May 1976), pp. 193–96, 231, included in Lerner, *The Majority Finds Its Past*; Bridenthal and Koonz; Mary S. Hartman and Lois Banner, eds. (New York: Harper & Row, 1974); and Berenice A. Carroll, ed., (Urbana, Ill.: University of Illinois Press, 1976).

found "methodological implications" for the field.[5] Far from simply retrieving women who had been omitted from the existing historical record, women's history as proposed in these essays—in the words of Olwen Hufton—"questioned the nature of the important issues, the value of potential source material, and the method of proceeding" for all historians. This founding decade of women's history in the academies of North America and Europe left a dual legacy: the first, a legacy of retrieval that sought to document the record of a silent majority omitted from the chronicles of the past; the second, a legacy of radical revision that called on historians to discard all their assumptions about the ordering of historical evidence, and indeed their assumptions about what constituted historical evidence, by rewriting a gendered history. Within a decade women's history had established academic credentials that traced what Hufton has called "a venerable tradition" stretching back at least into the nineteenth century in England.[6]

In Japan, the situation was—and remains—different. Institutionally, women's history is still not a widely recognized subfield of social history. There are as yet no departments of women's studies, and there is only one major research center: the Women's Studies Center at Ochanomizu Women's University in Tokyo. At this writing, a similar program is being developed at Waseda University as well. "Feminism," as the term is now used in social science, literature, and history in North America and Europe, is just entering Japanese intellectual discourse. The commonly understood Japanese phrase translated as "feminism" (*danjo dōken*) means "gender equality" or "equal rights between the sexes" and derives from the

[5] See, for example, Gerda Lerner, "Placing Women in History: Definitions and Challenges," *Feminist Studies* 3: 1–2 (1975), pp. 5–14; Natalie Zemon Davis, "'Women's History' in Transition: The European Case," *Feminist Studies* 3: 3–4 (1976), pp. 83–103; Joan Kelly-Gadol, "The Social Relations of the Sexes: Methodological Implications of Women's History," *Signs* 1: 4 (1976), pp. 809–23.

[6] See Olwen Hufton, "Survey Articles. Women in History I. Early Modern Europe," *Past and Present* 101 (Nov. 1983), p. 125. For a recent statement of the radical rethinking still required of women's historians, see Marilyn J. Boxer and Jean H. Quataert, "Overview, 1500–1700," in Boxer and Quataert, eds., *Connecting Spheres: Women in the Western World, 1500 to the Present* (New York: Oxford University Press, 1987), pp. 19–52. On the history of women's history in England, see also Joan Thirsk, "Forward," in Mary Prior, ed., *Women in English Society, 1500–1800* (London: Methuen, 1985), pp. 1–21.

suffrage movement. So when Ono Kazuko's essays on the history of Chinese women began appearing in Japan, they did not invoke a "venerable tradition" of feminist historiography. Still, the essays were not without precedent in the field of Chinese studies in Japan or China, as the References indicate, nor was she a lone voice. Her writings were also part of an age of rediscovery in the 1970's, an era that simultaneously rediscovered both the history of women and the history of the history of women (itself dormant for several decades in East Asia). Her book rings with the excitement and the radical sense of transformed consciousness that marked the era for historians of women around the world, regardless of their circumstances.[7]

The excitement came partly from defamiliarizing a familiar terrain, viewing it through a new lens, asking—as Kelly did—what did my field look like to the women who lived it? The excitement also came from making connections, often for the first time, between one's personal life experiences and feelings, one's political convictions, and one's scholarship. Women scholars who were active in this decade felt the profound force of the women's movement. They responded to pressures and appeals from their female students and, as Ono's case exemplifies, the appeals of sympathetic male colleagues as well. And they discovered an opportunity to respond to historical materials with an immediacy based on their own identity as women. As Carroll Smith-Rosenberg wrote, in speaking for women historians of the United States in the early 1970's: "We began as women and as historians to determine what concatenation of factors had decreed the particular assumptions of gender

---

[7] We have not touched on Japanese women's history here, nor for that matter have we looked at the history of Japanese feminism. There is a large literature on these subjects in Japanese, with much work remaining to be done in the West. Let us just mention two central figures in the postwar era. The author and novelist Inoue Kiyoshi wrote an important work shortly after the Second World War: *Nihon josei shi* [A history of Japanese women], which first appeared in 1948 and has since been reprinted (Kyoto: San'ichi shobō, 1954). And the feminist author, publicist, activist, and scholar of women's history, Takamure Itsue (1894–1964), in addition to numerous essays and books on various aspects of women's history and the women's movement in Japan, also wrote a monumental four-volume work *Josei no rekishi* [History of women], (Tokyo: Kōdansha, 1954–58). For a discussion in English of the women's movement from the Meiji period, see Sharon L. Sievers, *Flowers in Salt: The Beginnings of Feminist Consciousness in Modern Japan*, (Stanford, Calif.: Stanford University Press, 1983).

which the Western world imposed on its women and its men. For us the search was far from academic: these assumptions had shaped our own lives."[8]

Again, for Ono, writing in Japan in the late 1960's, this personal and political connectedness had its own peculiar shape and content. In her Preface to the Japanese edition, she refers to the personal pleasure she derived as a woman in studying women for the first time. Like Kelly, she originally made her reputation as a historian in a field where women were invisible—the intellectual and political thought of the Ming and Qing periods—and this has remained her major area of research. Her work includes a biography of the great seventeenth-century figure Huang Zongxi, his turbulent times, and his political theories,[9] as well as many essays on the fractious in-fighting among cliques in and around the late Ming government, in particular the Donglin party. She has also been a frequent contributor to several major historical encyclopedias. Her personal interest in Chinese women's struggles had another dimension: although she emerged as a major scholar in her field in Japan, she nonetheless failed to gain a regular professorial appointment throughout most of her career. For years she remained a Lecturer in the Research Institute for Humanistic Sciences at Kyoto University, primarily a research position. Only recently did she obtain a full professorial post at Mie University, despite the fact that her major publications span more than 25 years. Her own career testifies to the difficulties still faced by female scholars in the Japanese academy.

Ono's identification with Chinese women's struggles against discrimination went beyond her personal career path. She has felt a larger identification with the evolving struggle of the Chinese people as a whole. Every Japanese of leftist inclinations sympathized deeply with the Chinese Communist revolution, not just for reasons of political solidarity but also as part of an effort to redress the grievous wrongs committed in the name of the Japanese government and army against the people of China through most of the first half of this century: two wars, invasions, occupations, puppet governments, wholesale massacres, and endless derision. One common route to overcoming personally the enormous shame felt

[8] "The Feminist Reconstruction of History," *Academe* 69: 5 (1983), p. 28.
[9] Ono Kazuko, *Kō Sōgi* [Huang Zongxi] (Tokyo: Jimbutsu ōraisha, 1967).

by scholars of China for this Japanese past was through membership in the Japan Communist Party (JCP) in the years following the
Second World War. Ono and her husband, Ono Shinji, a scholar of
twentieth-century Chinese history, both joined the JCP as undergraduate students at Kyoto University in the early 1950's. Like
many left-wing Japanese intellectuals in the postwar period, she saw
in the rise of Chinese Communism a promise of that true democracy and egalitarianism for which the Chinese had been striving
since the beginning of the early decades of the century when the
women's movement had begun.[10] And, like many Japanese leftists
concerned with Chinese affairs, she broke with the JCP when its
allegiance to Moscow superseded continuing support for the Maoist
revolution. At the time of the Cultural Revolution, the JCP (following Moscow) directly attacked the direction Mao Zedong was
taking, and many Japanese China scholars left the JCP.

Idealizing the Chinese revolutionary experience was more common among Japanese intellectuals in the postwar period than it was
among American intellectuals. Where both shared an opposition to
the anti-Communist policies of their respective governments, many
Japanese were driven by a deeper sense of guilt from the war years.
Many felt personally committed to the success of the Chinese revolution, and some even fervently hoped that victory in China might
spark a revolution in Japan.

The reader will soon see that Ono's book is simultaneously a
work of detailed scholarship and a partisan account written on behalf of Chinese women and their battles in the century from 1850
to 1950. It is indeed more a history of women in the evolution of
the Chinese revolution than a modern history of Chinese women.
When the struggles of feminism and women's rights confront the
priority of the Chinese Communist Party, the observant reader will
also note a disturbing ambivalence and one that countless Chinese
women have no doubt faced.

Therefore, for Ono, personal and political convictions con-
verged in a particular way in her research in Chinese women's

---

[10] See the comments about the Chinese Communists' Eighth Route Army and its
extraordinarily democratic nature by Ienaga Saburō, "One of the most democratic
armies in the history of military organizations," in *The Pacific War: World War II and
the Japanese, 1931–1945*, trans. Frank Baldwin (New York: Pantheon Books, 1978),
pp. 89–96, quotation on p. 93.

history. Her study of the history of Chinese women also draws powerfully on her own previous scholarly work on critiques of absolutism in Chinese history. As Ono emphasizes in her chapters on the Chinese revolution in this volume, calls for democracy and demonstrations for people's rights all marked "absolutism" and "authoritarianism" as the enemy. Authoritarianism, according to the analysis of Chinese revolutionaries, was ultimately lodged in two major structures: the bureaucratic state and the family. Significantly, it was Huang Zongxi, the subject of Ono's splendid biography, whom the revolutionaries excitedly raised as the foremost critic of the state's authoritarianism. Huang's work was widely republished in the years around 1900, and he was accordingly dubbed the "Rousseau of China." Expanding on Huang's arguments, the revolutionaries insisted that revolutionary change could not end until the family and kinship system as well had been transformed. Equality for citizens meant equality for women. Much of Ono's book is devoted to tracing the historical roots of this linked struggle for equality in government and family affairs. Readers will appreciate the larger significance of her personal and intellectual quest if they understand its complex roots in Ono's own scholarship.

Research of recent years has challenged the validity of China's revolutionary goals and their accomplishments for women.[11] But the promise the Chinese revolution held out to women played a vital role in the historiography of the 1960's and 1970's. Indeed, few of us now will be able to read Ono Kazuko's history of Chinese women without feeling her own pride, and the pride of those women, in the struggle for women's rights in China. All of us can join her celebration of the courage and conviction of Chinese women who, as they were caught up in the nationalistic student-led movements of the 1920's, joined demonstrations to fight for their country and ended up fighting as well for education and for freedom in marriage. In those mass movements, as Ono tells us with genuine admiration, very ordinary women, who had been

---

[11] See in particular Judith Stacey, *Patriarchy and Socialist Revolution in China* (Berkeley, Calif.: University of California Press, 1983); Kay Ann Johnson, *Women, the Family and Peasant Revolution in China* (Chicago: University of Chicago Press, 1983); Phyllis Andors, *The Unfinished Liberation of Chinese Women, 1949–1980* (Bloomington, Ind.: University of Indiana Press, 1983); and Margery Wolf, *Revolution Postponed: Women in Contemporary China* (Stanford, Calif.: Stanford University Press, 1985).

untouched by the first revolution in 1911, were able to ask new questions, "questions that grew out of the contradictions they had encountered, as women, in their daily lives." Tracing this union of the personal and the political in the lives of ordinary women and describing their changing consciousness is the agenda of Ono's book. It remains a landmark in the development of the still young field of Chinese women's history.[12]

The history of the two extant translations of Ono's book deserves at least a brief mention. The book was translated over the past few years in the People's Republic of China by Chen Yuan-shan. However, even though women's history has recently been recognized as a "discipline" in China, the translation has not been published and may not be for some time. An assortment of publication problems confront it, not the least of which is the need for state funding. Subsidy remains unlikely for a book on Chinese history by a foreigner when no such book has been written in China since 1949.

Yi Dongyun, a scholar from the Republic of Korea, has also prepared a translation under the title *Hyŏndae Chungguk yŏsŏng sa* [A history of women in contemporary China] (Seoul: Chong'yusa, 1985). This edition includes the most radical segments of Chapter 8, praising the Cultural Revolution (which we, with Ono's consent, chose not to translate). When the present Chun regime came to power, the Korean translation was immediately banned as seditious, arguably because it supports the Chinese revolution and vigorously attacks the traditional East Asian family system based in popular Confucianism (as applicable to South Korea as it is to China). It was said to circulate in a kind of *samizdat* form among antitotalitarian elements in the South, a source of great pride for Ono, but there is no indication that the book is back on sale in South Korea.

---

[12] For more recent Japanese work on Chinese women's history, building on Ono's work, see: Nakayama Yoshihiro, *Kindai Chūgoku ni okeru josei kaihō no shisō to kōdō* [Women's liberation thought and activities in modern China] (Kita Kyūshū: Kita Kyūshū Chūgoku shoten, 1983); and the section on women's studies in Harigaya Miwako, "Japanese Studies of Post-Opium War China: 1983," trans. Joshua A. Fogel, *Modern China* (Oct. 1987).

Chinese Women in a
Century of Revolution,
1850-1950

Women Who Took to Battle Dress

The World of Love Songs

> Picking tea in the second month, the bushes sprout.
> Sisters go out together to gather the leaves.
> The elder picks a lot, the younger just a bit.
> They return home early, however much they've picked.
>
> Picking tea in the third month, on Tomb-Sweeping Day,
> Mother's at home, embroidering a handkerchief.
> On each of the two ends she stitches tea blossoms,
> And right in the middle a young girl picking tea.
>
> Picking tea in the fourth month, the leaves turn yellow.
> Women busily plow the fields with buffaloes.
> Once the plowing's done, the tea leaves have passed their prime.
> Once the tea's been picked, the rice is ready for harvest.
>
> —from a Hakka song

The Guangdong region of South China had a double-cropping system. Tea-picking began in the second month of the lunar calendar and continued through the fourth month, ending just before the harvest of early-ripening rice. Day after day, music-loving Hakka women, their songs echoing through the hills, picked tea leaves and plowed fields in the narrow mountain valleys. They were so skilled at their work that they could even handle a water buffalo with equanimity. This situation differed markedly from that of North China, where people abhorred women working outside the home, claiming that "when a woman labors in a field, three years of drought will be the yield."

Although the Hakka people are Han Chinese, they originally were not native to this region of South China, but immigrants who arrived there from distant Henan, Shandong, and Anhui over the course of several centuries. These newcomers settled on remote hill land of such low productivity that they could not possibly support their families through agriculture alone. The men therefore found employment outside the villages, and the women shouldered the burden of cultivating the land as well as of managing the household. In these virtually propertyless families, the men had no cause to dominate the women, and the women in turn had no reason to be dependent upon the men. Hakka women also did not practice footbinding, the symbol of the "cultured woman." With their bare, natural feet, they spent their days in demanding physical labor, sometimes in the company of men and sometimes in place of men who worked away from the villages.

Guangdong and Guangxi, the provinces where the Hakka lived, were also the homes of other minority ethnic groups, such as the Yao, Hmong, and Zhuang peoples. The Hakka and these other minorities were particularly fond of singing, and the unique tunes of their music continually resounded through the hills in this region.[1] On occasion, a single song could last for nearly half an hour—the leisurely verses and extended codas fading only to return full force as if there would be no end. The captivating lyrics and the tender emotions contained in them, it was said, were so powerful that they moved listeners to tears of joy or to tears of sorrow. Let us look at several Hakka folk songs.

Longing for Her

I have longed for her for years on end.
Burning incense at the old well, faint smoke rises.
My soul flirts with her in the hour before dawn.
But when I wake, another day separates us.

The phrase "old well" refers to a well in which the water has dried up and can no longer produce rippling waves. It thus symbolizes a virtuous girl whose heart has not been touched by love. A furtive glance in her direction seems to provoke some slight response. In the man's dreams before dawn, the two are on intimate terms; but when he awakes, she remains as unattainable as before.

This poem probably expresses a young man's yearning for a woman who is already engaged or married to someone else.

Greeting My Gentleman

Outside the front gate the dog barks noisily.
Inside the house I wait for the signal.
Shedding my embroidered slippers, in bare feet,
Slowly I go out to greet my gentleman.

Since this poem recounts a secret rendezvous, it, like the one above, concerns people who are not married to each other. Perhaps the woman is still single or perhaps she is the wife of a man who has gone to the South Seas to work. When the barking of the dog tells her that her lover has come to visit, she listens intently, her heart pounding audibly.

The Rooster Crows Early

The wild crowing of the rooster urges him out the door.
Bidding farewell is so difficult to do,
As irreversible as the westerly flow of the river.
I'm not raising any more early-crowing roosters.

The early-crowing rooster announces the time at four o'clock in the morning. If the woman is merely seeing her husband off to work, then why should she fear attracting the notice of others? Urged on by the crowing of the rooster, she hurriedly sends the man on his way before the break of day. Their relationship must be a secret love affair.

A great number of these Hakka love songs (called *qingge* or "songs of passion" in Chinese) have been collected. Of particular interest are the musical dialogues in which a man sings to woo his love and the woman sings her response. Many of these duets evoke erotic feelings.

Borrowing an Undershirt

Man: The north wind is blowing and I'm in a panic.
I want to borrow some winter clothing from you.
I don't want your short jacket or long padded gown.
What I want most of all is your undershirt.
Woman: An undershirt is an undershirt.
If I loan it to you, then I'll be cold.

>But I'll leave the buttons on my gown undone,
>And the collar on my jacket unfastened.

The man here wants the woman to give him an undershirt as proof of her love. Although she expressly refuses to do so, she impatiently awaits the day she can receive his love with her buttons undone and her collar unfastened.

Borrowing Three Items

Man: When the plum blossoms bloom, the chrysanthemums
        are fading.
     I want to borrow several things from you, younger sister.
     First, I want to borrow a conjugal pillow.
     Second, I want to borrow an ivory bed.
     Third, I want to borrow an elixir of life.

Woman: Beloved elder brother, why are you acting so crazy?
     How could I possibly have these things?
     The tailor will sew you a conjugal pillow.
     The carpenter will make you an ivory bed.
     And the doctor will give you an elixir of life.

Man: Beloved younger sister, I am not crazy.
     You do indeed have these things.
     Extended, your arms become a conjugal pillow.
     Your body is just like an ivory bed.
     And the love between us is an elixir of life.

Woman: Beloved elder brother, I now understand.
     I don't have those good things on my body now.
     And my body doesn't have anything especially good.
     But my parents gave me one treasure.
     And, beloved, I will gladly share that with you.

The large number of Hakka songs of passion suggests that relations between Hakka men and women who worked in the hills were extremely natural and open. Having attained an equal standing with men through participation in labor, Hakka women were not constrained by traditional Confucian norms and could express their love boldly.[2] Some argue that these songs reveal the passions of women raised in the subtropics.

Toward the Heavenly Kingdom of Great Peace

The Taiping Rebellion began in Guangxi, one of the resident provinces of the Hakka people. The supreme Taiping leader Hong Xiuquan (1814–64), a native of Hua county in Guangdong, was also a Hakka. While laid up in bed with despair over his repeated failures in the civil service examinations, he had a wondrous dream. He ascended to heaven and met a deity, who first instructed him to banish the demons and to castigate Confucius for his errors, and who then returned him to earth. Prior to this experience, on a journey to Guangzhou to sit for an examination, Hong had acquired a Protestant missionary tract entitled "Good Words to Admonish the Age." Now, when he reread the pamphlet, he discovered that it corresponded perfectly with his dream. The deity in his vision was Jehovah; Christ was God's elder son or the Heavenly Elder Brother; and he, Hong Xiuquan, was the second son of God. He believed that he was none other than the Heavenly Younger Brother, who had been sent to this world by Jehovah and Christ with the mission to expel all evil spirits from the midst of humanity. By combining his vision with Christianity, Hong Xiuquan thus established a unique religious system. In 1843 he organized a religious association called the Society of God-Worshippers and launched a fervent crusade to convert the infidels.

Besides revering Jehovah as the sole and absolute creator, the Society of God-Worshippers also envisioned the "Great Harmony" (*datong*) of Confucianism as their ideal future society. As Hong Xiuquan wrote in his "Proclamation on the Original Principle for the Enlightenment of the Age":

All men in the world are brothers, and all women in the world are sisters. Why, then, do we permit self-interest to set up boundaries among us? Why do we tolerate the idea that there must be a division of the people into the rulers and the ruled? Confucius said: "When the great principle prevails, the world will belong to the public. The people will not merely love their own parents and their own sons. The aged will have a place to complete their natural span of life, the able-bodied, a specific function to perform; the young will have their elders to look up to. The men will have their part to play, and the women a home in which to settle down. Goods will not be wasted, but neither will they be accumulated for selfish purposes; energy will not be kept unused within oneself, but neither will it be employed for the benefit of oneself. For this reason, the way to wickedness will be closed; there will be no robbers, thieves, or rebels, and the outer gates will not need to be shut. This is *ta-t'ung* [*datong*] (the Great Harmony)."[3]

In this manner, Hong Xiuquan used the Confucian idea of Great Harmony as the basis of his Utopian design, a design that he refined in 1853 in the "Land System of the Heavenly Dynasty."[4] A section of that document reads: "There being fields, let all cultivate them; there being food, let all eat; there being clothes, let all be dressed; there being money, let all use it." Private ownership of property would not be permitted; the land would be collectivized and distributed equally to all people, men and women alike. The result would be an agrarian, communistic society that guaranteed the people's right to sustenance and labor and generously protected the old and the weak. Insofar as this conception envisioned the realization of collective ownership on top of a system of individualized labor and small peasant management, it was a fantasy that neglected altogether objective historical processes. Yet, even so, Hong's Utopia reflected the ardent longings of a peasantry that had placed all hope in a future society.

The Taipings believed that only their Utopia, the Heavenly Kingdom of Great Peace, would fulfill the true teachings of Jehovah and furthermore that all the various secular irrationalities and inequities obstructing its realization were the handiwork of "demons"—the ruling elite. Accordingly, the God-Worshippers first smashed the Confucian mortuary tablets in village temples and then destroyed the images of all traditional deities—the Jade Emperor, the Buddha, the Great Lord Lao Zi, the King of Hell, and the like. Confucius and the various gods were judged to be no different from the King of Hell in that they, too, condoned the existence of so much absurdity and inequality in the world. The attack on temples honoring the gods thus signified a declaration of war against these divinities and an intention to replace them with a new spiritual authority.

The new deity, the sole and absolute creator Jehovah, had long condemned the egoism that discriminates among people and had forbidden any notion of rulers and ruled. The men and women who joined the Society of God-Worshippers were brothers and sisters entrusted with the mission of banishing the demons and ushering in the Kingdom of God, their Utopia. Every woman and man had to strengthen her or his faith and participate in the battle against the demons. Underlying this religious egalitarianism was, of course, the labor-based gender equality of Hakka society.

Barbarian Women with Big Feet

At the time of the Taiping Rebellion, the Manchus, an ethnically non-Chinese group, controlled China. After China's defeat in the Opium War (1839–42), increasing land taxes bore heavily on the peasantry, and the opium trade led to a large outflow of Chinese silver. Moreover, foreign-made cotton thread and cloth usurped the market for native products. Peasants and handicraft workers were ruined, losing their means of livelihood. Peasant revolts intensified with each passing year, apparently confirming the poet's premonition that: "Arising, I gaze upon the world; chaos is not so distant after all." It was in this setting that the Jintian uprising of Hong Xiuquan and his followers in Guangxi took place on January 11, 1851.

The members of the Society of God-Worshippers had assembled under Hong Xiuquan's command in eager anticipation of the revolt. Having sold what little land they may have possessed, entire families—old and young, men and women—took part in the uprising. The participation of whole families enabled men to share their fate with their wives and children and, moreover, strengthened the rebels' military potential through the inclusion of women. Hakka women, accustomed to relying on their own labor, also joined of their own volition.

Hong Xiuquan grouped the men and women who flocked to his banner into military organizations called the "male camp" and the "female camp." "At the time of the Jintian uprising, a great many people from Bobai County belonged to the Society of God-Worshippers. Generally, the entire family joined. Women and men lived separately; men resided in the male camp and women in the female camp. Children lived with their mothers. The members of a family got together once every seven days. Only at this time were they permitted to talk to each other freely."[5] Later residents of the area in which the Jintian uprising occurred related this reminiscence transmitted to them by their grandparents.

The camps were later renamed "male halls" and "female halls" and underwent some other minor changes over time, but they remained throughout the rebellion a kind of community, the basic unit of which was a group of 25 people under the leadership of a *liangsima* (sergeant). Above this level was a command structure composed of the positions of *zuzhang* (lieutenant), *junshuai* (general), and *zongzhi* (commandant). Women occupied the posts in the hierarchy of command in the female camp and men the positions in the male camp.

The Taipings dissolved nuclear families and segregated men and women primarily to build a military order capable of carrying out their revolution. Yet, as will be discussed later, they also upheld a puritanical canon that regarded illicit sexual behavior as the greatest sin of all. They therefore sought to eradicate all desire and concentrate all their energies against that most formidable enemy—the King of Hell.

Hakka women, having worked as hard as men in the hills of Guangxi, responded to these expectations in full. The writing of one supporter of the Qing describes their martial bearing and behavior: "Among the bandits there are female soldiers, all of whom are relatives of the Taiping kings. Being of vile minorities such as the Yao and the Zhuang, they grew up in caves and run around with bare feet and turbaned heads. They can scale steep cliffs with ease, and their courage surpasses that of men. On the battlefield, they carry weapons and fight at close quarters. Government troops have been defeated by them in battle."[6] Because they were so active, Taiping women bared their large (unbound) feet and preferred to wear pants instead of skirts. Their odd appearance—large feet, red-turbaned heads, and pants—probably caused the "civilized" people of the Chinese empire to regard them as an inferior race vastly different from the Han people, a race somewhere between monkeys and human beings on the evolutionary chain. But it was precisely these women who fought even more bravely than the men. (The Yao and Zhuang minorities mentioned in the source just cited took part in the Taiping movement, but they were not in its mainstream).

The Taipings produced several imposing women generals.[7] Su

Sanniang (Sanmei) was one of them, "Su" being her surname and "Sanniang" or "Sanmei" indicating that she was the third daughter of her family. She was literally nameless. A native of Guangdong, Su Sanniang had moved with her husband to Guilin in Guangxi province to farm the land there. Robbers later killed her husband; and Sanniang, because of her deep love for him, donned mourning clothes and vowed to exact revenge. Leading several hundred young men, she roamed the area in search of those who had murdered her husband. Before long, she accomplished her purpose and avenged her husband's death. Afterward, while being pursued by official troops, she evolved into a sort of knight-errant dedicated to eliminating the strong and assisting the weak and stealing from the rich to give to the poor. Her fame and influence spread throughout the Guilin region. After the outbreak of the Taiping Rebellion, Su Sanniang and the 2,000 troops under her command threw in their lot with the rebels.

> Drums and bugles sound clearly atop the city wall.
> Soldiers stand at attention, their flags and banners unfurled.
> Passersby push and shove each other,
> As they rush to catch a glimpse of Su Sanniang.

> The daughter from Ling Mountain is extremely skilled.
> Ten years with the bandits, she's called a valiant woman.
> Dressed in crimson before an audience, she receives an official rank.
> Dressed in white mourning clothes for her husband, she beheads her foes.
> Her arms have fought more than one hundred battles.
> She doesn't lower her spear until she's killed one thousand.

> The Qing general, hearing of her fame, summons his forces for war.
> Galloping on their horses, shouting loudly, their spirits running high,
> Five hundred stalwart youths under her command charge the enemy soldiers,
> Who flee like so many thousands of forlorn rats.
> Upon his return, the Qing commander washes his knife and curses madly.
> He shamefully lies about his losses and is promoted to a high position.[8]

During the advance from Guangxi into Hunan in 1852, the Taipings issued their "Heavenly Proclamation on the Campaign Against the Barbarians," which enumerated the many crimes committed by the Manchu dynasty against the Chinese people during its two hundred years of misrule. Upon receiving this order from heaven to subjugate the "barbarian" Manchus, the spirits of the rebels rose even higher; and the Taiping Army expanded its ranks enormously in Hunan, long an area of intense antigovernment protest.

The women's army also acquired many reliable fighters during the march through Hunan. Numbering 3,000 at the time of the rebel escape from the Qing siege of Yongan in April 1852, the female forces reached over 10,000 by the time of the attack on Wuchang, Hubei province, in January 1853. New recruits were called "new sisters" to distinguish them from the "old sisters" from Guangdong and Guangxi.

The ruling elite did not excuse the actions of these female soldiers simply on account of their sex. One Qing official, after scouting the situation in Nanjing, sent a letter of warning to his superiors in which he wrote: "After we recapture the city, all the Guangxi women should be executed. Absolutely no leniency or mercy should be shown them. For they have been just as courageous and fierce as male soldiers in defending the city."[9] Indeed, the female troops frequently humiliated Qing forces, and their bravery as well as their hatred and cruelty toward their enemies horrified the men of the elite.

In this manner, then, the Taipings incorporated intrepid women generals and soldiers under their banner, fought through Hunan, Hubei, Jiangxi, and Anhui, and in 1853 conquered Nanjing, dubbed by them the "little paradise." The rebels settled on this city as their capital, established a regime based on the power of the peasantry, and held their own against the Qing dynasty for the next eleven years.

A Community of Women

As mentioned previously, the female camp, although a military organization, was at the same time structured as a living communitarian order.[10] After the Taipings advanced into the lower Yangzi valley, the women found it particularly difficult to sustain the military character of their camp because of the need to incorporate as many as 100,000 Jiangnan women with bound feet. From that point, the female camp began to function more along the lines of a labor organization.

When the Taipings compelled women of the occupied territories to take up residence in the female halls that had been set up in civilian houses, they first forcibly removed the bindings from the women's feet. As is well known, footbinding was a custom that had shackled generations of women ever since it was introduced during the Five Dynasties period (907–960). The cloth that constricted the foot so tightly as to inhibit growth robbed women not only of their freedom of movement but of their freedom of spirit as well. The bound foot thus symbolized the sad plight of women forced to exist as the playthings of men.

The Taipings resolutely prohibited footbinding. Of course, one reason for this lay in the fact that the rebels needed an immense amount of labor power to pour into the all-out defense of Nanjing against the forces of the Qing government. For the Taiping women who had lived, worked, and fought in the hills of Guangxi with their natural feet intact, labor and unbound feet were, without question, elemental to human life. Though scorned as "big-footed barbarian women," Hakka women had not adopted this depraved practice, and they forcibly removed the cloth that bound the feet of others.

It was no easy matter, however, to change the consciousness of Jiangnan women who regarded bound feet, despite the great pain it had caused them, as their natural lot. After the prohibition against footbinding was issued, Guangxi women made rounds every evening to inspect the feet of women one by one. According to contemporary accounts, they frequently inflicted corporal punishment on women who had not removed their bindings, from the light penalty of flogging to the more severe penalty of cutting off the feet.

With their feet unbound, these women then began to participate in various kinds of labor. We have descriptions of women's labor from the side of the enemy—the ruling elite.[11] First of all, women made pickets by shaving the tips of a bamboo trunk into a sharp point. These spikes were then lined up on level ground or in a gully to impede the advance of the enemy. Every morning, the women set out on their journey of altogether about thirty *li* (ten miles) to cut bamboo. Each bundle was then carried back by two women tottering on their previously bound feet, perspiration streaming down their faces. After they returned, they lit a bonfire and worked the bamboo until well into the night.

Second, women twisted hemp into ropes. Each received a supply of hemp and a certain quota of rope to complete. When the women applied themselves assiduously to their task, callouses formed on their palms and blisters on their fingertips. Furtive inquiries about the purpose of these ropes revealed that the traps laid outside the city to ensnare the hooves of the enemy's horses had decomposed and that these ropes were to replace them.

Third, women measured out the grain in the Sacred Treasury. Although the Taipings forbade plundering of the common people, they treated wealthy families as a major source of supply and did not scruple to declare publicly that these households "are our storehouses." They placed confiscated goods in a warehouse called the Sacred Treasury and prohibited all private ownership. Every Sunday, each Nanjing resident received an allotment of grain determined on the basis of rank, sex, and age. Women were in charge of this weekly distribution. They left the halls under a canopy of stars in the early morning and returned after sunset, after an entire day of measuring grain. Since they had no measuring instruments, the women used their hands to scoop out the grain, suffering lacerations of the skin as a result. Rice chaff completely covered their hair.

Fourth, women transported bricks, which were used not only in public works but also for building earthen city walls and strengthening fortifications. The earthen walls were constructed with bamboo as the framework and bricks from the people's homes as the foundation. They formed solid structures, able to withstand a light rainfall undamaged. The transportation of these bricks became the work of women. The daily quota for one woman was to carry ten bricks the three *li* (one mile) from the women's hall to Xihua city gate and then the five *li* to the governor-general's office.

Fifth, women cut firewood. Initially the Taipings entrusted the task of ensuring a supply of fuel to the elderly. Older people had been absorbed into *paiweiguan* or "tag tail halls"[12] in groups of 25 and were engaged in light work, such as harvesting vegetables, maintaining the supply of fuel, and sweeping the streets. Ultimately, with the labor of the elderly alone, it was inordinately difficult to supply a sufficient amount of fuel during the winter months. Women therefore went to the islands in the middle of the Yangzi River to cut fuel. On those wind-blown islands, they busily plied their sickles until each had gathered several bundles of wood. Because the winter days were short, the evening star was twinkling brightly before they returned to the city.

In addition, women performed a host of other tasks—harvesting wheat, digging ditches, and the like. The removal of foot bindings did not mean that the feet reverted to their original state, and for women who had never engaged in physical labor, such a daily regimen of work was by no means easy.

The most wretched women were those from official-gentry families. Women of the first rank supposedly committed suicide rather than being forced into a female hall. Women of the second rank, after being placed in a hall and finding they despised it, took the first opportunity to kill themselves. Women of the third rank, unable to endure the coarse food, died of illness. And, women of the fourth rank kept delaying their suicides, meekly doing the arduous work demanded by the rebels. This commentary, of course, comes from the writings of a Qing supporter. To be sure, the sight of women staggering along under their burdens in the harsh sunlight, the skin on their shoulders so severely abraded that to onlookers it appeared to be red clothing, aroused much compassion. Wang Shiduo, the author of *Yibing riji* (A diary of the years 1855 and 1856), was probably expressing paternal love when he hoped that his daughter would commit suicide and even sent her a letter requesting her to do so.[13]

Yet were there no women who discovered in the halls a greater measure of ease than in their former lives as daughters-in-law who had been treated little better than beasts of burden? Were there no women who relished their first encounter with the outside world after having been virtually imprisoned at home because of the traditional dictate that "women must not go past the gate"? And, however strenuous the forced labor, were there no women who felt joy in being able to chat together while working? Unfortunately, we have no way of obtaining answers to these questions from the illiterate Taiping women.

Difficult though it may have been, a life of labor was the pathway to the Heavenly Kingdom. The "Land System of the Heavenly Dynasty," which outlined the Taiping agricultural program, pledged to distribute land to all people above the age of sixteen irrespective of gender. For women, land and participation in productive labor on that land were to form the economic basis necessary for their eventual emancipation, much as the "old sisters" from Guangxi had lived previously.

The military might that propelled the Taipings from the depths of the Guangxi hills through their sweep across eighteen provinces astounded not only the Qing but various foreign powers as well. The strength of the Taipings had nothing to do with any special technology or weaponry. Rather, the rebels "turned their lack of technology into a technique, their superiority of numbers into a technique, their courage in the face of death into a technique, and their disregard for hardship, hunger, and thirst into a technique."[14] In other words, the Taipings relied entirely upon basic human qualities in their effort to establish the Heavenly Kingdom on earth and, accordingly, had to attempt to draw from women all the ability they possessed. To that end, the rebels dissolved families and created a community of women, unlike anything that had existed before. Although this community got its start as a military unit based on a revolutionary asceticism, it soon evolved into an organization for the procurement of labor and the distribution of goods and also for ideological education. Eventually, the separation of the sexes was to be abolished; and, as can be seen in the "Land System of the Heavenly Dynasty," a kind of commune was to be formed around the basic social unit of 25 families.

Yet, whatever its military justification, the strict segregation of the sexes—including even husbands and wives—violated natural human emotions. The Taiping leaders reputedly had promised that if Nanjing could be captured and the "little paradise" established there, they would then permit husbands and wives to live together. The continued separation of the sexes after the occupation of Nanjing in 1853 therefore generated much discontent among the Taiping rank and file.

At that time, "old brothers" from the Guangxi days began to desert the movement. Some people have suggested that this flight of men once committed to the cause was due to the puritanical enforcement of sexual abstinence between husbands and wives. Finally, in 1855, the rebel leaders decided to open up the women's quarters and allow married couples to live together. Unmarried girls, however, were still housed within the protective walls of the female halls. Augustus F. Lindley, who served on the staff of Li Xiucheng in the latter years of the rebellion, related the following information:

Every woman in Ti-pingdom must either be married, the member of a family, or an inmate of one of the large institutions for unprotected females, existing in most of their principal cities, and superintended by proper officials; no single woman being allowed in their territory otherwise. This law is to prevent prostitution, which is punishable with death, and is one which has certainly proved effective, for such a thing is unknown in any of the Ti-ping cities. . . . The institutions for unprotected women are presided over by duly appointed matrons, and are particularly organized and designed to educate and protect those young girls who lose their natural guardians, or those married women whose husbands are away upon public duty, and who have no relations to protect and support them.[15]

Marriage Regulations and Registration

According to Lindley, Taiping marriages were generally love matches. The custom of a bride and groom not meeting until the wedding day gave way to free and natural associations between the sexes. Indeed, the assignment of unmarried men and women as individuals to the male and female halls, along with the repudiation of private ownership of property, naturally meant that traditional arranged marriages between families were no longer possible. Taiping weddings, while simple, were conducted with great solemnity. The rebels did not follow traditional practices such as the superstitious selection of an auspicious date or the exchange of engagement presents, a vestige of mercenary marriages. The only customs they retained were the refashioning of the bride's long braid into a chignon and the groom's journey out at night to escort his wife home. The actual ceremony itself, apparently an exact replica of the ritual of the Church of England, was, in all likelihood, brought into China by Hong Rengan (Hong Xiuquan's cousin), who had served as a minister with the London Missionary Society in Hong Kong.

Of particular interest concerning matrimony in the Heavenly Kingdom was the discovery after 1949 of a Taiping marriage license (known as a *longfeng hehui* or "dragon and phoenix flourish together") in Shaoxing prefecture, Zhejiang province.[16] When a wedding was to take place, the couple applied to the authorities in charge of such matters in the camps or halls to issue a marriage certificate. Recorded on this document were the names, ages, dates of joining the Taiping movement, and native places of the betrothed. After the authorities affixed an official seal with the Chinese characters *longfeng* (dragon and phoenix) on the license, they retained one half of the document and gave the other half to the couple. Later, the Marriage Law of the People's Republic of China provided for the implementation of marriage registration, but the Taipings had, in fact, introduced this new system a hundred years earlier.

The Taiping land law stipulated in its provisions regarding matrimony that the government treasury would supply the funds for wedding expenses and that property was not to be a consideration in marriage. In the communitarian society of the Taipings, the absence of both private ownership and its attendant family system enabled people to wed without having to take property and family status into account. In this sense, the complex of male and female halls as well as the Sacred Treasury laid the foundation for highly moralistic, monogamous marriages in which nothing other than love bound the couple together.

The Taipings regarded monogamy as sacred and banned all prostitution. People who operated brothels in defiance of this ban were to be executed along with their entire families. Those people who informed on them would be rewarded, while those who knowingly failed to report such violations would be punished. And those who knowingly violated the prohibition were to be decapitated. The Taipings thus maintained rigorous control over prostitution.

To the Taipings, strict observance of monogamy and prohibition of prostitution were closely linked, for marriages not based on love, they believed, were in reality no different from prostitution. Through the ages, Chinese women had been purchased more or less to be slaves of households, purveyors of sex, and producers of male progeny. Prostitution was but the most extreme form of this commerce in women. Its existence contributed not only to the misery of those women sold into it, but to the misery of all other women as well. By prohibiting prostitution, an action that no dynasty in China had ever attempted, the Taipings were seeking to restore to the relationships between men and women the equality and passion they had once extolled in song in the mountains of Guangxi. This great undertaking could be accomplished only in a social and economic system that offered no place, as Friedrich Engels once put it, for the "purchase of a woman's surrender with money or any other social instrument of power." [17]

A caveat must be added here. Despite the Taiping proscription of polygamy and prostitution, the rebel leaders, including Hong Xiuquan himself, kept a great number of concubines. Reportedly, Hong possessed 36 concubines by the time of the encampment at Yongan (September 1851 to April 1852) and some 88 concubines and 300 female servants later at his palace in Nanjing. The other kings such as Yang Xiuqing had similar numbers of concubines and attending ladies. The Taiping leaders thus exempted themselves from the prohibitions against adultery and lapsed into the licentious conduct common in the traditional Chinese monarchical system.

Women Officials

The novel *Jing hua yuan* [Flowers in the mirror] by Li Ruzhen explores the theme of civil service examinations for women. And legend has it that the Taipings implemented such a system. [18] Supposedly, the chief examiner was Hong Xuanjiao, the younger sister of Hong Xiuquan and the wife of Xiao Chaogui; and the assistant examiners were Zhang Wanru and Wang Zizhen. The examination question concerned the chapter in the *Analects* of Confucius that contains the line: "Only women and inferior men are difficult to teach." The woman who scored highest, or the Number One Woman Scholar according to this story, was one Fu Shanxiang. This information, though related in a plausible fashion, is hardly credible. To be sure, a woman named Fu Shanxiang did indeed exist. Well versed in letters, she was in charge of political affairs in the camp of Yang Xiuqing, the Eastern King of the Taipings.

Yet the more reliable sources that tell of the Taiping examination system make no mention whatever of tests for women. People of the time probably could not conceive of the possibility of anyone becoming an official without having passed through the examination system and concocted the notion of Taiping tests for women to account for the existence of female officials. False rumors thus abounded, eventually finding their way into writings that ridiculed the Taiping Rebellion.

Yet, even though the rebels did not hold examinations for women, there were female officials among them. For example, "old sisters" from Guangxi, such as Hong Xuanjiao and other wives and mothers of highly placed Taiping officials, commanded the women's army and exerted considerable influence in the central Taiping government.

Zhang Dejian's *Zeiqing huizuan* [Intelligence handbook on the Taipings], which relates the internal affairs of the Taiping rebels, contains a chart of women officials that suggests there was a systematic hierarchy of female bureaucrats.[19] Whether the Taipings actually employed such a great number (6,584) of women officials is highly doubtful.[20] Those scholars who accept Zhang's information at face value, however, point to the leaders of the female halls —that is, the organizers of the female community, as mentioned earlier. First, there were the sergeants, the heads of the 25-person women's halls. The leaders of groups of halls (ranging from several to more than ten separate halls) were called either *baizhang* or *zuzhang* (lieutenants). Above them were the positions of *junshuai* (general), *jianjun* (superintendant), and *zongzhi* (commandant). "Sisters" from Hunan and Hubei occupied the posts of *liangsima* and *baizhang*; and "old sisters" from Guangxi filled the positions of *junshuai* and above. The female officials played an active role in ideological education in the halls. And it was as organizers of the female community that these women were able to give meaning to their own lives.

If we define female participation in Taiping politics as the formal incorporation of women into the traditional dynastic structure of power, then this kind of participation did not exist among the Taipings. If we define politics narrowly as the management and control of people, then women did not ultimately escape being the managed and the controlled, and even if some women can be found on the side of the managers and the controllers, this was still a far cry from the emancipation of women.

The Repudiation of Eros

As has been mentioned frequently, the community of women created during the course of the rebellion was formed on the basis of a thorough repudiation of sexual love. The Taipings regarded physical intimacy to be the greatest sin and, until the occupation of Nanjing, did not permit sexual relations even between husbands and wives. Two famous stories illustrate their severity on this issue. During the rebel offensive in Hunan, Xiao Chaogui, the Taiping Western King, condemned his own parents to decapitation when he discovered that they were sharing the same bed; and Zhen Guohou and Lu Xianba were stripped of their titles for committing the same sin. The denial of the erotic, which might seem unnatural at first glance, was merely a manifestation of the asceticism being used to fortify the rebel ranks in their confrontation with the immense strength of their enemy.

The Taipings had ten regulations, known as Heavenly Commandments, patterned after the Ten Commandments of the Bible. The first four commandments concerned their religious creed, those beliefs that gave the Taipings their boundless courage and conviction and nurtured their sense of solidarity.[21] When the rebels charged into enemy camps shouting, "Kill the demons," their belief in the Heavenly Father Jehovah heightened the ordinary hatred they harbored against the elite, endowing them with a courage undaunted by the prospect of death. Like the Taipings, the ruling elite was comprised of human beings. Thus, this struggle between human beings was intensified through its transformation into a conflict between God and the demons.

The remaining Heavenly Commandments detail the precepts that Taiping adherents had to observe in their daily lives as preparation for the imminent struggle with the demons:

5. Thou shalt be filially pious to thy parents.
6. Thou shalt not kill or injure.
7. Thou shalt not commit adultery or be licentious.

8. Thou shalt not steal or plunder.
9. Thou shalt not utter falsehoods.
10. Thou shalt not conceive a covetous desire.[22]

Of the Heavenly Commandments, the seventh was the most strictly enforced. In contrast to the other nine, infractions of which were regarded as merely "violations of the Heavenly Commandments," adultery and licentious conduct were deemed "the greatest violation of the Heavenly Commandments." The Taiping leaders enforced this prohibition scrupulously among the rebel rank and file by sentencing to death all those who indulged in illicit sex.

As noted above, when Nanjing fell to the rebels, many women from families of the gentry hastened to kill themselves. A contemporary source relates the following about their motivation for doing so.

At that time, among gentry households, sometimes the entire family would commit suicide and sometimes several members of a household would do so. The total number of such deaths was no fewer than 120,000 to 130,000. But there is nothing worthy of particular note concerning female deaths because the bandits strictly prohibited rape and did not transgress against women. Thus, the suicides of women and girls were merely cases of daughters following their fathers and wives their husbands into death.

Fathers and husbands forced daughters and wives to protect their virtue—to become "virtuous women" (*lienü*)—by ending their own lives.[23] Yet, if the Taiping "bandits" did not commit rape, then how could these women and girls possibly establish posthumous reputations as *lienü*? The men feared imaginary bandits, and the women died as imaginary *lienü*.

Why were the Taipings so strict about the injunction of the seventh commandment against illicit sexual intercourse that they even prohibited physical intimacy between married couples? We noted that relations between the sexes among the Hakka poor of Guangdong and Guangxi (the birthplace of the rebellion) were natural and open, unrestrained by traditional Confucian ethics. Men sought the affections of women, and women boldly expressed their love in response. Work and love constituted virtually the entirety of their lives. Precisely because of this Hakka glorification of uninhibited sexual love, the Taipings regarded the denial of the erotic as tantamount to a renunciation of all worldly pleasures.

The Taipings maintained rigorous military discipline through-out their campaign from Jintian to their escape from the Qing siege of Yongan and from there through Hunan and Hubei to Nanjing. When they took a prisoner, they first examined his hands. If the palms were pink and soft and the fingers free of callouses, indicating that the captive had never engaged in physical work, then the rebels would summarily execute him for being a demon—that is, a member of the elite. In contrast, the rebel commanders did not permit any sort of mistreatment of laboring people; and to prevent the sexual abuse of the female populace, they forbade their troops from raiding houses in which women were present, in this way closely supervising relations between the sexes. Even people other-wise hostile to the rebels had to acknowledge the austerity of their military discipline. In order to overthrow the Qing and realize the Utopia of peasant egalitarianism, the Taiping leaders had to control their troops through a strict, revolutionary military regimen. In this respect, the Taiping regulations bring to mind the Chinese Red Army's "Three Rules and Eight Injunctions," which prohibited, among other things, the taking of so much as a single needle from the people.

To preserve such discipline, the Taipings carried out intensive ideological training. Customarily, every morning and evening, the residents of each hall recited the Heavenly Commandments from memory; any convert who was unable to do so after three weeks, it was said, faced possible decapitation. On Sundays, hall members would go en masse to chapel to receive another sort of religious instruction called "expounding the principles of truth." To arouse the masses, the Taipings had to effect a change in consciousness by explaining their revolutionary principles to each man and woman.

In this manner, the Taipings, though influenced by Christianity, did not accept it as given, but poured the experiences of their lives into it, transforming it into a weapon in their struggle for the realization of a peasant Utopia. This is not, of course, to deny their establishment of a new spiritual authority in China. But their God was specifically created to seize the world from the ruling imperial authority and the various traditional deities supporting this authority and restore it to the people. Through their belief in the Heavenly Father Jehovah, the rebels expanded to the utmost the range of human possibilities. And by projecting the conflict among people onto the conflict between God and the Devil, they inspired a sense of revolutionary zeal among the populace who had suffered at the hands of "demons." Their God bestowed upon the Taipings both a fearless religious conviction and a puritanical moral sensibility.

When women joined the battle against the demons, they could no longer simply be the objects of either discrimination or sexuality alone. All men and women were equal because each had a direct personal connection with God; and all men and women alike were to unite to wage the war against the demons and usher in the Heavenly Kingdom of Great Peace.

The Taipings organized men and women in a way most appropriate for this battle through the construction of a communitarian social order. This entailed the dissolution, however short-lived, of the traditional patriarchal family. This fact is of signal importance since the patriarchal family system, by instilling in people a slavish morality, provided the ideological foundation for autocratic monarchical rule and the dominant position of the landed elite. For these "slaves" to seek now to cast off their servitude was a fearful prospect to the ruling elite. Zeng Guofan, who was instrumental in the suppression of the Taipings, pronounced the rebellion to be "an unprecedented crisis in the history of ethical principles," a statement that he could only have made because he recognized the gravity of the Taiping challenge to Confucian morality.[24]

The Heavenly Kingdom of Great Peace, after holding its own for thirteen years, finally succumbed in 1864 to the combined forces of the Qing court and the foreign powers. Although unsuccessful, the Taiping Rebellion, a great peasant war that engulfed the Chinese people in its widespread revolutionary storm, served as the starting point for the next hundred years of revolution in China against imperialism and traditional society. The "historically unprecedented, glorious, and progressive liberation of women," as the Chinese scholar Fan Wenlan once put it, would become a reality in the unfolding course of this peasant revolution.[25] In marked contrast to the urban origins of the emancipation of women in Europe, it should be emphasized, the emancipation of Chinese women got its start in rural revolution. The "big-footed barbarian women" had thrown open the curtain on the modern history of Chinese women.

T W O

Between Footbinding and Nationhood

Participating in Productive Labor

Although the Taiping Rebellion was crushed, the Qing court found it exceedingly difficult to continue ruling China with their institutions unchanged. Thus, the ruling elite planned for the self-strengthening of China with the adoption of new weaponry and techniques from the West. The mouths of these new cannons were to be aimed at the Chinese peasantry (who were on the verge of rising in revolution) more than they were at the foreign invaders. This was the early Westernization (*yangwu*) movement, and at its center were such reformist officials as Li Hongzhang and Zhang Zhidong. The term *yangwu* connoted something related to the West and in its early period was limited to the area of munitions. Gradually, though, it came to apply to areas peripheral to weaponry and eventually expanded into the civil arena which was now seen as a source of funds for the state. The industrialization of China began under the leadership of these early Westernizing officials.

During this early industrialization, women laborers came into existence as a group.[1] At this point I should note one interesting fact about women workers in China. Even before the birth of the silk-reeling and spinning industries brought about by early Westernizing reforms, several silk mills had appeared in the city of Shanghai. In 1878 the French engineer Paul Brunat, who had been employed as the chief engineer at the Tomioka Filature in Japan, went to Shanghai on his way home from Japan and stayed to take over management of one of these silk mills, the Shanghai Silk Filature (or Baochang sichang). A diary of life in the Tomioka Filature, the *Tomioka nikki*, written by Wada Ei, is quite well known in Japan as a chronicle of women workers in the silk-reeling industry in the early years of Japanese capitalist production—and Chinese women workers emerged as modern laborers having learned the same techniques from the same French master technician.

Although silk-reeling was a mechanized industry, the machines were simple units, and the amount of capital needed to set up a filature was not excessive. As a result, numerous Chinese-owned filatures cropped up. By 1898 there were reportedly 36 silk mills, centered in Shanghai, with roughly 10,000 boilers and 20,000 laborers. Mechanized silk-reeling also developed in the Pearl River Delta region of Guangdong.[2]

In the case of cotton spinning, by contrast, the machines were extremely heavy, and the amount of capital required was enormous. Thus, this industry could only begin to develop as part of the larger Westernizing reform movement. China's first spinning mill was the Shanghai Mechanized Cotton Mill, which began operations in 1890; the Hubei Cotton Mill was founded in the city of Wuchang a bit later. It seems that women were not employed at the Hubei Cotton Mill, because, according to the newspaper reports at the time, Zhang Zhidong, the Huguang governor-general who had set up the Hubei mill, believed that hiring women workers violated Confucian morality. Zhang argued that China should make use of elements from the West for purposes of "utility" (modern technology), while retaining China's own learning for her "essence" (morality). The modern techniques of the West could be adopted, in Zhang's view, but Chinese morality—namely, China's age-old Confucian morality—required that women serve in the home, not in a factory. Such a conception of things was perfectly acceptable at the time.

Nonetheless, for some reason, in the silk-reeling filatures, which Zhang Zhidong set up later than the cotton mills, women were apparently employed from the start. Women laborers were invited from Shanghai and appointed to train others. It was difficult to replace women with men, for silk-reeling was considered women's work alone, and perhaps reformers did not want to upset the custom. The details on this matter are unclear, but beyond any discrimination between men and women, the establishment of a modern industry required the agile fingers of the female sex together with low-paying labor. This revealed a contradiction within the "essence-utility" formula advocated by the early Westernizers.[3]

The limitations of the military core of the early reforms became clear after the Sino-French War in 1884, and it was shortly thereafter that the Reform Movement of 1898 arose. The three leaders of the 1898 movement—Kang Youwei, Liang Qichao, and Tan Sitong—are discussed in this chapter.

Kang Youwei (1858–1927) was from Nanhai in Guangdong province. He saw that imperialism had grown fiercer ever since the Sino-French War and believed that if reform—meaning changes in political institutions—were not carried out, then China would be beyond salvation. He submitted memorial after memorial to that effect to the throne. His models for reform were the Meiji Restoration in Japan and Peter the Great's reforms in Russia. His advocacy of a route to liberal reform gained him wide support among Chinese intellectuals after China's defeat in the Sino-Japanese War of 1894–95. Study associations, which became the core of the reforms, were founded,[4] and journals such as *Shiwubao* were inaugurated. Through them, Kang and his followers acquainted Chinese readers with the social and political conditions in Europe and preached the inevitability of reform. As the movement rose to its full height in 1898 and Kang's ideas gained influence with the emperor, a major institutional reform effort was begun.

The 1898 Reform is also known as the Hundred Days Reform because it lasted only 103 days. In that period, a diverse program of change was formulated under the guidance of the reformers: reforms in educational institutions, the sending of students abroad, reforms in the bureaucratic structure, and the like. However, when the movement collapsed as a result of a coup d'état, all that remained were the paper memorials that had been issued in great numbers, packed as they were with reformist ideas. Both Kang Youwei and Liang Qichao became refugees. Tan Sitong and five of his comrades were executed, martyrs to the reformist cause. The route to bourgeois modernization from above had been frustrated.

Modern European ideas, such as the theory of evolution, were introduced in the course of the movement that culminated in the 1898 Reforms, and under the influence of such ideas bourgeois urban women's liberation was advocated for the first time. Later in this chapter, we will return to Kang Youwei and his views on women, but it is Liang Qichao who perhaps best illustrates the essence of the Reform Movement as it touched on women's issues.

Liang Qichao (1873–1929) was from Xinhui in the province of Guangdong. A well-known journalist who introduced European ideas to China, Liang wrote invigorating essays, bursting with emotion, that captivated many young people. As a young man he had studied with Kang Youwei, and he was active in the Reform Movement in 1898 as Kang's right-hand man. From 1896 through 1897 Liang wrote and published an essay entitled "Bianfa tongyi" (General discussion of reform) for *Shiwubao*, in which he developed the reformers' position on women's liberation, essentially as an argument for women's education.[5] According to Liang, there were two kinds of people: "those who produce profit" and "those who partake of profit." The former group consisted of people who produced goods through their labor; the latter were people who received and consumed goods.

Women, half the Chinese population, fell into the latter category. They did not take part in productive labor but simply consumed the portion allotted them. Far from supporting themselves, they had to rely on others. Thus, men cruelly mistreated women as animals or slaves, and women had to suffer this oppression. Even men, though, no matter how hard they might work, were unable to support their wives and children adequately, and so they all suffered together. If human beings produced for themselves, could clothe and feed themselves, then there would be no reason for such suffering. The reason for China's poverty lay in the fact that several people lived parasitically off the labor of one person. Although there were a variety of reasons for this, most important was the fact, Liang concluded, that women did not have occupations through which they could engage in productive labor.

Why among all human beings did women no longer have occupations? For a long time women had been disdained by men and had received no educational instruction. They had no alternative but to learn from men, and it was only natural that those who worked held a superior position. The inequality between men and women originated in this set of circumstances. In order to strengthen the country and enrich the people, Liang argued, the situation in which several people lived as parasites off the labors of a single person had to be fundamentally changed, and women had to be given work. To that end, the first order of the day was education for women—this was Liang's first reason for advocating women's education.[6]

Second, he strongly criticized the old view that "only the untalented woman was virtuous." According to Liang, learning was not something one used to appreciate the beauties of nature and to compose poetry or prose. Learning had to open up the mind and help one in daily life. If one could know history, both ancient and more recent, as well as the geography of the world, if one could learn how people lived their lives around the globe, and if one could then discover why certain countries in the world were strong and others weak, then there would be no reason to focus attention on affairs within one's household. His argument called for offering women education that would expand their field of vision and enable them to acquire professions.

Third, it was alleged that 70 percent of elementary education in the West was performed by mothers. If Chinese mothers understood the basis of learning and knew pedagogical methods, then children would be able to gain the rudiments of learning before the age of ten. Thus, what was needed was maternal education for elementary education and women's education for maternal education. Accordingly, women's education was the major issue, linked to the nation's survival or demise, its strength or weakness, through the education of children.

Liang's fourth point was prenatal care. He claimed that because of the need for a strong military, Western countries drilled women in calisthenics, concerned as they were with the health of children yet to be born. Men of learning now were anxious about the fate of their nation and were speaking of "preserving the nation," "preserving the race," and "preserving their teachings," but how could the state be preserved? It had to be strengthened. How could the race be preserved? It had to be pushed to evolve, and to that end one had to begin with education for men and for women, particularly women. To preserve China's moral teachings, the position of a Confucian religion had to be secured as the spiritual bond of the nation.

This was Liang's general position in favor of women's education. His first two points were linked to enriching the nation, and his third and fourth points were directly tied to strengthening the military. He understood the emancipation of women entirely in those terms—"enriching the nation and strengthening the military." Women's liberation was not something derived from rights women intrinsically possessed as human beings; this itself was not the objective. Rather, the aim lay in raising women's knowledge and improving their physical strength so as to develop their qualities as productive laborers or as child-bearing machines.

Despite this deficiency, Liang's argument did draw women into the arena of social labor, making his a rather unique viewpoint when compared to the views of such men as Fukuzawa Yukichi and John Stuart Mill. He probably witnessed economic development in Shanghai, Guangdong, and elsewhere, and, through his knowledge of capitalism in Europe, he firmly believed that the accumulation of capital and the guarantee of labor power were necessary for establishing a basis for modernization. Although the growth of domestic capital in China was still quite weak, he nonetheless seized on the logic of women's liberation in bourgeois society to prepare for the future bourgeois modernization of the country.

Even before Liang's advocacy of women's education, Christian missionaries had been active in the instruction of young women.[7] In 1844, shortly after the Opium War, Mary Ann Aldersey of the Society for Promoting Female Education in the East established in Ningbo what was apparently the first girls' school in China. Later girls' schools run by missionaries multiplied in the open Chinese ports, and in 1902 there were more than 4,000 women students studying in missionary schools for women. As we shall see later, though, popular antipathy to Christianity was fierce at the time, and an antimissionary movement repeatedly erupted with the burning of churches, the murder of missionaries, and the like. False rumors were spread to the effect that in the mission churches Christians gouged out the eyeballs of the dead and fed them to the children.

Those who studied at these missionary girls' schools were by and large the children of believers or the poverty-stricken. There was, of course, no tuition; expenses for food, clothing, and everything else were supplied for the students. The curriculum consisted of lectures on Christianity as well as domestic science; by no means was it a middle-class, general education for women. Furthermore, the practice of early marriage in China did not allow these young women to remain in school very long; most were compelled to leave before graduation.

The Methodist girls' school in Shanghai concluded contracts with parents at the time of the girls' entrance to the effect that the school retained the right of refusal for marriage until the young women reached the age of twenty and also required that the girls preserve their ties to the missionary groups. As a result the Methodists enjoyed great success in their evangelical work. Girls' schools of this sort, which sought to educate children of the relatively affluent middle or upper classes, began to appear in the 1890's and, it is fair to say, aimed mainly at training missionaries.

It was in these circumstances that the members of the Reform Movement of 1898 advocated the institution of women's schools. Liang Qichao's "Proposal for the Building of Women's Schools" is an example of such an appeal, and the "Rules of the Newly Established Chinese Women's School in Shanghai" was a virtual blueprint.[8]

The wives of many of the reformers raised a considerable quantity of money for the construction of women's schools. Their names and the amounts donated were printed through a number of the issues of *Shiwubao*. Yet, as in the case of Tan Sitong's wife, Li Run, the notice read that "Tan's wife Li Gongren [Li Run] donated 100 taels of silver and ten *yuan* for operating costs." The woman's name alone was not published, implying that she did not enjoy an independent existence under her own name. She was only known socially as the wife of someone else.

In any event, construction began on a girls' school built by Chinese (under the direction of Jing Yuanshan) in 1898. In June of that year it welcomed ten foreign visitors and sixteen students, and ceremonies honoring the formal commencement of classes were held. Maps and other visual materials published overseas were hung in the classrooms, and the school aimed at an ideal of having four students to a dormitory room.[9] The failure of the 1898 Reform Movement forced the school to close its doors. Jing Yuanshan incurred the displeasure of the authorities, and Liang Qichao had to seek refuge in Japan. The first women's school run by Chinese closed without producing a single graduate.

Stop Footbinding!

Woman with the small pair of feet—
To whose family do you belong?
The bow-shaped shoes beneath your dress are but three inches
    long.
Your body is so heavy a burden for your feet that you fear you may
    stumble in the wind.
And to move one step forward is as difficult as walking ten
    thousand *li.*
Leaning on the nanny's shoulder on your left and the maid's on
    your right,
A chance step on your foot will bring so much pain.
Why did you bind your feet like this?

When did she first have them bound?
When she was five or six years old, her mother ordered her to have
    her feet bound.
She screamed to heaven and earth, but her mother didn't hear.
Every night she cried in the middle of the night from the pain.
She cried to her mother from her bed.
When the daughter was sick, her mother felt so sorry,
And when the daughter had a headache, the mother was so
    frightened.

Now, the pain in the daughter's feet seems to go right to the
    marrow of her bones.
She's so pitiful, and her mother just doesn't care.
Instead, her mother laughs and consoles the little girl:
"When I was young, I was just like you.
I wanted you to walk in front of others with such small feet,
So I spent a lot of energy getting your feet bound."
But the feet are so small,
And her joints are uncomfortable,
And she's lost her appetite.
Many years she wept over fallen flowers.
The bow-shoe is just like a grave,
Listening to the singing of the morning birds.

The setting sun casts its light on the wretched hut
In which a woman as virtuous as Meng Guang dwelt.
She busied herself all day long gathering firewood and cooking,
With every step she sighs in distress,

Asking herself why her feet were so deformed.
She looks at her feet and tears pour down her face.
She regrets what she had done to them years before.
It was six or seven years since she lived by the side of the river.
The sound of a sudden flood roared like thunder.
Her husband still at the market and not yet home,
Her beloved son and daughter sound asleep.
Holding her son in her left hand and her daughter in her right:
"Where can we go, my children?
Your poor mother will stumble in the water,
And we shall be taken away by the current of the flood."
Nothing on earth is more miserable than bound feet.
Even now she trembles at the very thought of the incident.

She recently moved near the city.
The fire-bird screamed from the rooftop.
Her neighbors had a sudden fire and were terribly frightened.
She hastily threw her shoes away and walked along barefoot in the
    street.
Her toes broken and her heels cracked,
Her feet were covered with blood.
I exhorted people not to bind feet,
But the hearts of all the parents were like iron.
Now that they have heard her story of suffering,
They should change their hearts.

Here comes the cavalry on horseback,
Here they come,
Dust whirling in the wind as the bandits approach.
They go into each house, rob things, and kill people.
Most of the people run away.
The robust woman of the house to the east is barefooted,
Running with her son in her arms into the valley of South
    Mountain,
With a pan on her back and rice in her bag,
Disguised as a man, wrapping her head with a piece of blue cloth,
Hiding herself when the bandits arrive.

The woman in the house to the west is as beautiful as jade.
Not being able to run with her small feet, she weeps in panic.
Before her tears are dry the bandits appear,
Assaulting her in every horrible way.
She would have died anyway, despite such insults,
For the humiliations alone would have spelled her doom.

With her small feet she could hardly move.
Sometimes she even delayed her husband and son.
What we have just observed is truly pathetic,
Yet some people still say: "A lotus comes out of her every step.
Her shoe is as beautiful as a mandarin duck,
And the fibers of the shoe are as beautiful as a rose of Sharon."
This beauty, just like a goddess, has suffered so.
Can we ever make people understand even this little truth?
They all want small feet for their daughters.
Just wait for the robbers, and that will be the end of everything.

　　　　　　　　　　　　　　　　—*Shiwubao*, no. 49–50 [10]

This was a variety of song, entitled "New *Yuefu*," written by Lin Qinnan. Passed from mouth to mouth, from ear to ear by women who were unable to read, it denounced the suffering caused by footbinding.

Kang Youwei had begun an anti-footbinding movement when he became aware of the harm the practice caused.[11] As early as 1883 he created an Anti-Footbinding Society after having discussed the matter with Qu Eliang, who had been to the United States. Naturally, his daughters, Kang Tongwei and Kang Tongbi, did not bind their feet, a rather courageous act considering the scorn they received for it from certain of their relatives. The Society ended without any great accomplishments to its credit. Later Kang's younger brother, Kang Guangren, organized another Anti-Footbinding Society in 1895, using the rules set down earlier by Kang Youwei. Around the same time a Movement for the Natural Foot, organized primarily by missionary wives, was started.

The anti-footbinding movement began on a large scale in the year before the 1898 Reform Movement, when reformism was in the air. In his essay, "Discussion of the Anti-Footbinding Society" (published in *Shiwubao*),[12] Liang Qichao spoke of the atrocity of inflicting on innocent women the corporal mutilation caused by binding the feet. In addition to appealing for elimination of the custom, Liang offered a concrete plan for the movement in his "Concise Rules of the Experimental Anti-Footbinding Society."[13] Members of this Society were advised, of course, not to bind the feet of their female children and not to have their male children marry women with bound feet. For those who had already had their feet bound, those eight years of age or under were to unbind them; those nine or older were not to do so, and these items were registered in the membership list of the Society. The list was distributed to the members of the Society so that in the future the men could plan to marry young women within the Society who did not bind their feet. Since women who did not bind their feet ordinarily had little chance of marriage, Liang's innovations were enormously significant.

The Anti-Footbinding Society formally began in Shanghai on June 30, 1897, and reaction to the movement was tremendous. Letters and donations were sent in rapid succession to *Shiwubao*, and Anti-Footbinding Societies were set up in such places as Hunan, Jiading, and Fuzhou. With the rise of this movement, Kang Youwei submitted his "Memorial Requesting a Ban on the Binding of Women's Feet" in the following year during the Hundred Days Reform.[14] In the memorial, Kang argued his opposition to footbinding for the following reasons:

From the perspective of the government of the state, it punishes innocent women without justification. From the perspective of the kindness and love of the family, it is injurious to parental kindness and love. From the perspective of human health, it gives rise to a needless sickness. From the perspective of increasing military strength, it weakens the race hereditarily. From the perspective of the beauty of our customs, it invites the slander of those other nations known as "barbarians."

Through the abolition of footbinding and the restoration of women's capacities as human beings, Kang was clearly trying to mobilize women's strengths in order to enrich the nation and strengthen the military.

In any event, the reform movement of Kang Youwei and Liang Qichao disintegrated with the defeat of the Hundred Days Reform, and the various study societies organized as central to the movement were proscribed by the authorities. The Anti-Footbinding Society was closed down, and the movement for a time had to disband. Early in the twentieth century the anti-footbinding movement emerged a second time, and in the Empress Dowager's reforms following the Boxer Uprising, the Qing court itself, on December 23, 1900, issued an edict prohibiting footbinding.[15]

Sexual Liberation

We turn now to examine the views on women of the most left-wing thinker among the 1898 reformers—Tan Sitong (1865–98). This is not to say that Tan wrote anything that one might specifically call "views on women." In his 1897 book *Renxue* [On benevolence], however, he did develop a stinging critique of Confucian morality as well as ideas of human liberation.[16] He also touched on the most fundamental questions concerning gender and humanity. What then were his unique arguments?

Tan Sitong came from Liuyang in Hunan province. Under the influence of the reformist ideas of Kang Youwei and Liang Qichao, he took a leading role in the reforms under way in Hunan. After the failure of the movement in 1898, he refused to seek refuge and was executed at the age of 33. "Reforms have necessitated the spilling of blood in every country," he declared, "but I have yet to hear of blood flowing in China due to reforms. This is the reason China has yet to prosper. Let it begin with me."

Renxue was a distinct mixture of all sorts of ideas both new and old, Eastern and Western, drawn from such sources as Huayan and Chan Buddhism, the New Testament, Mozi's notion of "universal love," mathematics, physics, sociology, and such traditional Chinese scholars as Zhang Zai (1020–77), Wang Fuzhi (1619–92), and Huang Zongxi (1610–95). Tan wrote the book in an effort to break through the temporal blockade of his times. His shockingly unique conceptions and his reformist enthusiasm, which gush forth from the pages of this book, captivated his readers.

To begin with, Tan took the notion of *ren* (benevolence) in the title of this work from the established concept that "the benevolence of all things are of a single body," developed since Cheng Hao (1032–85) of the Song dynasty. To this he added Mozi's "universal love," Buddhist compassion, and Christian love. The main ingredient here was ether, the vaporous substance that filled everything from heaven to earth, and *ren* was none other than the workings of this ether.

This *ren* operated on the basic principle of "penetration" or "interconnectedness" (*tong*). Breaking through all enclosures, it moved toward an unrestrictedness and manifested itself in the form of equality. What sort of enclosures did this *tong* seek to break through? What sorts of interconnectedness would it achieve? The first was the *tong* between China and the outside world. In the Utopia Tan envisioned, national boundaries would be removed, and a sort of internationalism would emerge. The second was the *tong* between superior and inferior. The traditional hierarchical relations based on the Confucian notions of three bonds and five constant relationships would be broken down, and equality in human relations would emerge. The third was the *tong* between men and women, the external and the internal principles. Here, of course, sexual discrimination between men and women would be removed. The fourth *tong*, that between the self and others, provided the basis for the other three *tong* and removed the fences separating heaven and earth and all the things of the universe. One senses that here all of these interconnections come together into a single body.

Despite the fact that *ren*, or benevolence, as the workings of ether, took *tong*, or penetration, as its basic principle, at present, according to Tan, *ren* was in confusion, and humanity was bound firmly by traditional morality. How did this situation arise? According to Tan's way of thinking, it resulted from a disorder in "names." "Names" were linked to Confucian moral instruction, and as the latter became weakened, "names" swaggered about without a moral anchor. With his "name," the master fettered his servant; with his "name," the official yoked the people; with his "name," the father oppressed his children; and with his "name," the husband made his wife suffer. Older brother and younger brother, and friends as well, used "names" as pretexts to oppose one other. Thus, *ren* had ceased to exist.

For example, "sexual relations between a man and a woman" were called "lust," but "lust" was but a name, Tan argued. Because this name "lust" came into use after the birth of humanity, everyone understood it as something evil. For, at the very beginning of the human race, had "lustful" behavior become accepted as appropriate etiquette at receptions of state and been implemented at the court, in cities, and in the full view of the assembled masses (much as bowing with hands clapsed and kneeling and knocking were the ritual in China and as hugging and kissing were the ritual in the West) and had it continued down to the present day in this manner, then would anyone consider "lust" an evil thing? Some people held the theory that the male and female reproductive organs were hidden in a place where the eye could not see; thus, "lust" was easily conceived of as something evil. If that were the case, and from the very start heaven had not hidden the sexual organs but placed them on the forehead where they were readily visible, then "lust" would probably have become the appropriate ritual at a first meeting between two parties, and it would certainly never have been considered evil.

Generally speaking, Tan continued, the prevention of licentious behavior in the world had been far too extreme, and as a result this had led men and women directly back to it. The enactment of laws preventing adultery, the prohibition of pornography, and shyness at the use of lewd language were all examples of this. Even in the civilized world of Europe and the United States, people hesitated before using the language of the bed chamber, considering it an embarrassment.

Originally, Tan claimed, the disparity between the sexes was not particularly important. Both were made up of human beings with the only difference being several inches in the male and female sexual organs. However, what now strictly separated men and women lay in our having been taught that we must emphasize this gender gap of a few inches and esteem and covet it in others, and this distinction encouraged people to seek out licentiousness. Such a view regarded human beings solely as the objects of lust. Furthermore, while men had been able to enjoy the services of many wives and to become addicted to self-indulgence without the least hesitation, women were executed if they engaged in lustful behavior. Such honoring of men and disparaging of women had become increasingly more significant, and infanticide by drowning of female newborns had become an act parents performed with equanimity. Not bees, nor ants, nor even jackals and tigers would ever commit such irreparable crimes.

The dignity bestowed on men and the belittling of women were, Tan claimed, absent from Buddhist scripture, especially Mahayana scripture. Man and woman alike were the essence of heaven and earth. Both possessed numerous virtues and had many good deeds to perform. They were considered equal. They were assuredly not born into this world solely for the purpose of lust. "Feminine beauty" was nothing more than cosmetics and clothing. Take those things away and women were lumps of flesh and blood in no way different from men. Once that fact was recognized, men and women would become used to each other, would fully appreciate each other, and would come to act with spontaneity and calm in each other's presence. If people could forget that there was something called "the opposite sex" and treat each other equally as friends, then issues like lust would surely not arise, and an end to this whole business of "lust" would become possible.

Sexual "lust" itself was of no particular note, Tan argued, but merely the contact of two fitted sides of a machine. This "contact" occurred naturally, like the movement of a piston driven by steam: simple and unmysterious, not concerned with pleasure or the lack of it. Because women of the world did not understand the principle of these things, they believed beyond a doubt the fallacious arguments of those moronic scholars who advocated the prevention of lewd behavior. The fact was that "sexual relations between a man and a woman" was merely the activation of a two-sided mechanism. Once that fact became clear, people would probably set up research centers everywhere for the study of licentiousness.

Western medical science together with Chinese medical science would be able to chart—at the time of sexual intercourse—the conditions of the muscles, the movement of blood in the blood vessels, the saliva, and semen; and scientists could construct wax figures modeled on the human body for purposes of dissection and analysis. They would publish and distribute works explaining theories of sex and thus deepen people's understanding of it. Thus, by understanding the theory of "lustful" behavior, Tan claimed, labels like "lust" would eventually disappear.

In this way Tan used his innovative theory of ether to pull away the veil that Confucianism had used to cover sexuality. Using a scientific understanding of sex, he opposed seeing women as the instruments of lust. Had anyone ever proclaimed such a bold theory of sexual liberation?

Since the establishment of the school of Zhu Xi (1130–1200) as state orthodoxy, sex had been regarded as a human passion, and the destruction of the passions together with a return to the heavenly principle were to be the sole aims of life. The school of the Ming dynasty philosopher Wang Yangming (1472–1528), particularly in the development of its left wing, opposed this view and began the process of affirming passion as part of human nature. The valiant leader of that left wing Li Zhi (1527–1602) once said: "Wearing clothes and eating food are the natural laws of human relations." Furthermore, the early Qing thinker Wang Fuzhi developed Song scholar Zhang Zai's philosophy of *qi* (ether) arguing: "Heavenly principle lies within human passions. Without these passions, heavenly principle would not be manifest."

Tan Sitong unified these theories, inserted some knowledge from Western natural science, and fully liberated sex from the thrall of Confucianism. From our present perspective his theory may seem rather juvenile. However, when we consider that the women's liberation movement has deepened our concern for the female body and has moved toward building a new theory of sexuality while emancipating itself from past theories, then the fact that late in the nineteenth century, in a China still heavily under the sway of traditional Confucian morality, a man like Tan Sitong should proclaim sexual liberation with such courage and fit it out with a theory of sexuality makes him a remarkable pioneer.

In this way Tan expanded and developed the originally Confucian conception of *ren*, generally mobilized all the theories available, and with an energy to "burst through all strictures" set his sights on a more basic liberation of humanity. His attempt to establish the individual as the main actor in reform, through a distinctive philosophical system and a severe critique of Confucian morality, clearly far transcended the limits of the 1898 Reform Movement with the latter's primary concern for enriching the nation and strengthening the military. In Tan's own words, his execution "sacrificed a life for the fulfillment of benevolence (*ren*)." These words were a fitting end for the author of the *Renxue*.

Let me also tell the story of Tan Sitong's wife, Li Run. Li married Tan when she was eighteen. She was said to have read widely, and her points of view often gained Tan's assent. When Tan was executed in 1898, she was on her way back to her home village with Tan's father. On hearing the news, she immediately jumped off the boat into the river. She was soon saved, resuscitated, transported by palanquin to the city of Changsha, and placed at the office of the provincial governor. The governor at the time was Chen Baozhen, a man sympathetic to the reform movement. When he tried to bring her indoors, she lay prostrate on the ground and simply cried. At that point he said to her: "I really thought I was going to save Tan, but the court charged me with a crime and apprehended me. I guess I shall meet Tan again in the next world."

Before he could complete these words, Li Run pulled a dagger from her sleeve and thrust it into her own neck. Blood burst out onto Chen's body. His office went into an uproar, a doctor was summoned, treatment was immediately applied to her wound, and she was sent home. The next morning she seemed to want to say something. She asked her maidservant: "Who witnessed the killing of my husband?" When she was told that a certain grand secretary had seen it, she lay clinging to her bed, and with all the strength she could muster called out his name. Her wound promptly opened, and blood spurted out over a distance of nearly ten feet. From this she died. When she was moved to her coffin, her teeth were all broken and both of her hands remained tightly clenched. The blood she had spilled was said to have formed the Chinese character for "dagger" on her chest.

This rendition of the story follows the only biographical account we have of her ("Tan liefu zhuan"), which was carried in the newspaper *Tianjin guowenbao*.[17] The expression *liefu* denotes a woman whose sense of chastity is so firm that she must choose death (suicide) upon the demise of her husband. Given the traditional morality of the time, this was considered a woman's highest glory. Had he heard his wife referred to as a *liefu*, a woman of such extraordinarily chaste martyrdom, a bitter grin would probably have broken across Tan Sitong's face in the netherworld. Why did she follow her husband in death? Was she abiding by an ancient sense of morality? Was it because she loved him so much? Or was it due to the hatred and despair she felt for the murderer of her spouse? We get none of these answers from this story. Beyond this, a few of the biographies of Tan Sitong mention only that his wife, Li Run, ran a Chinese Women's Study Society; most of Tan's biographies scarcely even give her name. Perhaps the portrait of Li Run painted in this one extant biography is simply what was expected of a woman, the wife of Tan Sitong, as her husband met his final, glorious end, and hence not an accurate portrayal of the truth. In any event, one cannot fully comprehend the sadness of this woman who lived under the shadow of the revolutionary Tan Sitong.

The World of the *Datong shu*

I have postponed discussion of Kang Youwei's view of women, which properly speaking might have been introduced first, to follow the examination of Liang Qichao and Tan Sitong. Kang's work, *Datong shu* [The book of great harmony], which we shall analyze at this point, was in fact completed only after the 1898 Reform Movement and was not published until even later, during the Republican period.[18] Kang developed *Datong shu* on the basis of principles deriving from the 1898 Reforms, and its ideas go far beyond the realities of China in its day, for Kang constructed it as a kind of Utopia.

The expression *datong* (great harmony) in the title comes from the chapter entitled "Liyun" [Evolution of rites] of the classical Chinese text on rites, *Liji*. We have already noted how Hong Xiuquan dreamt of a society based on this notion of "great harmony." According to Liang Qichao's modern rendition of an important passage from the "Liyun" chapter, which he cited in painstaking detail, the concept of *datong* should be interpreted in the following manner.

When the Great Way was pursued, a public spiritedness ruled all under heaven. They chose men of virtue and capability (democracy); their words were sincere and they cultivated harmony (the League of Nations); and thus men were not solely close to their parents, nor did they treat just their own children as children (the public rearing of children). The aged were provided for until their death, employment was provided for the able-bodied, and an upbringing was secured for the young. They took care of widowers, widows, orphans, the childless, and the diseased (sickness and old-age insurance). Men had their work, and women were to be married. Although they did not like to throw goods away, they certainly did not wish to keep them for themselves (communism). Although they did not like that their own labor should fail to be used, they certainly did not employ it to their own gain (sanctity of labor). . . . This was the [principle of] "great harmony" [in action].[19]

Kang Youwei integrated this concept of "great harmony" with the theory of "three ages," which he had taken from the Gongyang school of *Chunqiu* [Spring and autumn annals] studies. This theory argued that history progressed through three stages or "ages": disorder, ascending peace, and great peace. The last age of great peace accompanied the world of "great harmony." Kang's concept of historical progress regarded development toward a constitutional form of the polity as a historical necessity and claimed the inevitability of political reform. Kang thus offered a powerful theoretical basis for the future he envisioned.

The *Datong shu* was divided into the following ten chapter headings:

1. Entering the World and Witnessing Universal Suffering
2. Doing Away with National Frontiers and Unifying the World (the extinction of nation states)
3. Doing Away with Boundaries of Class and Making [All] Peoples Equal (the extinction of class)
4. Doing Away with Boundaries of Race and Rendering [All] Races the Same (the assimilation of races)
5. Doing Away with Boundaries of Sex and Protecting Individual Independence (the liberation of women)
6. Doing Away with Boundaries of Family and [All] Becoming People of Heaven (the abolition of family)
7. Doing Away with Boundaries of Wealth and Creating a System of Public Ownership (the abolition of private property)
8. Doing Away with Boundaries of Administration and Creating an Age of Great Peace (administrative reorganization)
9. Doing Away with Boundaries Between Kinds of Living Things and Lovingly Protecting All Living Things (the prohibition on killing animals)
10. Doing Away with Boundaries of Suffering and Reaching Great Happiness (the phase of great happiness)

In this way he gave expression to a kind of communistic Utopian world in his concern for sweeping away the sufferings of all living creatures around the globe—including complete outcasts—and bringing salvation to all sentient beings. To that end he particularly saw the need for rescuing women who had sunk into obscurity in a world of suffering. In that context he wrote a section early in the book entitled "The Suffering of Women, Summary" in which he described in great detail the unfair, "horrifying, appalling, lamentable, bitter" circumstances in which Chinese women found themselves.[20] Kang here considered the individual to be the key to this lamentable situation. The concept of the individual implied for Kang freedom, equality, mutual love, the natural rights of humanity, and personal emancipation. With this as his model, he cast light throughout the darkness of the contemporary world in which Chinese women were still treated as slaves, prisoners, accessories, and playthings. His profound knowledge of the world, past and present, East and West, combined with penetrating insights to make this perception of the position of women unprecedented in China.

The state of women in China at that time was certainly, he argued, in the age of disorder, and it had first to be drawn into the age of ascending peace, the norm then for the West. He then enumerated the conditions for the liberation of women in the age of ascending peace,[21] which generally entailed an adoption of bourgeois Western society, with the exception of one item. The one differing element was the eventual uniformity of male and female garb; differentiation in clothing discriminated between men and women, he argued, on the basis of shape. Kang did indeed offer a fascinating conceptualization.

Ultimately, the age of ascending peace was to develop, according to this schema, into the age of great harmony. The key point of the *datong*, in Liang Qichao's view, lay in the abolition of the family, and here Kang developed fully his thesis of the discontinuance of the family. According to Kang, such forms as husband-wife and the like were products of the age of disorder. Conjugal relations had become fixed: the father's blood line alone was recognized, and father-son was deemed the real blood tie. Since this requirement was an egotistical male one, women were of necessity coerced into an entire life paired with one man. However, because human beings possess their own individuality, they also have their own tastes. As often happens, if the content of one's work changes over a long period of time, then one's position will change as well. If a man marries with the aim of getting a beautiful bride, several years later autumn will come and he will fall for someone more beautiful—this is only the workings of human nature. That a single male-female couple could endure an entire lifetime together happily was itself, in Kang's estimation, a ridiculous demand to make.

In the age of great peace, however, men and women would be equal, and human beings would be able to find independence, each in his or her own fashion. People would be raised by society, and they would become citizens of the world. There would no longer be any need to maintain a rigid father-son relationship. There would be no need to compel lifelong marriage and cause people suffering. The male-female relationship could be founded solely on love.

Kang Youwei thus advocated marriages of specified, limited duration. Once the two parties involved reached a mutual understanding on the basis of their individual wills, a marriage would be contracted in a document called "a contract of intimate relations." This contract was to be from one month to as long as one year, and never for an entire lifetime. The old expression "husband and wife" would no longer be used. If the love of both parties endured perpetually, the contract might be renewed, and if the love dissolved, the contract could be nullified at any point. People thus could exhaust the pleasures of love and enjoy the feeling expressed in the song of the ancient Chinese classic *Shijing*: "Enjoy the felicity of harmonious married life, an enjoyment which knows no limit."

In this way the ossified husband-wife bond would dissolve, and men and women would enter free contractual relations. Thus, the Chinese family system could no longer exist. To begin with, the family was the root of all evil, for it permitted the selfishness of one individual family to take precedence over the common good. At the same time, however, the family had functioned as the means by which human beings protected each other during the ages of disorder and ascending peace. Human beings were born into a family, which nurtured them to adulthood, protected them in difficult times, assisted them in times of poverty, cared for them in times of ill health, attended to them at the time of their funerals, and saw to their place of rest after passing into the realm of spirits. Once the family ceased to exist, society would have to replace it in seeing to these protective functions. But it would not be just a matter of replacing the family with society's assumption of these protective functions, for these functions would now be realized to perfection.

Thus, Kang Youwei conceived a grand plan from the cradle to the grave. His concept began within the mother's womb prior to birth. Because childbirth is a public act in which a mother, as heaven's surrogate, gives birth to a human being, the surroundings naturally have to be prepared in full by society. The suitable environment was to be supplied by a "human roots institution."

Pregnant mothers would enter it soon after conception and receive appropriate care there for medical problems and for their daily livelihood. Prenatal care was to be fully attended to, and education in these matters was to be given to the mothers. Abortion would be prohibited. During the difficult period of weaning three to six months after birth, mothers would play music; they would be honored for their great deed, and then they would leave the human roots institution.

After weaning, the infants were to be placed in a "child-rearing institution" (a nursery) near a human roots institution. All concerns would be fully planned for—environment, ventilation, and lighting. Growing trees and raising animals within the institution would stimulate the loving minds of the children from the age of six months to two years. After the children reached the age of two, teachers would work with groups of two or three children for two-year periods. Once the period of teaching was completed, the teachers would be honored for their meritorious work of rearing the children in place of the mothers, and they would be given decorations. When the children reached the age of six, they would leave the child-rearing institution and enter primary school.

Primary school covered ages six to ten, and only women would serve as teachers and principals there, for women's disposition was (in Kang's view) more refined, more compassionate, more loving, and more patient than men's. At age eleven, children would enter middle school. At age sixteen, they would graduate and proceed to college. Their education would be completed at age twenty.

After age twenty, each graduate was to be employed at a profession. Those who did not have work would enter an institution to aid the poor. Entering such an institution and receiving relief was to be seen as exceedingly dishonorable. People at the poor house would be separated by the number of times they had dwelled there, and they would be made to feel a sense of disgrace.

Should one become ill, one would be brought to a hospital, and society would cover all medical fees. Both male and female nurses would be hired with one-year periods of employment. Work reports on the nurses would be written up on the basis of letters of recommendation by their patients.

After age 60, people would enter "institutions to care for the aged." Having exerted themselves on behalf of society over a period of several decades as members of the society, they would now be justly repaid for their work. Employees at these institutions to care for the aged would be both male and female and would serve one-year terms. Work reports on these employees would be written based on letters of recommendation by the old people, and those fired as a result of these reports would never be allowed to hold a high position for the rest of their lives. All men would be permitted promotion to a high post only after they had served either in an institution to care for the aged or a hospital; all women would be allowed promotion to high position only after having served either in a human roots institution or in a child-rearing institution.

When a person died, the remains were to be removed to an "institution for consideration of a whole life." The chief mourners would be the father and mother, sons and daughters, brothers and sisters, friends, acquaintances, and teachers. Men and women who were very close and teachers and disciples who enjoyed good relations would express their sadness on this occasion. Except in extraordinary cases, cremation of the corpse was deemed the best manner of dealing with the remains. Despite opposition to cremation, in the age of great harmony machines would be so thoroughly precise and electrification so advanced that there would be no cause for concern about such things.

If the extinction of the family could be realized, then in 60 years, Kang felt, families would cease to exist among all the peoples in the world. The selfishness between husband and wife and between father and son would disappear. Since property would no longer be passed on to descendants, land, factories, and commercial products would become the public property of society. The system of private property would be abolished, and the world of great harmony would become manifest. Kang Youwei was a man of extraordinary optimism.

Kang's pursuit of freedom and equality for the bourgeois individual led him into the realm of "great harmony." In laying the groundwork for an advanced material civilization and a system of public ownership, Kang believed the individual would prosper and achieve perfection. Kang's conception of a universe of great harmony, his plan for reforming the world, truly astounded people, both in the massive conceptual energy with which his plan enveloped the entire world and in the exceptionally detailed preparations that he painstakingly elaborated in the text. The real problem lay in how to bring about this society of great harmony. As Kang argued:

If people throughout the world try to abolish the evils of the family, then they should begin by making men and women clearly equal with each person enjoying independence. This is a right which heaven bestows on humanity. If people throughout the entire world try to abolish the evil of private property, then they should begin by making men and women clearly equal with each person enjoying independence. This is a right which heaven bestows on humanity.

"If people try to abolish fighting between nations . . . if people try to abolish fighting between ethnic groups . . . if people try to attain the world of great harmony"—in each of these cases, Kang argued, they should begin with gender equality. Sexual equality was itself a passport—a passport to a society of great harmony. As we shall soon see, however, as long as inequality between men and women and the family system remained inseparably tied to the social system of landlord control, changing male-female relations without changing society was impossible. Ultimately the passport was invalid.

As author of the *Datong shu*, Kang Youwei was fearful of the dangerous role his ideas might play—like a flood or wild beasts—and he did not rush to see it published. In the revolutionary movement that overthrew the Qing dynasty, the Republic of China (which would have corresponded to Kang's age of great peace) ignored his developmental stages of history; first, one had to pass through an era of constitutional monarchy (his age of ascending peace). Thus, Kang took an antirevolutionary position. Perhaps it was to be expected that, as Mao Tse-tung put it, "Kang Youwei . . . did not and could not find the way to achieve Great Harmony." [22]

中
國
婦
女

The Red Lanterns and the Boxer Rebellion

From our brief journey into the Utopian world of Kang You-wei, we must now return to the realities of modern Chinese history. Following its defeat in the Sino-Japanese War of 1894–95, China was forced to sign the humiliating Treaty of Shimonoseki. The treaty signaled a new stage in China's decline toward colonial status. With it, Japan seized control of Taiwan, and China with her immense territory now faced the danger of partition by the imperialist powers. Germany occupied Jiaozhou (Kiaochow); Russia seized Port Arthur; and France grabbed Guangzhou Bay. Soon England leased Weihaiwei and the New Territories opposite Hong Kong, and all the great powers had established spheres of influence in China.

The Treaty of Shimonoseki also recognized the Japanese right to open factories in the treaty ports of China, though this right was not exclusively for the Japanese. By virtue of the "most favored nation" clause in the treaties, all the imperialist powers acquired the same privilege. The establishment of factories—that is, the export of capital—was what world capitalism then most needed as it entered its imperialist stage. The powers competed to open factories and banks and to build railways. Furthermore, through the large loans issued to pay the war indemnity to Japan, the powers gained control over the key to China's finances. In this way China was trampled by the imperialist powers, and the people of China were exploited by world capitalism.

At the vanguard of this imperialist invasion were the Christian missionaries. In their efforts to spread the gospel, missionaries had penetrated the interior of China where no white person had been before. Following the missionaries came gunboats and foreign businesses. These missionaries and some of their converts presumed upon the power and might of imperialism to seize peasants' lands and property for their churches and to intervene in lawsuits. No matter how perverse the demands of the missionaries might be, officials could do nothing to resist them. In this situation, disputes between Chinese and Christians broke out across the land. From stoning and beating missionaries, incidents escalated to burning churches and killing the foreign proselytizers. "Missionary cases" (*jiaoan*), as these anti-Christian disturbances were called, increased with each passing year and spread to all parts of the country. The Boxer Uprising developed out of these anti-Christian activities to become a full-scale anti-imperialist struggle.

The Boxers were originally called "Boxers United in Righteousness" (*Yihequan*). Their "boxing" was a kind of martial art, but with a significant magical component. They believed that once they had mastered this form of "boxing," spirits would take possession of their bodies and make them invulnerable to bullets. Lacking any real weapons and armed only with this faith, the Chinese peasants confronted modern Western guns. With their faith, they organized the populace and went forth to do battle with imperialism.[1]

As the national crisis deepened following the Sino-Japanese War, the Boxer movement spread rapidly across North China. Fearing that this movement would turn into an attack on the Qing dynasty, some officials even tacitly recognized it and thereby sought to evade the thrust of the Boxer attack. In this semitolerated form, the Boxer movement raised the anti-imperialist slogan "Support the Qing, Destroy the Foreign." Then in August 1900, Japan, Russia, England, France, Germany, the United States, Austria, and Italy joined in the Eight-Nation International Expedition and set out to suppress the Boxers. The Qing court declared war on the foreign powers, and China entered a state of war with the imperialists.

The cities of Beijing and Tianjin were occupied by people who studied the new boxing techniques, believed in their invulnerability, and set forth to do battle with imperialism. The main participants in the Boxer movement were peasants, craftsmen, and transport workers who had lost their lands and jobs with the inroads made by imperialism and China's endemic natural disasters.

The Boxers lacked a unified organization. Usually each village formed its own band or *tuan* which operated independently, although in some cases bands from separate villages united to take part in joint operations. Their leaders were called "Senior Brother-Disciple" (*da shixiong*), and often there were assistants called "Second Brother-Disciple" (*er shixiong*).[2] They lived collectively in public buildings, eating a simple coarse fare and drinking only hot water; they were not permitted to touch any liquor, tobacco, or meat. Like the Taipings before them, the Boxers also forbade contact with women.

When the men set out to do battle with the foreigners, there was no reason for the women to stand aside quietly. Young women organized the Red Lanterns (*Hongdeng zhao*, literally "Red Lanterns Shining"), middle-aged women formed the Blue Lanterns (*Landeng zhao*), and elderly women organized the Black Lanterns (*Heideng zhao*). Particularly famous among these was the Red Lanterns group. Its members worked tirelessly, looking after injured Boxers, serving as lookouts, and gathering intelligence on the enemy.

The Red Lanterns were an organization of young women between the ages of twelve and eighteen. Occasionally they even included girls as young as eight or nine. Their leaders were called by names parallel to those of the Boxers: "Senior Sister-Disciple" (*da shijie*) and "Second Sister-Disciple" (*er shijie*). These young women neither arranged their hair in the traditional manner nor bound their feet. They wore red coats and trousers, red hats, and red shoes. All red from top to bottom, they tied up their sleeves to make it easier to work, and each carried a red lantern. It was said, "The men practiced United in Righteousness Boxing, and the women practiced the Red Lanterns Shining." The Red Lanterns' training in wielding swords and waving fans was extraordinarily rigorous. Their round red fans were shaped like an evergreen shrub, and they believed that when they waved these fans they could leap up to heaven.

> Wearing all red,
> Carrying a small red lantern,
> Woosh, with a wave of the fan
> Up they fly to heaven.[3]

It was said that having flown to heaven, the Red Lanterns would cross the Yellow Sea to Japan to take back their country's stolen land. This sort of belief—that the small-framed Red Lanterns could roam the heavens and reach the heartland of the imperialists—expressed the fantastic hopes and ambitions of the day. A wave of their fans was even credited with starting fires.

Stories such as the following have been passed down from Boxer times. In Tianjin were located well-fortified foreign buildings that even the Qing armies despaired of ever taking. The Red Lanterns, clad all in red, appeared close to these buildings, each carrying the precious fan in the right hand and a flower basket in the left. Rumor had it that with the flower basket the women caught the bullets of the foreigners' guns, and with a wave of the fan they could ignite a blaze. The French and the tiny Japanese soldiers trembled in the foreign enclave, while the Red Lanterns steadily increased in number. "Burn!" "Burn!" they cried out in thundering voices. Every place the Red Lanterns reached, the flames would immediately rise up. "This looks bad!" cried the French; "let's get out of here." But the tiny Japanese replied: "No, let's watch things for a while longer." "However we shoot at them, none of the bullets or shells seems to have any effect. With just a wave of their fans, they can set off such a blaze! With another two waves of the fan, we're going to get cooked alive! This looks bad! Let's get out of here!" When the French looked again at the tiny Japanese, they had already withdrawn.[4]

Every day the young women would practice with swords and fans. Then every ten days, or perhaps every seven or eight days, they would form bands and circle through the villages, running and waving their swords as a kind of demonstrative warning. They called this "walking the city" (*caicheng*), and it was similar to the Boxer practice of "walking the streets" (*caijie*). In addition to practicing every day, the Red Lanterns would also join the Boxers in burning foreign buildings and killing foreign devils.

> Standing on the street corner, eighteen good men,
> Burning the foreign buildings, the Red Lanterns Shining.
> Burning these buildings is not a big deal,
> But until the foreign devils are all driven off, our efforts will not
> cease.

> The women do not comb their hair.
> They cut off the foreigners' heads.
> The women do not bind their feet.
> They kill all the foreigners, laughing as they go.

The Boxers and the Red Lanterns, though, did not merely confine themselves to antiforeign beliefs and activities.

> The emperor demands our grain.
> The foreign devils steal our treasures.
> But as long as we have our big swords,
> They'll get neither grain nor treasures.

The Boxers and the Red Lanterns were prepared to spare no one who stole the fruits of their labor, be they foreigners or the emperor himself. "Share the grain equally" and "Rob the rich and give to the poor" were the sorts of slogans that appeared at the time. After they attacked the foreign legations in Beijing, talk spread of killing "a dragon, a tiger, and three hundred rams." The dragon was the emperor; the tiger was the powerful Prince Qing; and the three hundred rams were the officials of the central government. It was said that only eighteen members of the central government would escape their wrath. The Qing court's declaration of war against the foreign powers derived partly from fear of the antidynastic impulse of the Boxer movement, which the court hoped to appease. But immediately after the termination of hostilities with the foreigners, the court then turned against the Boxers themselves.

The members of the Red Lanterns were all young women, and hardly any of their names survive. A look at the two leaders whose names have come down to us, Holy Mother of the Yellow Lotus (Huanglian Shengmu) and Azure Cloud (Cui Yun Jie), may provide some insight into their movement.

The Holy Mother of the Yellow Lotus was married to the son of a boatman by the name of Li You.[5] Nothing is known of her background except that she was just twenty years of age and that her original name was Lin Heier. Another story has it that she was a prostitute on board a ship. In 1900, the year of the Boxers, Li You had some sort of dispute with a foreigner and was thrown in jail, which caused the young woman to nurse a deep hatred of the foreign invaders. By arrangement with the Boxer leader Zhang Decheng, she entered the city of Tianjin, established an altar on a salt boat along the Grand Canal, and there organized young women. From the mast of this ship flew a flag on which was written in large characters: Holy Mother of the Yellow Lotus. There she was said to cure the sick, and great numbers of patients flocked to the boat to receive her remedies.

This woman devoted herself to caring for injured Boxer soldiers, but she also maintained contact with the Boxer leaders and worked over battle plans with them. Thus, when the International Expedition pressed closer to Tianjin, she led the Red Lanterns into battle at the Laolongtou Station and at Zizhulin. After Tianjin fell, she was captured and executed, but it was said that the calm she maintained to the very end inspired an instinctive respect among onlookers. Even after her death, red lanterns continued to hang from the boats along the Grand Canal. When foreign soldiers would see them, they would immediately flee—such was the fear engendered by the fighting spirit of these young women.

The second Red Lantern leader was Azure Cloud.[6] Her original name is not known. She was about seventeen or eighteen years old. Her feet were said to be small, so possibly they had been bound. Her build was slight, and she allegedly could leap over ten feet in the air. She was also an expert in karate. Once when she had been doing acrobatics in Shanghai, her father was arrested, but the foreign courts never allowed any defense. She developed a ferocious enmity for the foreigners. Later she joined the Boxers and acquired the name Azure Cloud. So beautiful that she could be taken for a goddess, she was envied by everyone, and Azure Cloud seems a most appropriate name for a young girl who hoped to roam the heavens.

When the International Expedition entered Beijing, Azure Cloud urged on the people who were about to flee. In one day of fierce street fighting, she struck down many foreign soldiers. Almost all of her followers were killed or wounded at this time. Some of the leaders of the remaining Boxers went over to the foreigners and committed all sorts of vile crimes. She was ashamed of having ever made common cause with them, so one evening she invited them to a banquet and lectured them: "I would never have believed you could be such beasts. It is your fault that the country is on the verge of collapse. I will cut you down as an apology to heaven." Having executed them, she left, disappearing forever without a trace.

After the Qing and the International Expedition had suppressed the Boxers, the court signed the Boxer Protocol with eleven nations and openly sold out the country. With the customs and salt tax revenues as security, 450 million taels of silver in indemnity was assessed. Foreign troops were stationed in Beijing's legation quarter. Thus, the Qing dynasty became "the foreigners' dynasty," the agent of imperialism resting on the backs of the Chinese people. The Boxer movement made it clear that the enemies of the Chinese people were the imperialist powers and their agents, the Qing. No longer would "Support the Qing, Destroy the Foreign" be the slogan; now it was necessary to "Sweep away the Qing, Destroy the Foreign." In this way the Boxers served to clear the way for the development of Sun Yat-sen's revolutionary movement to overthrow the Qing dynasty.

As one piece of Boxer propaganda put it:

> The red lantern shines,
> Lighting the path for the people.

Women in the 1911 Revolution

Shimoda Utako and Women's Education in the Late Qing

After the Boxer Uprising, the Qing court, realizing that its own survival was at stake, embarked on what are known as the Empress Dowager's reforms. As part of this new program, students were sent overseas, and from this period many young people, with public and private funding, went to Japan to study.[1] The first young woman to do so entered the Girls' Practical School in Kōjimachi, Tokyo in 1901; and four or five more requested entrance there the next year. These women students were wives and daughters who accompanied their fathers, brothers, and husbands to Japan, and they had at best an incomplete knowledge of Japanese. They were admitted by the school's principal, Shimoda Utako,[2] a well-known scholar of the time and a good friend of Konoe Atsumaro and Itō Hirobumi.

Earlier Shimoda had once met the revolutionary Sun Yat-sen in the foothills of Futarayama in Nikkō and had presented him with a poem that read:

> Futarayama,
> The night, dwelling in the clouds of the foothills,
> Lost on the road of dreams,
> In the heart of the land of China.

For some years she had dreamt of setting out from Japan for the "heart of the land of China," the mainland. In her capacity as an educator, Shimoda planned to realize her dream through women's education. The Girls' Practical School reported to the Japanese Ministry of Education its "Educational Principles for Overseas Chinese Students" and set up a separate classroom in Hinoki-chō in the Akasaka section of Tokyo, for classes to begin in 1905. In 1908 a "Chinese department" was founded on the school grounds in Tokiwamatsu, and by 1914 well over 200 overseas women students had graduated from the school.

At the first commencement ceremony, Shimoda told the graduating students:

The Qing state has maintained its feudal institutions until the present. When those living under its monarchical autocracy travel abroad and all of a sudden observe a free attitude toward life, they are most likely to become ardent supporters of popular rights. Long-awaited knowledge may invite the danger of engendering traitors and rebels. I used to worry about this, but by exercising severe control over thought I would have been excessively cruel with you young women. . . . Although it is now time for us to part, if our wills be united, then even though our bodies may be separated, our spirits can never change. Do not forget that you leave Japan in tears. Please keep it always in your minds that although the country that reared you was China, the country in which you received an education was Japan.

Her words may strike us now as fairly arrogant. Through the education of these overseas students, Shimoda sought to nurture Chinese women to regard Japan as their spiritual motherland and to establish Japanese leadership over Chinese women.

Contrary to Shimoda's expectations, however, students from the Girls' Practical School became increasingly aware of the crisis in their own motherland. When Imperial Russia in 1903 laid bare its ambition to invade Manchuria, the Mutual Love Association (Gongaihui),[3] an organization of overseas women students, called an emergency general meeting, and the members resolved to fight in a war of resistance against Russia. In tears, these students appealed to Shimoda: "We can exist only when we have a country. If it ceases to exist, then we will be no more, and there will be no learning at all." Furthermore, from among the graduates of this school there did in fact emerge one of the sort Shimoda most feared would become "a traitor or a rebel," "an ardent support of popular rights"—Qiu Jin. We will have more to say about Qiu later.

The Empress Dowager's reforms in the aftermath of the Boxer Rebellion included a program of educational modernization, but the primary targets of education in these reforms were not women, as they were ultimately to receive only domestic education.[4] Arguing for the necessity of women's public education to the conservative Qing authorities was Hattori Unokichi, professor at the Daxuetang (the forerunner of Beijing University) in Beijing. He had recommended Shimoda to the Empress Dowager and sought to have the education of Chinese women entrusted to her. Doubtless the Qing court was completely amenable to Shimoda's educational ideal for women: to demonstrate all the more the "beauty of East Asian female virtue" through the new sciences.[5]

Allegedly, upon hearing this report of Shimoda's ideal, the Empress Dowager began confidential negotiations in which she sought to bring Shimoda to China and entrust her with the education of Chinese women. However, with the death of the Empress Dowager in 1908, her promise to Hattori came to naught, and the Japanese government for its part was thoroughly indifferent to a tedious program of furthering educational enterprises. Thus, Shimoda's dream of going to "the heart of the land of China," of assuming predominance in women's education there, was crushed. Nonetheless, new education for Chinese women was about to begin, albeit of a kind completely unrelated to that undertaken by Shimoda Utako or the Qing court.

One of the first women's magazines in China, *Nübao*,[6] began publication in 1902 in Shanghai, and with it began revolutionary propaganda for women. In her piece "Duli pian" (On independence), which ran in the pages of *Nübao*, Chen Xiefen argued that first of all women had to be independent. Although men had been promoting women's education and women's rights, their advocacy amounted merely to women's education convenient for men and women's rights convenient for men. They were unreliable, for independence was essential. This meant more than resistance against male oppression and obstruction. It necessitated the decision not to cooperate or negotiate with men at all. You could speak of men, but high officials were controlled by the court; lesser officials were controlled by high officials; the people were under the control of the lesser officials; and above it all the nation was under the thumb of foreign powers. Among all these, who for certain would uphold republican thought? It was useless to rely on such men. Women themselves had to promote women's education and restore women's rights.

Liang Qichao and others had argued that, since the emancipation of women from above was primarily for the benefit of men and the state or the nation, women should liberate themselves from below. Of course, women had never made their own emancipation an objective. In order to secure the liberation of the nation and the people, women first, Liang and others claimed, had to begin by gaining their own independence; and liberation from above was the very opposite of this. The importance of this stance was enormous, for women, who until then were merely objects of men or the nation, were now for the first time seen as central to the revolution. The first issue of *Nübao* also carried a letter from Fukuda Hideko.[7] She denounced the brutality of Western imperialism and argued that women in China and Japan had common sympathies and possessed a united spirit of resistance to Western imperialism.

In the same year in Shanghai, the Patriotic Girls' School was founded.[8] Jing Yuanshan was responsible for its planning, and Lin Xie and Cai Yuanpei participated.[9] It was established under the auspices of the Chinese Educational Society. Initially teachers were unpaid, and the "students" were principally the family members of the founders, some dozen or more people. At that time Cai Yuanpei (1847–1940) believed that revolution required violence and assassination: through military training in the Men's Patriotic Society, he and his associates were sowing the seeds of violence, and inasmuch as women were to play a role in assassination, they tried to plant ideas among them concerning the utility of assassination. The courses taught included the history of the French Revolution and the Russian Nihilist movement. Also emphasized was the science of making bombs. In short, this was education distinctly for the making of revolution. In addition, a women's handicraft center was set up where women were able to make preparations for their own material independence.[10] The education imparted at this school was way ahead of its time, and it was rather different, to say the least, from the aims the Qing court had in mind for women's education.

Somewhat later a booklet entitled *Nüjie zhong* (A tocsin for women) was published in Shanghai.[11] It was apparently a propaganda pamphlet of less than one hundred pages, but the original is no longer available. The author, Jin Tiange (1874–1947), used the pen-name "Jin Yi who loves liberty." Jin's work was possibly the first document in China to deal specifically with the issue of women's liberation, and he was hailed as "our women's Rosseau."

Jin argued that since virtue and knowledge were originally bestowed on human beings by nature, there was no reason to differentiate between men and women in this regard. Although women had tried to study, they were not allowed; even though they tried to enter schools, they were forbidden from so doing; they tried to have companions but were not allowed; and they tried to travel but were not allowed. In the end they became engrossed in reading trivial literature and drama, visiting temples, and joining new religions. The present character of women was formed in this manner. Accordingly, women had to regain six rights: (1) the right of entrance into higher level schools; (2) the right of companionship; (3) the right to engage in business; (4) the right to control property; (5) the right to freedom of movement; and (6) the right to freedom in marriage. In order to recover these rights, women's education was demanded, and this had extremely important ramifications. Jin offered the following eight points as objectives for women's education: (1) to realize a refinement and purity that would bring forth women's full natural endowments; (2) to rid women of oppression in order to attain freedom and independence; (3) to develop their thought in order to furnish them with a temperament like men's; (4) to reform their spirit in order to make them forerunners for all women in the world; (5) to strengthen their physical constitution so they can bear healthy children; (6) to furnish them with pure virtue so they may set a standard for the whole nation; (7) to give them a public-mindedness so they will have sympathy for all humanity; and, (8) to firmly preserve their integrity in order to stimulate revolution.

Hence, Jin Tiange's position on education did not see women simply as wives and mothers, but recognized them as independent, free human beings. In this portrayal, the ideal woman was a human being who resisted oppression and was devoted to the revolution. Jin appealed to women:

At present China is an autocratic monarchy. Even if you try to oversee the government and you can't do it, it's still appropriate to thrust demands before it. Even if you try to organize a revolutionary government and you lack the ability to do so, it's appropriate to act with violence. Thrusting demands is the responsibility of us men, but destroying and rebuilding are duties to be borne by both men and women. You rack your brains, stupefied into silence, and write away with your pens, but if your brains dry up, your tongues become exhausted, and your pens wear out, then let your tears gush forth. Once your tears are spent, pour forth your blood. Once inundated by blood, take up the sword. If you run out of swords, use bullets and guns. Thus, destruction shall proceed. Women! Do not be surprised! This is the incantation by which we fight for the rights and freedom of our comrades!

Apparently this appeal found many sympathizers among the women students of the time. Lin Zongsu, a student at the Girls' Practical School, wrote a piece entitled "Nüjie zhong xu" (Preface to *A tocsin for women*) in response to Jin's booklet in which she called for an uprising by women students: "Mr. Jin is truly China's Rousseau. However, rights are something to be fought for; they will never be conceded. If we let Mr. Jin alone plead on behalf of women and plan for the restoration of our rights, this is the same as expecting the government peacefully to promulgate a constitution without our shedding blood and overthrowing it."[12] Women, who had said practically nothing at all in the 1898 Reform Movement, gradually began to break through their silence and mobilize their numbers. Into this milieu Qiu Jin, "the woman revolutionary in male garb," was born.

Qiu Jin, Woman Revolutionary

We have already noted that Qiu Jin (1875–1907), a native of Shanyin, Zhejiang, studied at Shimoda Utako's Girls' Practical School in Japan.[13] After an unhappy marriage, Qiu suffered a tremendous shock when she observed the aftermath of the Boxer Uprising in Beijing. Contact with new ideas set her mind on overseas study, and eventually, leaving her two children behind, she traveled to Japan.

It was Hattori Unokichi's wife Shigeko, a former student of Shimoda Utako, who found the opportunity for Qiu to study in Japan. Shigeko led a women's conversation group when she was in Beijing with her husband and at one of her sessions she met a beautiful young women dressed in the clothing of a man. As she remembered Qiu Jin later:

Was this person before me a man or a woman? A tall slender body bent slightly forward in Western male dress with a full head of trimmed black hair. A blue hunting cap sitting sideways on her head covered half her ears. A dark blue, secondhand business suit didn't fit her at all. The sleeves were too long and from her cuffs one could see just her white, delicate hands. She carried a slender walking stick. Beneath her baggy trousers, worn-out brown shoes peeped through. A green necktie hung loosely over her chest.

Why did she walk around dressed like a man? Qiu Jin explained to Shigeko:

My aim is to dress like a man! As your husband well knows, in China men are strong, and women are oppressed because they're supposed to be weak. I want somehow to have a mind as strong as a man's. If I first take on the form of a man, then I think my mind too will eventually become that of a man. My hair is cut in a foreigner's style, something Chinese aren't supposed to do, and I'm wearing Western clothes.

Qiu Jin often visited Shigeko, and they spoke in a mixture of English and Japanese. At some point their conversation always came to the following impasses.

Qiu Jin: If I might be so bold as to ask for your instruction, are you a conservative or a radical?

Shigeko: Oh, no, no. I am a follower of Confucius.

Qiu Jin: A follower of Confucius?! So that means you're a follower of [the Confucian dictum that] "women and petty men are difficult to educate."

Qiu Jin: What's your opinion of revolution?

Shigeko: Revolution? Miss Qiu Jin, my country of Japan is a nation crowned with an Emperor of the same line for ten thousand generations. It is abominable for me to hear the sound of the word "revolution."

Although Qiu Jin had at first wanted to study in America, Shigeko eventually convinced her to abandon that idea and set her mind on going to school in Japan. Qiu had joined the Chinese secret society known as the Triads, which advocated overthrowing the Qing dynasty and returning control to the Chinese. Apparently Chen Xiefen was also a member of the Triads when she was publishing *Nübao* in Shanghai. At the time of the suppression of the radical newspaper *Subao* in 1903 Qiu Jin escaped to Japan. Arriving in Japan in 1904, she first entered a Japanese language school in Surugadai in the Kanda area of Tokyo and later transferred to Shimoda's practical school.

Among the overseas Chinese students in Japan at that time there was a variety of revolutionary groups—such as the Huaxinghui, the Xing-Zhonghui, and the Guangfuhui—organized along provincial lines. In 1905 they came together to form a united body known as the Tongmenghui (Revolutionary Alliance), which became the force that drove the revolution forward. Its program had the following points: "Expel the barbarians, revive China, establish a republic, and equalize land rights." Qiu Jin was charged with responsibility for Zhejiang Province within the Revolutionary Alliance.

Surprised by the cohesiveness of this revolutionary force, the Qing court urged the Japanese government to promulgate a series of "Regulations Supervising Overseas Students from China." Claiming that it would control student activities outside of class and expel any student for irregular behavior, the Japanese government did try to regulate the political activities of Chinese students on Japanese soil.

In response about 8,000 students protested by leaving school en masse in December 1905. A major Japanese newspaper, the *Asahi shimbun*, evaluated their action at the time: "With the base intent and self-indulgence characteristic of Chinese, these Chinese students arose out of discontent with the supervisory regulations, which they understood too narrowly." This assessment came as a great blow to the Chinese students. Ridiculed for self-indulgence and meanness, why couldn't they simply continue their happy-go-lucky life studying, implied the *Asahi*? Leaving an ardently worded will appealing to the students to revolt, the revolutionary propagandist Chen Tianhua threw himself into the sea off the shore near Ōmori, in what has now become a legendary act of self-sacrifice.

At that time the overseas students were divided into two groups. One group wanted to return to China immediately and join the revolution. The other group called for patience, for remaining in Japan in preparation for the future. Qiu Jin opted unflinchingly for the former. At a meeting of Zhejiang students at which this issue was debated, she thrust the dagger she always carried on her person into the podium and said: "If I return to the motherland, surrender to the Manchu barbarians, and deceive the Han people, stab me with this dagger!" And so she left Japan in 1906, together with some 2,000 other students.

Before this incident, Qiu had poured considerable energy into revolutionary propaganda through her reorganization of the Mutual Love Society and in her activities organizing Chinese women students in Tokyo. She stressed two principal means for her revolutionary work: speeches and the colloquial written word. Essays in Chinese were ordinarily written in a literary style radically removed from the spoken language. This made the written medium extremely difficult for even somewhat educated people to read, to say nothing of those who were illiterate. Thus, Qiu Jin tried through her speeches to appeal directly to the minds of her listeners.

In an article entitled "The Advantage of Speeches," she made the following points. The first advantage of speech-making was that one could do it freely anywhere and anytime. Second, many could come to listen without incurring any cost. Third, anyone who heard would understand, even women and youngsters who were unable to read. Fourth, one could organize an army and mobilize the masses with eloquence. Fifth, everything under the sun could be explained. Her own speeches were said to be full of energy and packed with an intensity "sufficient to jolt people's spirits and make them burst into tears from an excess of excitement."

Qiu also edited a journal by herself in Tokyo by the name of *Baihua bao* (Colloquial magazine). The movement to write articles in the colloquial or spoken language developed in a major way later, during the May Fourth era, beginning about 1915. Already, in the revolutionary movement of the late Qing, a number of issues of *Baihua bao* were published using the colloquial as a medium of revolutionary propaganda.

In an issue of *Baihua bao*, Qiu Jin wrote a manifesto entitled "A Respectful Proclamation to China's 200 Million Women Comrades." She began this piece as follows: "Oh, the most unfairly treated people in the world are we 200 million fellow women. Once born, it's better to have a good father; but if your father is a hot-tempered obstinate sort, when you open your mouth and shout, 'You good-for-nothing,' it will seem as though he's sorry he can't grab and kill you." Women suffered from bound feet and from problems of marriage, and after cataloging how they had to suffer as wives and mothers, Qiu addressed each woman individually.

Grandmothers, you mustn't say that you're useless because you're old. If your husbands are really good men and they build schools for you, don't hinder them in any way. Middle-aged women, you mustn't oppose your husbands, diminish their fighting spirit, make them incapable of accomplishing deeds, or seek your own fame. If you have children, please send them to school by all means. Girls, no matter what, never have your feet bound. Young women, if possible it's best for you to go to school; but even if you can't, then read at home and study your characters all the time. . . . Everyone, the nation is on the verge of collapse. Men can no longer protect it, so how can we depend on them? If we fail to rouse ourselves, it will be too late after the nation perishes.

This article addressed concretely in very simple language what each woman should proceed to do. Qiu Jin herself had had bound feet and had endured a dull marriage that had been arranged by her parents, but the pain had been overwhelming. She explained this in her article and elicited an overwhelmingly sympathetic response among her readers. She also wrote the words for a musical piece entitled "Labor in Vain" and "Song for Women's Rights," both weapons of revolutionary propaganda.

In these ways she intimately and individually addressed women who were unable to read and who lived empty lives as the slaves of their husbands, themselves slaves of the Manchus. Although she sought an awakening, what did she actually expect of the women to whom she was appealing? She wanted women to enter schools "to study women's arts to become independent and self-supporting." Thus, "by prospering in your work, gaining the respect of men, and ridding yourself of the name of 'good-for-nothing,' you will enjoy the blessings of freedom."

If you seek to escape the shackles of men, you must be independent. If you seek independence, you must gain knowledge and organize. Women's education is becoming more popular in Japan, with each woman becoming expert in her own business and building a life for herself. They [Japanese women] are trying to rid themselves of a life without work of their own in which they are dependent upon their husbands. And, as a result, their nation is getting stronger.

The foregoing appeared in a letter Qiu Jin wrote promoting overseas study to women students from the Number One Women's School in Hunan. By ceasing to rely upon their husbands and by consciously participating in society's labors themselves, she hoped that women would improve their position and help to make the Chinese nation strong.

In 1907 Qiu inaugurated the publication of *Zhongguo nübao* (Chinese women) in Shanghai. This magazine aimed at "advancing civilization, promoting women's education, uniting their emotions, solidifying an organization, and some day establishing a Chinese Women's Association." Qiu did not, however, expect that at the time she would be able to organize all of China's women and press them into revolutionary action to overthrow the Qing dynasty. She knew only too well the present condition of women in China.

Of course, given that current situation, good fortune for women was impossible without toppling the despotic Qing dynasty. By the same token, the success of a revolution was impossible without concentrating the power of women and preventing them from becoming a burden of this same revolution. In order to create the necessary conditions for such a movement, freedom to the extent that it could exist for women within the family had to be secured. This is what Qiu Jin had in mind in her often-used statement: "The revolution must begin inside the family. This means equal rights for men and women."

In addition, though, Qiu hoped that from the women to whom she was appealing there would emerge heroines prepared to die for the cause. "Come forth successors to Madame Roland! Come forth successors to Sophia!" she called out to them. Undeniably, a kind of heroism constituted part of her expectations; not that the masses would rise up and secure their freedom but that heroines would appear to emancipate women and, hence, China. Without this sort of heroism, though, how were they to cut through the muddled circumstances of the time? Qiu Jin herself planned to follow in the footsteps of Madame Roland (who was guillotined) and Sophia Perovskaya, the Russian Nihilist. Calling herself the Female Knight of Lake Jian, she intended to transform herself into a female knight-errant.

To that end she became a teacher in the Datong School for

women in Shaoxing, Zhejiang province, and began to publish *Zhongguo nübao*. The main point of all of her activities was less as an activist for women than it was as a woman revolutionary. There was something awe-inspiring in the look of this woman—sitting dashingly astride a horse and wearing a man's dark blue long-sleeved gown—that did not generally make one think of women.

Presiding over the Datong School, which she used both as a contact point for like-minded associates and as a military training ground, Qiu kept in touch with the local secret societies while she slowly but surely prepared for an armed revolt. She also organized a Restoration Army for the uprising. When every detail of the preparations had been made, the plans for her revolt leaked out, and her comrade Xu Xilin in Anhui Province committed an act of terrorism. Although in danger, she did not try to flee and was ultimately captured on the grounds of the Datong School. Even after being apprehended she revealed nothing. She left to posterity the sublime phrase: "Autumn rain, autumn wind, they make one die of sorrow." She was executed at the age of 32 on July 15, 1907. Her execution pierced the hearts of others as an act of propaganda far more powerful than any written works.

Anarchists of the Late Qing Period

At roughly the same time as the death of Qiu Jin, the Society for the Reinstatement of Women's Rights was organized in Tokyo and began to publish the journal *Tianyi* (Heaven's justice).[14] The Japanese journal *Sekai fujin* (Women of the world), run by Fukuda Hideko, introduced its readers to the Society for the Reinstatement of Women's Rights and explained that the Society had the following guidelines:

1. *Principles.* While keeping firm in our divine task in the cause of women, strive to change age-old customs that honor men and belittle women.

2. *Methods.* There are two methods for women to use. They are the two methods for the world: first, to force men with violence; and second, to intervene on behalf of women who are suffering oppression.

3. *Rules.* Never rely on the government. Never follow the orders of men. Several women should never be in the service of one man. A woman's first marriage must never be to a man who already has a wife.

4. *Morality*. Endure pain, be courageous, have a sense of shame, honor the public, be of upright character.

5. *Privileges*. Upon entrance into the Society, you obtain three privileges. Generally speaking, if you report to the Society any repression at the hands of males after your marriage, we will be able to avenge it. Those who die as a result of opposition to male privilege or in social struggles will be exalted. Those who get into trouble resisting male privilege or in social struggles have the right to receive this Society's assistance and protection.[15]

Thus, the Society for the Reinstatement of Women's Rights promoted social destruction by force as well as opposition to rulers and capitalists. Its concrete program entailed resistance against the control of women by men. For this reason its guidelines spoke of separate means of assistance. In fact, serious doubt has been raised as to whether the Society actually organized women to become active in aiding those who suffered under male domination. Apparently, publishing the organ *Tianyi* and encouraging revenge against men constituted the entirety of its activities. *Tianyi* was issued twice monthly under the joint editorship of Liu Shipei and his wife He Zhen. Its stated objective was "to destroy the old society and to implement equality of all human beings. In addition to supporting a women's revolution, we also support racial, political, and economic revolutions."

Liu Shipei (1884–1919) was a nativist scholar of the highest caliber who left major works in the field of Chinese classical research. In 1903 he met Zhang Binglin and Cai Yuanpei in Shanghai, and the three set their minds on an anti-Manchu racialist revolution. Intent on reviving the Han race, Liu even changed his given name to Guanghan ("revive the Han people"). When he escaped to Japan in 1907, he became a member of the Revolutionary Alliance and a frequent contributor to its organ *Minbao* (People's paper). At the same time he became closely associated with the Japanese anarchist Kōtoku Shūsui through Zhang Ji and rapidly was drawn to an anarchist position. Eventually internal contradictions aggravated relations within the Revolutionary Alliance and the publishing staff of *Minbao*. The revolutionaries splintered, and just about this time *Tianyi* began to appear in print.

Liu's wife He Zhen[16] (born He Ban) had studied at the Patriotic Girls' School, but in 1907 she escaped with her husband to Japan.

Not only was she the nominal publisher of *Tianyi*, she frequently published essays in it and spoke out strongly for the return of rights to women. Yet her writings were more about revenge than the return of rights. One of her essays, "On Women's Revenge," which embellished the cover of *Tianyi*, best illustrates this position.

Since the issues of *Tianyi* are now scattered or lost, only a fragment of "On Women's Revenge" survives. It strongly criticized the slavish subservience Confucianism compelled women to endure. Undoubtedly assisted by Liu Shipei's extensive knowledge, she laid out a critical view of the discrimination against women to be found in many Confucian texts. These Confucian views, she argued, were all rooted in male egoism, but this did not mean that women had no responsibility for the discrimination that men had carried on unchallenged as the norm. Was not Ban Zhao (40?–115?) of the Latter Han, author of *Nüjie* (Admonitions to women), a woman? Ban Zhao (or Ban the Traitor, as He Zhen was fond of calling her), although a woman herself, had been deceived by Confucian fallacies and brought harm and shame upon her fellow women; she was a slave to men, a great traitor to women. After the Latter Han, He continued, women's rights had not been extended because men made use of Ban Zhao's text and because women were influenced by it as well. Although He lashed out at women's internalization of gender discrimination, the real sin of this "Ban the Traitor" was something Confucianism had created.

Chinese scholarship had humiliated women; Chinese scholarship had wronged women; Chinese scholarship had fettered women. Failure to eradicate Confucian learning would ultimately, she argued, make their emancipation impossible. The force of her critique of Confucianism was extremely sharp, a forerunner of the full-fledged critique to come during the May Fourth Movement. This was also a feminist position that had emerged abruptly in late Qing society, a fact that stands in stark contrast to the virtual absence of articles on women's liberation in *Minbao*, the journal of the revolutionaries.

Thus, He Zhen understood the oppression of women as a function of gender relations, and she frequently incited women's sense of revenge against men, though she paid scant attention to the actual, concrete tasks confronting women's liberation. This point will be made clear by looking at two of her articles: "The Problem of Women's Liberation" and "Women Should Know about Communism," both of which appeared in *Tianyi* (joint issue 8–10). Recently, she argued, one often heard of women's occupational independence, but only a minority of rich people, the bourgeoisie, monopolized the means of production; and even if women had jobs, they were after all merely serving the bourgeoisie. This by no means spelled the attainment of freedom or emancipation. To obtain true freedom and liberation required the implementation of communism.

Furthermore, she continued, the women's suffrage movement had now become an international movement, but "parliamentism" was the main source of evil in the world. Insofar as classes existed, the poor (or proletariat) had to curry favor with the rich (or bourgeoisie). Naturally, the bourgeoisie were selected to fill the seats in parliaments, and the same situation prevailed in the world of women. Thus, even if women had the franchise, for poor women this would only mean that an additional layer of oppression, by upper-class women, would line up alongside oppression by the government and by men. Accordingly, He argued, rather than fight against men, women now had to enact a fundamental transformation by overthrowing rule of people by people. They had to change their goal from campaigning within the government to crushing it from without.

She thus denied the two objectives of the bourgeois women's liberation movement: women's attainment of the franchise and of economic independence. Her much grander ideal was to invoke the destruction of government and the realization of communist society. It appears that this position was greatly influenced by Kōtoku Shūsui's views of the time—for example, his article, "Women's Liberation and Socialism."[17] She clearly struck at the heart of the limitations of women's liberation in capitalist society. Yet, inasmuch as she provided no concrete program of action for implementation of this communist society, not only did this advocacy remain a pipe dream, it averted people's attention from contemporary reality and functioned actually to undermine the developing feminist movement. One wonders if she ever seriously considered a program aimed at the genuine liberation of women.

The journal *Tianyi* carried an article entitled "On the Destruction of the Family," which was also published by Chinese anarchists in

Paris in *Xin shiji* (New Century).[18] It was signed by one Han Yi, whose real name is unknown. The original in *Tianyi* (volume 4) is no longer extant. Li Shizeng published a number of articles along similar themes—such as "The Male-Female Revolution" and "The Revolution in the Three Bonds"—for *Xin shiji*. Li argued in these articles that society was comprised of human beings, and humans beings were born of men and women. Thus, it was first essential for the purposes of a social revolution to institute reform at the roots, and a social revolution had to begin with a revolution in male-female relations. In short, he claimed, it had to begin with the destruction of the family.

For anarchists the family was the root of all evil. The family gave rise to egoism. Where there were families, women fell under the control of men; because of families, the common humanity of the world had become privatized by individuals. Once the family disappeared and the basis of the old morality—the three bonds—were gone, then for the first time freedom, equality, and universal love could be realized. A revolution first in gender relations and then in the family would be carried out by an intellectual revolution and the destruction of the old, false morality. It was really quite easy, Li concluded. Anarchists at the time all premised their arguments on the elimination of the family (a family revolution) and a revolution in male-female relations.

Qiu Jin had also argued that revolution had to begin with the family, but in her case the revolution was the objective in and of itself; equality between men and women was not pursued as a separate goal. The anarchists, though, raised the idea of social revolution or communism only to relegate it to the imagination, thus placing it far in the future; there was the danger that the gender revolution itself would become their sole objective. This can clearly be seen in the principles of the Society for the Reinstatement of Women's Rights, the parent body of the journal *Tianyi*, and in He's article "On Women's Revenge."

Thus, the anarchists opposed women's occupational independence, and they almost completely vitiated the perspective that had been argued consistently since the time of Liang Qichao and the reformers: women's participation in societal labor, proceeding to economic independence, to fulfillment of national (or state) strength, to national (or ethnic) self-reliance. Furthermore, they stressed the abuse of women workers by capitalists in contemporary society and explicitly addressed the hatred and derision visited on laborers.

As for women's suffrage, in a China that still lacked representative government, the question was not necessarily one of the franchise. Political participation by women meant participation in the revolution. He Zhen and others labeled the Manchu government "a coercive, oppressive controlling power" and advocated the overthrow of autocratic government. The Society for the Reinstatement of Women's Rights never became concretely involved in the return of rights to women. Rather, while stressing a gender revolution and advocating absolute gender equality and absolute liberty, members of the Society became deluded by the idea that men were ultimately the enemy. Understanding women's issues in this way sidestepped and minimized the painful source of the problem that faced women at the time. In addition, it served to diffuse, in fact to negate, the pressing issues of "overthrowing the court of foreigners, overthrowing the Manchu dynasty."

Housewives and the Rice Riots

In 1906, the year after Sun Yat-sen and others formed the Revolutionary Alliance in Tokyo, the Qing court announced in an edict that it would launch preparations for a constitutional government. The constitution was to be modeled after the Meiji Constitution, and after a nine-year period of preparation the court planned to convene a national assembly. The aim was clearly to use the constitutional system to reshape the Qing court and stifle the revolutionary movement.

Even with these plans, though, the court proved unable to patch over the critical situation of the day. Besides the immense indemnities incurred as a result of the Boxer Incident, the Qing government's repayment of loans to foreign powers took up 40 percent of the annual state revenues. The central government responded with tax increases on top of surcharges, which drove the people to the limits of starvation. Natural disasters made matters worse, and, in addition, commodity prices were generally on the rise at that time.

Ordinarily, one *sheng* (1.0355 litres) of rice fetched 20 to 30 *wen* in the city of Changsha in Hunan province, but in the spring of 1910 the price soared to 80 *wen*. On April 12 one old woman reportedly went to buy rice with 74 *wen*, but the price had already risen to 76 *wen* by the time she arrived. She hurried home and took 76 *wen* but by that time the price had risen to 78 *wen*, and she was unable to buy the rice she wanted. How was a family to survive if for one day's work a laborer could not afford to buy even a liter of rice? Several days before this, an incident occurred in which a family of four, unable to purchase enough rice in the market outside Changsha drowned themselves in a river. The reason was not simply a poor harvest. In a situation that was already bad, evil officials and avaricious merchants took the opportunity to buy up what little rice there was, hoarded it, and then raised the price further. Shops run by foreigners even exported rice to other provinces.

No longer able to remain silent, the people of Changsha besieged the officials and demanded the release of rice because of famine. The officials not only failed to respond to this demand, they enacted further oppressive measures. The anger of the starving masses then exploded. A large group of people, swelling to 20,000, simultaneously rushed on the rice shops, attacked the churches, and struck at the shops of foreign merchants. Foreign consulates and the yamen office were also set ablaze, and the rioting eventually extended throughout the entire province of Hunan.

With the help of foreign imperialists, the Qing brutally crushed these rice riots in Changsha, but similar riots motivated by famine became chronic in the middle and lower reaches of the Yangzi basin. Ninety such incidents, small and large, have been counted for the period from 1907 to 1910. Just as the rice riots in Japan were sparked by the wives of fishermen in Toyama, in these Chinese rice riots women seething with anger took part everywhere. In certain cases women alone apparently stormed the rice shops. The *North China Herald* for September 23, 1911, carried the following item.

RICE TROUBLES

. . . About the same time as the last trouble we noted at Pootung in connexion with the dear rice, a second raid was being made some miles off by another crowd of women. On this occasion the affair occurred at a village called Yangchin, which is just opposite Yangtszepoo [in Shanghai]. Here as in the other case, the women, to the number of about a hundred, led the trouble, and going to the rice shops with bags and baskets, they helped themselves, taking away a considerable quantity. The thing was done as peaceably as such a type of robbery could be, and during the rest of the day nothing happened.

On the following day a crowd estimated at between 500 and 600 proceeded to the rice shops in the vicinity of a temple known as Tsing Poo Yang Di. Here all that fell to them was seven piculs of rice, and they then turned their footsteps farther down the river to Chingdoo, which is nearly opposite the Point. The shopkeepers had notice of their approach, however, and by the time they arrived they had all the places of business in the village shut up. . . .

Since these occurrences there have been no further reports, but with a class of women fully up to the standard of the suffragette, and in these cases having the sympathy of the men, the neighbourhood is obviously in a state of unrest. The extraordinary feature of the whole affair is the ease with which the women have scored their victories.[19]

Under these circumstances, armed struggles led by the revolutionaries grew more violent with each passing day. A string of uprisings provided a momentum toward revolution: the Ping, Liu, and Li uprisings in 1906; the Huizhou and Zhennanguan uprisings in 1907; the Qinzhou and Lianzhou uprisings in 1908; the New Army Uprising in 1910; and in 1911 the Huanghuagang Uprising.

Among those actively participating in the transport of weapons and ammunition at the time of the Huanghuagang Uprising was a woman by the name of Xu Zonghan, from Xiangshan, Guangdong province.[20] After her husband's death, Xu converted to Christianity under the influence of Dr. Zhang Zhujun and became deeply concerned with the new tides of thought. She joined the Revolutionary Alliance in Penang, Malaysia, in 1907, and after returning to China, became involved in the revolutionary movement in Guangdong. In installments hidden in cans of foodstuffs, she transported three hundred pistols and a huge quantity of ammunition from Hong Kong. She had the weighty responsibility in Hong Kong and, on the eve of the Huanghuagang Uprising, in Guangdong, of procuring ammunition and distributing it to her comrades.

On the day of the uprising, a pair of red banners announcing a wedding ceremony hung as camouflage on either side of the door leading to the revolutionaries' secret headquarters. With the red banners as a sign to her comrades, Xu successfully carried out the difficult task of passing the weaponry hidden in the sedan chair of the "bride." Springing into action at the sight of the red banners was the revolutionary Huang Xing. Together with two hundred compatriots, Huang attacked the office of the governor-general. They were badly defeated by the Qing army, and Huang himself suffered the loss of two fingers. Fighting deep into the night, he sought out a hiding place; coming upon the red banners, he dashed inside. But if the enemies' search extended to his hiding place, all the revolutionaries would be in danger. Xu Zonghan went and bought some merchants' clothes for Huang, and pretending to be man and wife, they escaped to Hong Kong. He needed the signature of a relative to obtain medical treatment for his injuries at a hospital in Hong Kong, and still playing her part, Xu signed as his wife. They actually did marry at this time, and in the smoke of the revolution the red banners hanging before that hiding place served as a blessing to the newly wedded couple.

Organizing the Women's Army

As revolutionary circumstances matured, the Qing court became increasingly isolated and ever more reactionary. With the realignment of the Manchu Cabinet in May 1911, there was announced an order for the nationalization of the railways, as the court attempted to break its financial deadlock. On the pretext of building railways, the regime wanted to take out a loan from a foreign nation. This move only served to turn even the constitutionalist monarchists against the Qing court.

The fiercest fighting in opposition to the nationalization of the railways took place in Sichuan. To suppress it, the Qing hurriedly mobilized its troops in Hubei and sent them to Sichuan. Just at this time, on October 10, 1911, there was also an uprising in the city of Wuchang. Nearby Hankou and Hanyang soon fell, and the revolution quickly spread to Hunan, Shaanxi, Jiangxi, Shanxi, Shanghai, Zhejiang, and Guangdong. On January 1, 1912, the Republic of China was formed with Sun Yat-sen as interim president. In February the Qing emperor abdicated, and the dynastic system of the past two thousand years came to an end. The 1911 Revolution had triumphed.

When the uprising broke out in Wuchang, the people rushed to join the forces of the revolution. Their spirits soared, and recruitment of new troops almost immediately exceeded four bri-

gades. In this revolutionary upsurge a proposal for the organization of a women's army was put forward by Wu Shuqing from
the city of Hanyang. Military Governor and Commander-in-Chief
of the Revolutionary Army Li Yuanhong, in a roundabout rejection of this proposal he received from her, argued that because
the troops were composed entirely of men, the incorporation of
women would be too difficult. She wrote back to say that in fighting a revolution there was no difference between men and women.

Were they to hear that the nation was conscripting troops, farmers would
lay down their hoes and laborers would abandon their tools. In high spirits
they would go off and become soldiers. Even teachers and students in
school would all have to become troops. The people are the starting point
for society, and society is the point at which the state begins. The people
are thus of major importance in terms of the victory or defeat of the state.
If we do not now come to the aid of the great Han people and wipe out the
Manchu bastards, we will assuredly earn the slander of foreigners. In the
north sit powerful Russia and majestic Great Britain. Our country faces
great dangers on that front. I seek no instant glory. I merely want to join
the troops in fighting northward, giving my life in pursuit of the enemy,
killing the Manchus. Only then will our Han race be avenged.

To confront the Qing forces, the Taipings had established a
women's army, which was organized by resolute peasant women
with considerable training in labor. By contrast, the women that
the revolutionaries were now trying to organize were middle class
and primarily students. There were apparently even some women
who had bound their feet previously. Were these women going to
be useful fighters?

This was a consideration for the most part beyond the consciousness of these women. As a whole they ignored the existing
physiological differences between men and women, the gender discrimination inflicted by society, and the self-restraint that women
themselves felt as the weaker sex. They considered themselves citizens of the nation before they were women. Furthermore, they
were not dealing with a long-established nation. As citizens of an
infant republic, they took it as incumbent upon themselves to resist
the forces of both imperialism and traditional Chinese social strictures. Most important, they felt, was to fight as individual soldiers.

Li Yuanhong accepted their later request and organized a

women's regiment. Perhaps as many as several hundred women signed up. Wu Shuqing led the troops, trained them, and conducted them in combat as well. In the fighting for Nanjing in particular, they reportedly adopted a stratagem to occupy the fort at Shizishan and thereby opened a route for the advance of the revolutionary army.

A number of women's forces were born in rapid succession. In Shanghai, there were a women's military guard, a women's northern expeditionary regiment, and a women's military training regiment. The women's northern expeditionary regiment was known by the name "Northern Expeditionary Dare-to-Die Regiment." Led by Shen Jingyin, who was then roughly twenty years of age, the troops numbered over seventy women soldiers.[21] Among them were many student volunteers from the Beiyang Number One Women's Normal School in Tianjin. These women had been stirred by Qiu Jin's death and had set their minds on participating in the revolution.

There had originally been a revolutionary group in Tianjin known as the Gonghehui (Republic Society) which was organized within the Women's Normal School. On its instructions, women students there helped transport pistols and ammunition to the revolutionary forces, knowing that the authorities did not check the packages of women visitors to the school. The principal, Wu Dingchang, tried to control the revolutionary activities of these women students by punishing those near to graduation. In response the students rose in a protest strike, and when the administration decided to push up the school vacation, the students moved to Shanghai en masse and joined the Northern Expeditionary Regiment.

Du Wei, an educational official in the landing forces of the Chinese navy, cooperated in training women's forces. He spent half of every day guiding them in rudimentary military knowledge, strategy, tactics, and live ammunition practice. After receiving this training, the Women's Northern Expeditionary Regiment proceeded to Nanjing and demanded that they participate in the fighting to the north. Soon thereafter, however, they were disbanded because a compromise was reached between the forces of Yuan Shikai in the north and those of Sun Yat-sen in the south.

Around the time of the Women's Northern Expeditionary Regiment in Shanghai, a similarly named group was organized in Guangzhou as well.[22] Like Shanghai, Guangzhou was an area in which women's activities were most vigorous. According to the memoirs of Zhao Liancheng, a member of the Revolutionary Alliance, the Alliance used the Girl's Practical School in Hong Kong to carry on revolutionary work. In addition to the Revolutionary Alliance slogans, they hoisted such placards there as "Oppose the despotism of the family," "Freedom of marriage," and "Oppose footbinding." They also engaged in direct propaganda work among the young women. Many young women, unable to bear the oppression of the traditional family, left their homes to join the revolutionary cause, and the Girls' Practical School became a center for receiving such women.

When news of the Wuchang Uprising reached Guangzhou, popular forces there rose in revolt too, and a group of women at the Girls' Practical School joined in as members of the southern branch of the Revolutionary Alliance in Hong Kong. These women walked the entire way to Guangzhou, refusing to ride in the palanquins specifically prepared for them. It was still extremely rare for women to participate as soldiers, and they were continually stared at with curious eyes that seemed to say, "If women are now rebelling, the world really has changed!"

After the capture of Guangdong, the Guangdong military government organized a Guangdong Northern Expeditionary Army, and the formation of the Women's Northern Expeditionary Regiment also began. However, because of poor weaponry and insufficient training, the Women's Regiment missed the departure of the first group of the Northern Expeditionary Army. Only five women, Zou Xingmin and four others, joined the first group of the Northern Expeditionary Army and were active in Red Cross work. Zou Xingmin claimed she was dissatisfied with working on the home front with the Red Cross, and she took an active part at the front lines in the fighting at Suzhou in February.

The more than twenty remaining women of the Northern Expeditionary Regiment—one-third of whom were teachers and students of the Girls' Practical School in Hong Kong—received short-term military instruction in equestrian strategy, shooting, and the like. According to Fernand Farjenel, author of *A travers la révolution chinoise*, who visited Canton at this time, the women in male uniforms who were receiving training on military parade grounds were burning with ardent enthusiasm, prepared to risk their lives in the battle for a new society. On February 22, 1912, the Northern Expeditionary Regiment set out for Nanjing from Guangzhou. But because of the north-south compromise, they returned home in April.

Roughly at the same time as the departure of the Guangzhou Northern Expeditionary forces, the Ministry of War ordered the dissolution of the Women's Army. The revolutionary forces had found wide popular support for their cause of eradicating the Manchus, and when they surrounded Nanjing and launched an attack on the troops of Zhang Xun, women fought right at the front lines. However, even though only women with "natural feet" were selected, women were considered physically unsuitable as soldiers; they were better placed as hospital nurses on the home front.

Women, for whom frailty was regarded as appropriate from the day of their birth, would not necessarily make good soldiers, it was widely argued. However comical or absurd it may have seemed at the time, there was no doubt at all that those women who did choose to become soldiers were expressing their deep revolutionary passion. Bai Wenwei, under whose command the Women's Army was placed, encouraged the troops under him by saying: "They may be women, but they are persevering in their patriotic enthusiasm." That even such supposedly frail women took up arms in the fight served as a great impetus to others. Even though women troops did not play a terribly important role as a fighting force, there can be little doubt that they provided a strong impulse to the revolutionary struggle overall.

Some women, such as Dr. Zhang Zhujun from Guangdong, did not concur in the organization of a Women's Army.[23] For that reason she put her technical capacities as a medical doctor to good use by organizing a Red Cross and working hard in relief activities on behalf of the wounded. She cared for over one thousand injured soldiers in the two-month period in which she was stationed in Hankou and Hanyang, and she subsequently saw to the needs of another thousand or more wounded troops when the rear guard moved from Zhenjiang to Nanjing. In addition, a women's brigade was active in preparing clothing and bedding for the wounded soldiers. Perhaps this was anticipated by Qiu Jin, who had translated "A Course in the Science of Nursing" (published serially by *Zhongguo nübao*). In any event Qiu Jin's dying wish had borne fruit in this form.

The Revolutionary Alliance had earlier constructed a bomb factory in Yokohama and invited some Russian anarchists to teach them how to make bombs. A number of women had participated in this work, including Qiu Jin, Fang Junying, Chen Xiefen, Lin Zongsu, Tang Qunying, Cai Hui, and Wu Mulan. Many of them had contacts in the Women's Army and took part in the women's suffrage movement.

Two of Qiu Jin's disciples, the sisters Yin Ruizhi and Yin Weijun, engaged in liaison work between the bomb making and the revolution.[24] Yin Ruizhi joined the Guangfuhui at the age of thirteen and with her younger sister did contact work for that organization, principally in Shanghai. Later they ran a school together, the Ruijun Academy, named after them both. It was ostensibly a cultural center where people read newspapers and magazines, but this was a camouflage, for in fact it housed the general headquarters of the Guangfuhui. At the time of the uprising in Shanghai in 1911, the command center of the army of the Guangfuhui was the Ruijun Academy.

After the Shanghai uprising, Yin Ruizhi helped produce bombs and was seriously injured by an explosion. She was thus unable to join the fighting in Nanjing, but her sister Yin Weijun played a major role in commanding the Dare-to-Die Corps. When a telegram reporting the revolt in Nanjing reached Shanghai, people lauded Weijun as a second "Maria," and she has been revered as a shining light in the history of the Republican Revolution ever since. ("Maria" was a woman fighter in the Italian popular movement; together with Garibaldi, she was honored as a pioneer of national liberation by revolutionaries in her day.)

In the midst of all this, it was the prostitutes of Shanghai who demonstrated the most tragic resolve in the gathering of intelligence. These women organized the Chinese Women's Espionage Training Institute[25] and tried to educate spies for the collection of intelligence. Requirements for entrance into this spying group were that one had to be between the ages of 16 and 30 and have some reading ability. Their manifesto read as follows:

We were unhappily born as women and have unhappily been forced into prostitution. Our lives have been very sad, but though we have ended up in brothels, if we look back to find the root cause of our situation, it is not because we are not descendants of the Yellow Emperor. Because we have not been given the advantages accorded others from birth, we must not die without having gained those advantages. Thus, we have chosen the kind of work that women in China's better families either cannot possibly do or would never consent to doing, and we have thus created a women's spying brigade. We pray that in some small way we may fulfill an obligation as one element of our nation's people. From the past we take as our model Liang Hongyu's beating of the drum, and more recently courtier Fei's stabbing a tiger. Ordinary women also have responsibilities in the world. What difference does occupation make when it is a question of duty?

In this way these women, trying to do their part for the revolutionary cause, used their unhappy circumstances as prostitutes to engage in spying activities, the kind of work impossible for the women of better families, where the concept of propriety remained quite strong. Liang Hongyu was the wife of Han Shizhong of the Song dynasty. When Han was fighting the Jurchen invaders, she was said to have beaten a drum as encouragement to the troops, preventing advances by the Jurchen troops. She too had been a prostitute. Courtier Fei was a palace lady in the late Ming court. Did she in fact really dazzle an invading Manchu "bandit" with her charms, then proceed to stab him and cut off her own head? It remains unclear.

In any case, there is in this prostitutes' manifesto both a sense of pride at being among the descendants of the Yellow Emperor, namely members of the Han race, and an intense hatred of the Qing dynasty, which had turned them into slaves of the Manchus. However, there is no animosity toward those who had actually turned these women into sexual slaves. Rather than living as individual human beings or individual women, in this manifesto they had chosen the path of living as one element of the nation. Perhaps in so doing, these women were at least redeeming their pride as human beings, despite the fact that in actuality they had not been allowed to enjoy life as such. Thus, while making full use of their situation as sexual slaves, these women tried to act as spies for the revolutionary cause. Their tragic determination illustrates the extraordinary awareness of these women who devoted their lives to the 1911 Revolution.

In the process of the Revolution, women tried to fulfill their obligation as one element of the population, principally in the sort of military activities described above. They believed that, if it was a question of uncovering information or of training body and spirit, men and women could display the same capacities in military or any other matters. Gender differences and femininity were irrelevent here. The revolution had liberated women's thought to this point.

For the women who took part in the military arena, their demand for rights—for the franchise—as citizens of a republic, was something self-evident. For that reason the women's movement developed as a suffrage movement after the establishment of the Republic of China. Women of the 1911 Revolution sought equal treatment in the military as well as the right to vote, for these were important elements, they believed, in gender equality.

The Women's Suffrage Movement

Following the victory of the Wuchang Uprising, the first organization to pursue the women's suffrage movement was Jiang Kanghu's Chinese Socialist Party.[26] Shortly after its founding, the party formed a Women's Suffrage Alliance in Shanghai in November 1911. At the center of it was Lin Zongsu, author of "Nüjie zhong xu" (Preface to *A tocsin for women*), who had called for an uprising of women.

The Women's Suffrage Alliance aimed, as its name indicated, at the enfranchisement of women. Its members, who were to be at least sixteen years old and "equipped with common sense," decided to promote their movement with the following slogans:

1. Reform the methods of women's education to achieve gender equality in the school curriculum and school system.
2. Create a suffrage institute, invite lecturers, and offer supplementary classes in politics and law.
3. Join various political organizations and associations.

4. Communicate to the provisional government our demand for the right to vote.

5. Make contacts with comrades in other countries for mutual support.

On the basis of these resolutions the Women's Suffrage Alliance soon began its activities.

First, Chairman Lin Zongsu, representing the Alliance's membership, went to Nanjing to visit Provisional President Sun Yatsen. She explained the state of the Chinese Socialist Party and the circumstances surrounding the creation of the Women's Suffrage Alliance. Sun Yat-sen at that time recognized women's suffrage as perfectly appropriate,[27] and he declared to Lin: "In the future, women's right to vote will surely be affirmed. Women too should gain knowledge of law and politics and strive to understand the truth about freedom and equality. Of course, opponents to women's suffrage may appear, but I will intervene on your behalf. I recognize that your association represents women comrades from the entire nation, and I fully respect your objectives." Having gained Sun Yat-sen's approval, Lin Zongsu published their conversation in a variety of newspapers. She believed that this agreement effectively achieved women's suffrage for the movement.[28]

On January 28, 1912, a parliament was established in Nanjing, and on February 7 deliberations began for a provisional constitution. To this parliament was presented a petition, "Letter from the Women of the Republic of China to the Parliament," which offered the following arguments. In the beginning, men and women together formed human society. Although there was a distinction between the roles of husband and wife, there was no differentiation in the respect each received. In the realm of obligations and rights, men and women were identical. However, the worthless Confucians raised their theory of the three bonds, and from then on women became enslaved to men. Now, the political revolution has succeeded, and the social revolution is about to follow. If you are to avoid the tragedies of a social revolution, you must establish social equality. To that end you must enact equality of the sexes and recognize women's right to vote. In the text of the constitution, you must specify an item that "Equality is uniform, regardless of sex; this appertains in the right to vote and the right to be elected to office." Even if this is not so specified in the text of the constitution, you can offer the supplementary explanation that, where the text speaks of equality of the people of the nation, it means to include both men and women, and you can then publish this explanation of the official text of the constitution as proof of women's right to vote.

Before this petition was sent to the Parliament, however, revolutionary forces in the south had compelled the Qing government to compromise, and on February 12, 1912, it issued an edict of abdication. The system of monarchic autocracy that had lasted two thousand years collapsed, and the first republic in Asia came into existence.

The Qing, however, was replaced in power not by the revolutionaries, but by Yuan Shikai, who ironically sought to revive the imperial system. As a result of the north-south compromise, Sun Yat-sen relinquished the provisional presidency to Yuan. On March 10, 1912, Yuan Shikai became provisional president of the Republic of China. On the following day the constitution of the new republic, the Provisional Constitution, was promulgated in Nanjing, proclaiming that sovereignty of the Republic of China belonged to the people as a whole and that *the people* had the freedoms of speech, publication, assembly, and association. This was China's first constitution to stipulate popular rights in law, and Sun Yat-sen and the revolutionaries tried to bind Yuan Shikai to this Provisional Constitution by law.

Were women actually included among "the people," to use the expression of the constitution? Article 5 of Section 2 (entitled "The People") of the Provisional Constitution read: "The people of the Republic of China are uniformly equal, without distinction as to race, class, or religion." It did not specify, as the women had earlier requested in their "Letter," that there was also to be no gender distinction. The request had been ignored. The women immediately organized and convened a conference of the Shenzhou Women's Assistance Society, where they appealed for the acquisition of women's suffrage and declared that they would begin activities devoted to the appropriate training of women as female citizens of the Republic of China.

One group of women was unhappy with this tepid approach. On March 19, 1912, when the parliament in Nanjing was deliberating on the issue of women's suffrage, they resorted to force.[29]

At 8:00 A.M. Tang Qunying and ten or more others from the Women's Suffrage Alliance, in "an armed state," broke in on the parliament. "Armed" probably meant that they were carrying pistols. The clerk in charge tried to show these women to the visitors' gallery, but they refused, rushed into the parliamentary chambers, and planted themselves down among the delegates. When the question of women's suffrage came up for discussion, they jeered so loudly that the proceedings could not continue.

At 11:30 the women withdrew for a while. When parliament reconvened in the afternoon, they again barged into chambers and occupied the entrances. The bell announcing the resumption of parliamentary session sounded, but the women blocked the delegates from entering. The speaker of the parliament called the guards into action and forced the women back into the visitors' gallery. At that point, a certain delegate addressed those assembled: "It is not necessarily the case that we in this hall disagree with women's right to the vote, but you must await the formal establishment of the parliament before that issue is resolved. When we observe women behaving in the present manner, we see that there are all sorts of women, and we may resolve to oppose you."

Yet another delegate stood up and detailed the history of the women's suffrage movement in Europe. And, criticizing the women's use of force, he declared: "One absolutely did not find such barbarous and illegal behavior on the part of women in civilized countries."

The Provisional Constitution was temporary by its very nature, and as a result of these debates the delegates promised to raise the issue as a topic for parliamentary deliberation again once the government was firmly established. At this, the women finally withdrew. We shall see later, though, just how halfheartedly this promise was carried out.

The next day, March 20, 1912, Tang Qunying and her cohorts again invaded the parliament. However, on this day they were anticipated by the parliament, which had taken stringent precautions to prevent them from entering parliamentary chambers. The women protested and broke the glass windows, drenching their hands in fresh blood. The guards who tried to keep them from entering were kicked and knocked to the ground.

At 9:00 A.M. of March 21, Tang Qunying and her associates for the third time broke in on the parliament in an "armed state." Sixty members of parliament were congregated there. Because parliament that day had taken strict precautions, Tang and her followers were unable to enter the main hall. Thus, the women went to the office of the president and sought an audience with Sun Yat-sen (who had relinquished this post eleven days earlier). Complaining that they had been repeatedly obstructed from entering parliamentary chambers, they demanded that they be protected with guards upon entrance there and that Sun Yat-sen attend a session of parliament and raise the issue of women's suffrage again. The Provisional Constitution provided that only the president could raise a proposal a second time.

Sun Yat-sen consented to mediate the two parties, and since the Women's Suffrage Alliance had presented their petition once, he agreed to return it to the parliamentary agenda. (Actually, however, once Sun Yat-sen had resigned the presidency, there was no reason to believe Yuan Shikai would ever have this issue brought up for discussion a second time).

The use of force was unprecedented for the women's suffrage movement. What drove the women to resort to such violence? In the previous few months, women had fought beside men equally on the battlefields, in their Red Cross activities, or in the collection of war funds. Had not Qiu Jin, above all, fought side-by-side with men in the revolution and given her life in the cause? This event had filled these women with a firm conviction, and once the revolution had succeeded they immediately burned with rage at anyone who sought to betray them. It is not too difficult to imagine why they were driven to radical action. For the first time contradictions of gender, which had scarcely been contemplated with the obligations of the revolution so prominent, now were plain to see.

At the same time, these women were strongly encouraged in their use of force by the radical women's suffrage movement far off in England. The Women's Social and Political Union, led by Emmeline Pankhurst, had adopted extreme tactics in the struggle for women's suffrage in Britain at that time.[30] Their strategy from 1905 to 1909 was to bombard members of Parliament with questions and to send delegates to sessions of Parliament, but in 1909 they adopted the public tactics of breaking windows and hunger strikes in prison. In 1911 Parliament passed a Franchise Bill that did not once mention women's suffrage, and their discontent exploded. Thus, in 1912, the same year these events were taking place in China, the tactics of the English suffragette movement escalated further, even to committing suicide in public. In particular, in early March of that year, windows in England were broken on a large scale. It was patently not the case, then, that "one absolutely did not find such barbarous and illegal behavior on the part of women in civilized countries."

Chinese newspapers and magazines reported almost hourly on the British women's suffrage movement. The smashing of windows and protests before parliament by Chinese women was a result of a conscious emulation of their English counterparts. That Chinese women had resorted to the use of force eventually was conveyed across the seas to England, and the Women's Social and Political Union sent the following message praising their bold actions: "The radical English group that demands the franchise expresses its respect for the courageous actions of the Chinese women. In addition we hope that you will achieve success in opposing male monopolization of the franchise and that with the establishment of the Republic of China the enjoyment of political rights for women will become the model for the civilized world."[31]

The radical tactics adopted by the English suffrage movement were already being criticized from all sides. They provided a tremendous stimulus in the use of force, though, for Chinese women in an era when the 1911 Revolution had been successful but the pathway to politics had been closed to women. Yet, as women were becoming more conspicuous through the suffrage movement, the political arena in which they sought a role was moving more and more in an antirevolutionary direction. It was on April 1, 1912, that the man in whom the women activists had placed such hopes, Sun Yat-sen, announced his resignation; on April 5 it was decided that the Nanjing provisional government was to be disbanded and the parliament moved to Beijing. Thus, the revolutionary government transferred all control into the hands of Yuan Shikai. The future for women was to be difficult indeed.

After the defeat of the Nanjing parliament, a group of women's rights groups came together in Nanjing on April 8 to reorganize the Women's Suffrage Alliance. Among these groups from a variety of places in China were the Women's Suffrage Alliance of the Chinese Socialist Party, the Women's Assistance Society, the Women's Military Society, the Jinling Women's Union, and the Women's National Society of Hunan. These women's rights associations merged out of their desire to have one united organization to promote the movement for women's suffrage. The new Women's Suffrage Alliance adopted a nine-point resolution.

1. Equal rights for men and women.
2. Spread of women's education and facilities for it.
3. Improvement in the position of women in the home.
4. Monogamy.
5. Freedom in marriage and a ban on divorce without reason.
6. Encouragement of careers for women.
7. A ban on the keeping of concubines and the buying and selling of women.
8. Improvement in the political position of women.
9. Reform of the licensed prostitution system (which, it is worth noting, had not been abolished).

These demands for gender equality had never previously been brought together by women's groups. One might imagine that the defeat of the women's suffrage movement caused them to turn their attention to specifically feminist demands. However, the actual activities of the Women's Suffrage Alliance remained thoroughly tied to obtaining the franchise for women.

In March the Revolutionary Alliance, the organization that had propelled the 1911 Revolution, became a public political party, and to that end it affirmed a pledge to "stabilize the Republic of China" and to "realize the principle of People's Livelihood." At the same time, it adopted a political program from the nine-point resolution, including "equal rights for men and women" (point 1). The principle of people's livelihood was aimed at the "equalization of land rights"—that is, fixing the present value of land—and the return to the state of all future increases in its value. Subjectively this sought to overcome the economic inequality at the root of capitalism and all at once to realize socialism. Also, "equal rights for men and women" aimed at recognizing the equality of all human beings in a republic and at acquiring political equality for all, including women. With its pledge and its program for economic and political equality, the Revolutionary Alliance assumed the posture of deepening the revolution.

Meanwhile, deliberations aimed at the formal inauguration of a parliament—over laws concerning the composition of the parliament and the election of delegates to an upper and lower house—were being conducted. The Women's Suffrage Alliance, however, could not find a representative to introduce their resolution. On August 10, 1912, an election law for delegates to the lower house was promulgated; it stipulated that only male citizens of the Republic of China, minimum age 21, who had been living in their election districts for at least two years, with certain property and educational restrictions as well, could vote.

At the same time the Revolutionary Alliance was reorganized into the Nationalist Party (Guomindang). Considering the revolution to be over, it now began planning to expand its influence as a political party within the parliament. To that end it merged with such groups as the Unified Republican Party (Tongyi gonghedang), the National Progress Society (Guomin gongjinhui), and the Republican Real Progress Society (Gonghe shijinhui). This marks the Revolutionary Alliance's abandonment of its role as a revolutionary association; for, as a result of its compromise with right-wing political parties, the level of its principles and policies dropped. Two items were then expunged from the party program: the principle of people's livelihood and equal rights for men and women.

The conference at which an amalgamated Guomindang was formed took place on August 25. Three to four thousand persons attended, of whom forty or fifty were women. The temporary chairman responsible for running the proceedings was Zhang Ji, who had introduced the women's petition to the assembly. From the very start the floor of the conference was in an uproar over the issue of "equal rights for men and women."

First, Zheng Shidao (a man) asked for an explanation of why the article of "equal rights for men and women" had been excised. Then, Tang Qunying, Wang Changguo, and Fu Wenyu each in turn asked questions. In response Zhang Ji and others explained that "inasmuch as even members of the Revolutionary Alliance are not equal, it was only natural that voting rights for men and women not be equal." The conference then fell into complete chaos. At that point, in order to save the situation, Zhang Ji took down a piece of paper on which was written in large characters "equal rights for men and women," and he asked the entire assembled body whether this item should be included in the party program. In the ensuing commotion only thirty or forty people raised their hands, and "equal rights for men and women" was buried by an overwhelming majority.

Finally, Sun Yat-sen rose to deliver a speech. Touching on the issue of "equal rights for men and women," he explained that this item had not been included in the new program because the various parties with which the Guomindang had merged did not agree with it. He concluded, however, that "equal rights for men and women" was fully in line with the truth and that if the civilization of the nation was to progress, it had to realize this principle.

The fact that the principle of people's livelihood and equal rights for men and women were removed from the party platform because of the Guomindang reorganization is extremely interesting, for just like people's livelihood, equal rights for the sexes was something these various political groupings feared was linked to social change. In the process of the revolution, one group had already heightened their wariness with respect to the "equalization of land rights." The Gongjinhui changed "equalization of land rights" to the "equalization of human rights," and the general body of the Revolutionary Alliance's center dropped this slogan altogether. Yet, it became evident that "equalization of human rights" in fact was only "equalization of male rights," and "equalization of male rights" meant only the rights of men selected from a minority by virtue of property and education.

While the principles of people's livelihood and equal rights for men and women appear unrelated at first glance, in fact they both had to be removed because they were regarded as linked to the transformation of society as a whole. "Equal rights for men and women" was never only a gender question, for it was connected both to the reality of men's rights and to the essence of political and economic equality of all people.

Later, in November, the Women's Suffrage Alliance again filed a petition, but this time debate ensued over whether or not to consider it. In the end, the members of the upper house decided not even to entertain it for discussion because they could not constitutionally raise this issue for deliberation a second time and because of the insulting language referring to the upper house that ran throughout the petition. And, just as planned, elections aimed at the establishment of a formal parliament began.

The Guomindang, with its policies watered down, won an overwhelming victory in the elections and commanded a definite majority in the parliament. Circumstances seemed to be moving forward just as Song Jiaoren, a leader of the Guomindang, had anticipated, when in March 1913 he was assassinated in Shanghai by one of Yuan Shikai's henchmen. Even with their great electoral victory, the Guomindang still had not defeated the brute force of counterrevolution. Song's death spelled the complete bankruptcy of the right-wing parliamentarist line and, at the same time the defeat of the women's suffrage movement, which had sought gender equality within the structure of parliamentary rules. In November 1913 an order for the dissolution of the Women's Suffrage Alliance was issued by the government and its eleven provincial branches were disbanded. The women's suffrage movement, which had lasted for over a year, came to an end for the time being in the midst of the defeat of the revolution itself.

The First Women Delegates to the Guangdong Assembly

Before these last events, the public trial of Mrs. Pankhurst over the window-breaking incident in March of 1913 began in the Central Criminal Court of England. Arguing the propriety of women's suffrage in a reasoned fashion, she appealed from the dock: "Is there anything more marvellous in modern times than the kind of spontaneous outburst in every country of this women's movement? Even in China—and I think it somewhat of a disgrace to Englishmen— even in China women have won the vote, as an outcome of a successful revolution." The source for her information about China is unknown, and needless to say Chinese women had not been able to enter politics at the national parliamentary level. However, China's first women delegates were in attendance at the provincial assembly of Guangdong.[32]

The province of Guangdong had been one of the revolutionary centers. Under the leadership of the Revolutionary Alliance, a military government was organized there, and Hu Hanmin assumed the position of provincial military governor. At a conference of representatives from various groups that convened at the end of 1911, abridged regulations for the provisional assembly of Guangdong were set down. Before this took place, women there had organized a study group on women's rights and continued their movement for the legal enactment of gender equality; and the abridged regulations enacted on this occasion for the most part satisfied the demands of these women. For example, the only requirements for delegates to the Guangdong provincial assembly were that one be a minimum age of 21 and either a native to Guangdong or a Chinese resident there for at least the previous five years; there were no restrictions on the basis of property, education, or sex, as there were in the national franchise law.

In addition, this election, coming as it did on the heels of the Revolution, had a certain transitional quality: various spheres were allocated a specific number of delegates, and each group elected its delegates. As a result, of the total 165 representatives to the assembly, ten positions were allocated to women. These ten, each elected by various women's groups, included Zhuang Hanqiao (a teacher at the Girls' Practical School in Hong Kong and bomb commander in the Revolutionary Alliance), Li Peilan (of overseas Chinese origin), and Zhang Yuan (a principal of a girls' normal school). This marked the first appearance in Chinese history of women delegates and, it is perhaps needless to say, the first instance of elected women delegates in Asia.

In the provisional constitution for the province of Guangdong, gender equality was clearly codified. Article 2, Section 3 stipulated that all of "the people are uniformly equal." And Article 8, Section 47, stated that "the people as designated in this constitution includes both men and women." The demands of the Women's Suffrage Alliance at the time of the enactment of the national provisional constitution were fulfilled in the provisional constitution of Guangdong.

Women's right to vote at this time was recognized in only a handful of countries around the world, including New Zealand, Australia, and Finland. Even such developed nations as England and France had still not given women the franchise. Thus, the appearance of women delegates in Guangdong was quite a newsworthy event. Despite this, Chinese women still did not have the right to vote at the national level, and hence the position of these women representatives in Guangdong was extremely tenuous. Then, with the promulgation of the provincial assembly election law on September 4, 1912, women delegates in Guangdong were excluded from the provincial assembly.

Having once had the franchise in hand, the women of Guangdong naturally resisted this new law. It was inordinately unfair, they argued, to have used women at the time of the revolution only to revoke sexual equality once the revolution had succeeded. The demand was voiced to the provincial assembly that its upper house request the admission of women delegates, as had been the case in Guangdong, in each provincial assembly. This proposal was defeated by a margin of 65 votes to 38, and the franchise for Guangdong women, the first in Chinese history, vanished.

Thereafter, the counterrevolution marched forward and outlawed women's activities altogether. In March 1914 "Police Regulations on Public Order" (following the example in Japan) were issued, and women's admission into political associations and their participation in political campaign meetings were forbidden. The ban extended to the private Women's Legal and Political Academy, which also received an order to shut down. The authorities dreaded the possibilities unleashed by women obtaining political education, women who were supposed to cultivate the knowledge and skills appropriate to becoming good wives and mothers. And the national and international concerns of women who had arisen like a flood tide in the course of the revolution were completely frustrated.

We can trace the women's movement in the period of the 1911 Revolution—from the Wuchang Uprising to the second revolution of 1913—as it developed from military activities to a women's suffrage movement. While the 1898 Reform Movement had advocated the emancipation of women for the purposes of modernization, we can count scarcely a single woman activist. The 1911 Revolution, however, produced a small group of women activists who participated alongside men and engaged in the same sort of activities.

Behind this impressive activity of a minority of Chinese women, 200 million ordinary women lived under diverse conditions that prevented them from becoming active even had they desired to do so. Because of the strictures of the family system, women lacked the freedom to live according to their own designs. The 1911 Revolution overturned the autocratic dynasties of the previous two thousand years, but it did not touch the autocracy to be found in countless families throughout China, and it was extremely rare then for anyone to be conscious of this fact.

Revolutionaries in the period of the 1911 Revolution saw the family primarily as something from which to be extricated. Father, mother, wife—these were merely roles to be overcome. One apocryphal account tells of the wife of Hubei revolutionary Yang Yuru who committed suicide because she feared she would become an impediment to her revolutionary husband;[33] this story, however unreliable, symbolizes the tragic conclusion to which such logic extended. Women were expected to die in the cause of the revolution if they fought beside the men or, if they did not fight, to deny their own existence. In fact, to put it bluntly, there was no room for women to exist as individual human beings in service to the nation. For those ordinary women—women who were not the sort to commit suicide because of their inability to participate in the revolution—the Revolution of 1911 brought an objective awareness of the actual circumstances confronting women, though it was unable to provide them with the strength to forge their own pathway through those circumstances.

中
國
婦
女

FIVE

Casting Off the Shackles of the Family

The "Two Bonds" and "Four Relationships" Undermined

As we have seen, the Revolution of 1911, which overthrew two thousand years of autocratic rule in China, almost immediately took a reactionary turn under the leadership of Yuan Shikai. In 1913 Li Liejun, the military governor of Jiangxi, led a movement to oust Yuan and started what became known as the Second Revolution, but this uprising could not hold out for even two months. Sun Yat-sen and his revolutionary faction became refugees, and the women who had participated in the "revolution outside the family" had no choice but to return once more to families where they no longer had a place. Wrote one of these women to a friend: "There is no way to revolt against the autocracy of the family; the only way to escape the point of its sword is to run away." In the depths of their despair, some women threw themselves into lakes and drowned; others entered Buddhist convents.[1]

The darkness of that era cast a particularly deep shadow over women. However gloomy things seemed, though, the significant fact remained: two thousand years of authoritarian rule had ended. The 1911 Revolution had undermined both the traditional structure of gender discrimination and the value system that supported it. The scholar and writer Wu Yu (1872–1949) described the temper of his time in this way: "In the Republican era, the gentry class has smashed the three bonds and the five relationships, which were once held in awe as heavenly laws and earthly duties. Now all that remains are two bonds and four relationships. . . . And," he continued, "the foundation of these two bonds and four relationships is being profoundly shaken."

The "three bonds" and the "five relationships" supplied the groundwork for traditional Chinese morality. They consisted of the ties that bound subject to ruler, son to father, and wife to husband, together with the relationships between father and son, ruler and subject, husband and wife, elder and younger brother, and friend and friend. With the exception of the relationship between friends, all these bonds placed individuals in a hierarchy of superiority and subordination. As Wu pointed out, with the overthrow of the Qing dynasty, the cornerstone of the five relationships—the relationship between ruler and subject—had been torn away, leaving only "two bonds" and "four relationships." As a result, the raison d'être of these remaining principles was also called into question. That, he argued, spelled the ruin of the entire traditional value system.

It is widely acknowledged that traditional Chinese kinship was a patrilineal joint family system. The authority of the family head was absolute, and the entire family structure was based on hierarchical kin relationships between father and son, husband and wife, and elders and youth. Thus, the family unilaterally imposed a moral code of deference and submission on those who occupied subordinate positions within it. Moreover, the foremost aim of this family system was the perpetuation of the male line of descent, and in order to ensure the purity of that line, female chastity was rigidly enforced on the one hand, and a system of plural wives to facilitate the birth of many sons was widely adopted on the other. (Female children were not counted as heirs—only male children.) Sexual discrimination therefore lay at the very heart of the family system because a gender hierarchy was built into its structure.

The servile morality fostered in such a kinship system, according to Wu Yu, supplied the ideological foundation ensuring that no peasant would ever rise in opposition to his landlord. Moral standards inculcated by the family served as a cloak to mask the conflicts between landlord and tenant. As a result, family morality provided the foundation that had enabled prolonged domination of peasants by landlords, and the lengthy period of autocratic monarchy in China as a whole.

The fall of the Qing dynasty in the 1911 Revolution, however, brought the morality of China's traditional kinship system under attack as well. The youth of the May Fourth Movement found themselves in a new environment, the Republic of China, which had been laid open for them by the Revolution, and they sought to clear away the despair and gloom of that time. Bringing down autocratic rule, which had been the root cause of the republican movement, brought with it no less than a total transformation of every human being who supported the structure of autocracy. Such were the origins of the May Fourth and New Culture Movements.

In 1915, the journal *Xin qingnian* (New youth) declared its rejection of all things "servile, conservative, retiring, isolationist, formalistic, and imaginary, " and proposed that as a guiding principle young people embrace everything that was "independent, progressive, assertive, cosmopolitan, utilitarian, and scientific."[2] The loathsome qualities that had to be eliminated were all Eastern; the admirable qualities that had to be adopted were all Western. Writers for *New Youth* set East and West in direct opposition to each other, and they insisted that the fundamental principles of familism in the old patriarchal society had permeated both the Chinese family and the Chinese nation, which acted together to oppress the individual. Compared with the individual in the West, an individual in the patrilineal society of the East was no more than a slave to the dictates of the three bonds. His or her own individual identity was obliterated. For two thousand years, every man and woman had been forced into this slavery. Whether as a subject, or as a son, or as a wife, *everyone was a slave*. This was the painful realization youth came to at the time.

What, after all, was this family system that nurtured slavery? It was Wu Yu who tackled this question directly, and it was he who wrote most perceptively about the mutual reinforcement of authoritarian structures and the family system. His essay, entitled "The Family System is the Foundation of Authoritarianism" (published in *New Youth* in 1916),[3] set forth a detailed analysis of the reasons why the family system was "intimately bound up" with the structure of despotism, for which the family in turn endlessly reproduced the right kinds of people. Accordingly to Wu, Confucian thought and the forms of action and behavior it required were entirely summed up in the two ancient classical texts: the *Chunqiu* (Spring and Autumn Annals) and the *Xiaojing* (Classic of Filial

Piety). The *Spring and Autumn Annals* clearly described the hierarchical relationship between ruler and subject, between domination and subordination. The *Classic of Filial Piety*, which regarded filiality as the essence of morality and virtue and the fundamental principle of education, depicted the proper mode of behavior before one's ruler and one's parents. Thus, the two—authoritarian structures and the family system—were inseparable.

The reason was that "family morality" demanded unlimited subservience toward superiors, and this servile moral code—one that required filiality (*xiao*) toward one's father and respect (*ti*) for one's elder brother—permitted no defiance of one's superiors. Such conditions made rebellion unthinkable, and day by day over time they fostered a slave-like mentality. It was a moral code conducive precisely to maintaining the structure of the autocratic monarchy and to preventing rebellion. Consequently, rulers took wholehearted advantage of this family morality of "filiality and respect," and the two words "filial" and "respectful" had, in Wu Yu's view, became the fundamental bonds joining an authoritarian government with the family system over the previous two thousand years. Confucian family morality—that is, this ideology of inequality—which had been so extensively utilized in this way by autocratic rulers, was precisely the reason China had remained for so long a familistic society, unable to develop into a modern nation-state. It was a national disaster more fearful than flood or pestilence.

So wrote Wu Yu. With these arguments, he explained how, of the three bonds and five relationships that formed the basis of traditional Chinese morality, the moral code governing ruler and subject and that governing father and son (as well as elder and younger brothers) had a mutually reinforcing, complementary relationship. The family system had been used as an instrument of authoritarian control, and the servile morality that it had nurtured in the populace over time was the single factor most responsible for two thousand years of acquiescence under despotic rule. Filiality was the establishment's ideology for producing a people submissive toward authority; the family system was nothing more than the means of production (and reproduction) of such a people.

Wu Yu's attack on the family system was inspired by ideas of individualism of Western bourgeois thinkers such as Mill, Spencer, and Montesquieu. However, Wu was not using Western individualism to criticize Eastern familism. Instead, he endowed with new meaning certain values and patterns of Chinese thought outside the Confucian tradition; and by a critical comparison with these non-Confucian values, he revealed how Confucianists had become so closely intertwined with political authority and Confucianism an ideology of control. Thus, he concentrated his energies on exposing in minute detail the ideological functions of Confucianism: as a guardian of the "class" system (naturally by "class" he meant the social hierarchy with the monarch at the top, and not "class" in its social scientific sense) in which the family system played a distinct role. As Hu Shi once put it, Wu Yu served as the "street cleaner" for the old patterns of Chinese thought.

"Virtuous Women" and Nora

Although Wu Yu launched a frontal assault on the traditional family system, his critique did not probe deeply to the roots of the gender inequality inherent in the role prescribed by the autocratic state and by the family. The person who pressed such questions most sharply was Lu Xun.[4] Lu Xun published a number of essays in *New Youth*, among them a piece entitled "My Views on Chastity." In this essay he vigorously attacked the ideas of "chastity" and "virtue" that had been considered a woman's highest moral behavior in the past.

"Chastity," he noted in this essay, referred to a woman "who does not remarry or run off with a lover after her husband's death." "Virtue" implied that she "kill herself when her husband or fiancé dies" or "commit suicide when confronted by a rapist or meet her death while resisting." Even in the Republican period, a woman's "chastity" was still being rewarded. Or, to put it more accurately, precisely because it was the era of the Republic, it was necessary to recognize "chastity" and "virtuousness" in order to repair the unraveling ties that might still hold the family system together and to support and maintain the social order.

Lu Xun went on to make the following historical observations about the glorification of "chastity."

The more loyalty the emperor demanded of his subjects, the more chastity the men required of the women. . . . When the country is about to be subjugated, there is much talk of chastity, and women who take their own lives are highly regarded. For women belong to men, and when a man dies his wife should not remarry; much less should she be snatched from him during his life. But since he himself is one of a conquered people, with no power to protect his wife and no courage to resist, he finds a way out by urging her to kill herself.

The references to a subjugated people in this passage point to China's 260 years of rule by the alien Manchus. Certainly, the Qing dynasty, in which a Manchu minority had to establish its predominance over the Han people, made extensive use of Confucian ideology to strengthen the hierarchical order of society.

Under these conditions, as oppression from above increased and social hierarchy was strengthened, the effect was also to enforce the control of men over women. "Subjugated" men sought an object on which to pass the oppression they felt and their own complicity in it. "Chastity"—the emblem of women's oppression—was the indirect result of the oppression of *men*. The oppression of subjects by the ruler led inevitably to the oppression of women by men; what rulers demanded of their subjects—loyalty—led to the demand for chastity that husbands made of their wives.

Women, however, had no object upon which to pass these demands further. As a result, they raised not a single question about what Lu Xun called this "warped morality"—warped even in its spirit—that had been forced on them. Discrimination tended to be completely internalized by women. In scathing terms, Lu Xun condemned the society that had given rise to this "warped morality" and the ignorance and brutality of the men who forced it upon women.

Lu Xun brilliantly depicted the sadness of such women in his fictional writings. Consider as an example one of his characters, Xiang Lin's Wife, who appears in the story "The New Year's Sacrifice." After her husband dies, she goes to work as a maid in the household of "Fourth Uncle Lu" in Luzhen (Lu village). One day, she is seized and, without being told where she is going, taken to a home deep in the mountains. There she is sold by her mother-in-law as a bride and forced to remarry.

Xiang Lin's Wife, weeping and cursing as if her throat were being crushed in the bridal sedan-chair, strikes her head on the corner of the ancestral altar during the marriage ceremony to protest her fate, but all to no avail. As it turns out, her new husband is a hard worker, and they are blessed with a son, so that for a time it appears that her second match has been a fortunate one. But this good fortune is not to last. Her second husband dies of typhoid fever; her beloved son is eaten by a wolf; and the woman, a shadow of her former self, returns to the Lu household.

But the villagers believe that a twice-married woman is polluted, and when she dies and goes to hell, the King of Hell will take a saw and cut her in two so that each of her former husbands can have his share of her. As atonement for her sins, Xiang Lin's Wife pledges to donate all her earnings for one year to the city god's temple. But the people continue to look coldly on this "polluted" woman, and she is still not allowed to participate in the New Year's festival. Thus, she becomes a beggar, wandering and stopping everyone she meets to ask: "After a person dies, does he turn into a ghost or not? . . . Then there must also be a Hell?" Finally, she collapses and dies in the street.

The solitary death of Xiang Lin's Wife, surrounded by the village festivities for the New Year, beautifully captured the tragedy of a woman murdered by the virtue of so-called "chastity." She never protested the idea of chastity; striving to live a chaste life, she was in fact destroyed by it, and that makes her tragedy even more poignant. A woman like Xiang Lin's Wife, although she had no exposure to Confucian education, was nonetheless raised according to Confucian morality; she could not escape the pernicious influence of "chastity" in the eyes of the world and in the eyes of the city god. That deity represented precisely the dominance of religious authority to which Mao Zedong was referring in a passage to be discussed below.

In June 1918 *New Youth* published a special issue on the Norwegian dramatist Henrik Ibsen, and Hu Shi penned the lead essay, entitled "Ibsenism." It included translations of *A Doll's House*, *An Enemy of the People*, and *Little Eyolf*, along with a biography of Ibsen. (*A Doll's House* was first performed in Japan about seven years earlier and starred the renowned actress Matsui Sumako).[5]

A Doll's House made a tremendous impression on young people. Soon after it appeared in translation, it was performed on stage around China, where lines such as "don't become a man's plaything," "recognize individuality," and "demand freedom" created a sensation. Young people, deprived of free aspirations and individuality and living as if they were so many discrete dolls within a joint family system suffused with falsehood and hypocrisy, saw in Nora not just a woman, but an individual human being. More specifically, in the figure of this woman leaving her family, they may have seen themselves being liberated from the family system itself.

Later, as the title of an essay, Lu Xun posed the question: "What Happens to Nora After She Leaves Home?" He speculated that only one of two things could happen to her: either she would sink into depravity or she would return to her family. This led him to recognize the importance of women's economic independence. Then, in his short story, "Regret for the Past," he described the death of a woman named Shijun, who had left her family for her lover but had to return to her parents when her romance failed. Shijun had been one of the "new women" who talked about Ibsen with her lover. But in the character of Shijun, who—unlike Nora—failed to extricate herself from the family and was forced instead to return to her parents, we can see Lu Xun's vigorous efforts to confront directly the fate of women fleeing one family, then another.

In November 1919 the suicide of a bride named Zhao Wuzhen in Hunan province was widely reported in the press.[6] This event sent shock waves through the country; a young bride, protesting the marriage her parents had arranged for her, had stabbed herself to death in her bridal carriage with a dagger. In his story "A Madman's Diary" (published in *New Youth*), Lu Xun once wrote: "Our education in the rules of propriety is an education that eats people alive." This is precisely what had happened in the tragedy that befell Miss Zhao.

At the time of the incident, Mao Zedong was living in Changsha, the capital of Hunan. Upon reading the news report in the Changsha papers, he immediately wrote an essay entitled "A Critique of Miss Zhao's Suicide," which provoked a storm of indignation as people discussed her death. In the ten days that followed, Mao published seven articles in the leading Changsha daily *Dagongbao*; and scores of commentaries were reported to have poured in to the newspaper office from all parts of the country. From this outpouring we can judge how profoundly concerned young people of the time were about freedom in love and marriage.

In the fiery articles he wrote in the aftermath of the suicide, Mao blamed Miss Zhao's parents for forcing her into a marriage against her wishes, placing responsibility for her death squarely on their shoulders: "All parents who are like Miss Zhao's should be thrown in jail." At the same time, though, he emphasized that the ultimate cause of their criminal act lay in the society that enforced a marriage system so benighted and so barbaric. As long as such a society remained intact, he pointed out, even if Miss Zhao had taken an activist stance and left her family, what awaited her were only "rejection," "scorn," and "ridicule": "Because the causes of Miss Zhao's suicide lie in society itself, such a society is extremely dangerous. If it could kill Miss Zhao, it can also kill Miss Qian and Miss Sun and Miss Li, can't it? If it can kill women, can't it also kill men?" Qian, Sun, and Li are surnames found throughout China. Mao Zedong understood that society's threat to Miss Zhao was a threat to all women and to all men. The young people who collectively suffered the oppression of the family thus experienced the death of one young woman as their own pain, and they joined to forge a solidarity in opposition to their society.

A still more explicit statement of the attitude of young people of the May Fourth generation appears in the following excerpt from an essay by Li Dazhao entitled "Women's Liberation and Democracy": "True democracy is only realized with the liberation of women. If women are not liberated, there can be no genuine democracy. . . . There is a potential for transformation in all classes of society; it is only in the single relationship between a man and a woman that a permanent barrier exists, and one which is impossible to move. Therefore democracy between the sexes is our first and foremost priority."[7]

Without a doubt, women's liberation formed an essential part of the democracy these young people sought. Journals such as *New Youth*, *Xin chao* (New tide), and *Jiefang yu gaizao* (Emancipation and reconstruction) all debated "the woman question" and "the family question." In women's magazines too—*Funü zazhi* (Ladies' journal) and the avant-garde *Funü pinglun* (Women's critic)[8]—writers such as Chen Wangdao, Mao Dun, and other vibrant spirits contributed polemical articles that demonstrate how the youth of the May Fourth generation made the woman question their own personal question.

Freedom in Love

In the May Fourth era, young people worshipped romantic love. An example is the essay entitled "Independent Love" by Gao Xian.[9] What did he mean by "independent" love? According to Gao, the two most fundamental human needs were love and hunger—that is, the acts of loving and of eating. Of the two, he argued, love was more basic, because the act of eating was essentially a technique or a method. However, as it turned out, the order of these two basic needs had been reversed, and hunger—a means to an end— had actually become the dominant driving force in human life.

How had this come to pass? Because without jobs, women were unable to support themselves, and so they of necessity had become dependent on their husbands. To obtain support from their husbands, they gave their bodies; for them, marriage was the same as prostitution. In fact, marriage without love was nothing more than long-term prostitution. In this way, young people of that era, like Gao Xian, bitterly criticized the hypocrisy of the traditional Chinese marriage system.[10]

How was one to purge marriage of this taint of "sex for hire?" To remove the mercenary aspect of marriage, argued Gao, marriage had to be based on romantic love, and that in turn required that women be able to work and support themselves. As long as a woman remained dependent on her husband for support, "independent love" was impossible; when women became self-supporting— that is, when women had their own jobs—then and only then, Gao insisted, would sex for sale end and marriage based on genuine love become possible.

Even if one married for love, though, love was extremely difficult to sustain over a long period of time; thus, arguments such as these inevitably gave rise to a critique of the system of marriage itself. Many intellectuals were influenced by the anarchists' attack not only on the traditional joint family system but on the nuclear family as well. An example is the essay, "On the Problem of Abolishing Marriage," by Shi Cuntong.

According to Shi, the "family" was the root of all evil, and it came into being because of the Chinese system of marriage. Originally, individuals were not bound to one another by any political, coercive, religious, or formal structures; instead, they lived in absolute freedom. The family was the mechanism whereby these absolutely free individuals were brought into bondage. Even assuming that a marriage was based on true love and was not contracted for the traditional purpose of joining one family to another, then—disregarding the problem of keeping love alive—any marriage still meant that one specific person monopolized the emotional and sexual love of another. No individual, argued Shi, should be attached to another individual in this way. Hence, the anarchists called for the abolition of marriage—namely, the dissolution of the nuclear family.

Essays like Shi's on abolishing the family formed a piece with another theme at the time: public day care for children. This theme involved the debate about whether children should be taken from the home and placed in public day-care facilities, such as nursery schools. However, day care was not simply a children's issue. The controversy developed in the context of a debate about whether the family should be dissolved, and so it was connected to the attack on the family.

One important figure in this debate was Yun Daiying. He too was an ardent supporter of the attack on the family, but he envisioned a system of both free marriage based on love and free divorce. Only when freedom of divorce was achieved, he argued, would there be any protection for a married life based on genuine love. People who opposed public child care, he said, maintained that family life was highly refined and based on pure love; in fact, as long as a woman had to take care of children day and night, could not support herself, had no choice but to remain utterly patient, and could never get a divorce—how could anybody call this a "life of love?" Marriages in which emotional love no longer existed, Yun argued, had to be dissolved immediately; and that made solving the child-care question all the more urgent, for child care ensured freedom of divorce.

In making his argument, Yun stressed that the "family" had not existed since the time of primitive society, but rather had come into being for the first time at a specific stage in history. Thus, the family as a social form was neither necessary nor inevitable. Moreover, at the present time the family was playing a negative role by providing children with an inferior education: in the family system, children were raised to suppress their individuality. This made public day care necessary for the benefit of the children as well.

Yun Daiying was not the only one to put forward the argument that children should be rescued from the evil influence of the family. It was echoed loudly by other young people at the time. After the age-old family had been destroyed, they believed, children could be raised according to purely nurturant techniques—for anarchists had faith in science. Their ideal plans envisioned children raised in nursery schools that were scientifically programmed and staffed by nursery school teachers well trained in child development.

This is how the theme of public child care, which originally sought a way to save children from the pernicious influence of the family system, contributed to the debate over the abolition as well as the very significance of the family. Adopting an extreme position in support of the dissolution of the family led other young people to call for a still more radical reexamination of the meaning of the family. Thus, in expanding the realm of individual freedom, the anarchists proved to be a vigorous inspiration for a spirit that rebelled against both family and society.

In contrast to those people who, under the influence of anarchism, moved from small-scale issues like the family all the way to larger questions about the transformation of society as a whole, the Marxists moved from a broad consideration of society as a whole to focus on the narrower "woman question." The following two paragraphs are a summary of Li Hanjun's essay, "The Key to the Woman Question."

First of all, human survival involves the preservation of the individual and the preservation of the race. For the preservation of the individual, it is necessary to produce the necessities of life; these are the fruits of the labor of workers in production. The preservation of the race requires bearing and rearing children, and these are unavoidably tasks borne by women. However, both productive laborers and women are controlled by people who do not produce, nor give birth, nor nurture. This is the result of economic exploitation, and it is one of the roots of women's oppression.

The bourgeoisie, Li continued, believes that women have lost their economic independence because of political, legal, educational, and occupational inequality. Therefore, it seeks gender equality first. But its way of thinking confuses cause and effect. We of the proletariat believe that when women lost their economic independence, they also lost—as a result—their equality with men in politics, law, education, and jobs. Women lost their economic independence because of society's exploitative system of private property. When private property is abolished, therefore, women will be able for the first time to achieve equality in politics, law, education, and jobs. The economic independence we advocate will mean that every man and every woman will have the right to live and to work, and that no one, during his or her lifetime, will rule or be ruled by others. In fact, the existence of a proletariat that labors in production makes possible both a ruling class which controls the lives of people and an underclass which will liberate society through its own efforts.

People influenced by Marxism in this way went far beyond the others by arguing that sexual discrimination did not derive from individual gender relations, but rather from the structures of private property and class rule. Here was a concrete definition of that "society" condemned by Mao Zedong as the murderer of Zhao Wuzhen. The women's liberation movement after May Fourth—particularly after the establishment of the Chinese Communist Party in 1921—began to wage a war, seeking the abolition of private property and the destruction of class rule, in order to revolutionize a society steeped in sexual discrimination. Li Hanjun and the other youth of the May Fourth era, however, ultimately failed to understand the relationship between society and gender discrimination in the context of material conditions in China—that is, the realities of landlord control in rural society.

Participation in the Patriotic May Fourth Movement

The youth of the May Fourth era adopted as their own the theme of women's liberation, and they developed this issue in countless ways. They lived at a time of wrenching upheavals; or, to put it more accurately, in the tension-packed confrontations between the youth of the May Fourth era and the new political conditions they were facing, their debates grew ever sharper.

In the year 1915, in the midst of the First World War, Japan presented Yuan Shikai with the famous Twenty-One Demands. Because the demands called not only for Japanese acquisition of German leaseholds in Shandong Province, but also for the recognition of Japanese sovereign authority in China's political, economic, and military affairs, they were an utter humiliation in the eyes of the Chinese people. Worse yet, the regime of Yuan's successor, Duan Qirui, who assumed power in 1916, strengthened its ties with Japanese imperialism by "gladly agreeing" to the Japanese demands.[11] As these events unfolded, alarm over a nation in crisis—with students and intellectuals at the forefront—swept the country.

Shortly thereafter, though, the war ended, and peace treaty negotiations began in Paris. At those talks, President of the United States Woodrow Wilson was a vigorous advocate of national self-determination. As negotiations progressed, the Chinese representatives demanded the direct return of former German leaseholds to China. Chinese had high hopes for a favorable settlement, but their hopes were dashed. On May 4, 1919—under banners that read "Defend our national sovereignty abroad and punish traitors at home!" "Tear up the Twenty-One Demands!" "Ignore the Treaty of Versailles!"—students marched into the great square in front of Beijing's Gate of Heavenly Peace. In the ensuing demonstration, they invaded the residence of Cao Rulin, whom they dubbed chief spokesman for the "Pro-Japanese Traitors," and beat up the Chinese Minister to Japan, Zhang Zongxiang, whom they found in Cao's home. Then a group of students set fire to Cao's residence. The spark of the May Fourth Movement had burst into flames.

The news from Versailles brought the masses of women to their feet as well.[12] Everywhere, Women's Patriotic Associations were formed, and through neighborhood discussion groups and house-to-house visits, women spread the word to "Resist Japan and save the country," "Boycott Japanese goods," and "Tear up the Twenty-One Demands." Particularly after a massive repression of students by the Beijing government on June 3, 1919, the movement spread across the country, with students and workers joining strikes and shopkeepers closing their doors. Many female students joined these actions, and even the mill girls, lashing out against their manifold hardships, went out on a political strike.[13] Young women students cut the tips of their fingers to write in blood the slogan: "Boycott Japanese products!" In the endless rows of marching demonstrators were women teachers and students in large numbers; sometimes they were arrested, sometimes injured. Some female students who were jailed refused to eat the Japanese produce, mostly kelp and vegetable gelatin, commonly served as prison fare.

Amid this rising tide of activism, on June 10 the government removed Cao Rulin and others from office, and on June 28 the Chinese delegate to the Paris Peace Conference refused to sign the accords. The movement had achieved its first victory.

The most violent confrontations of the May Fourth Movement occurred in Tianjin. Among the leaders of the movement there were Deng Yingchao of the Beiyang First Girls' Normal School and Liu Qingyang,[14] a graduate of that institution. Even so, at the out-set of the movement, the traditional Chinese sense of differentiation between the sexes ran high, and the Tianjin Student Union there-fore created a separate women's organization: the Tianjin Associa-tion of Women Patriotic Comrades. It began with 600 members in all, from school girls of thirteen or fourteen years of age to women in their sixties and older, but as the movement continued to grow, the sense of gender discrimination was overcome. In October 1919 women students joined the Student Union to promote the national salvation movement alongside men, and the Association of Women Patriotic Comrades disbanded. Once again demands for women's independence arose in their calls for free relationships between the sexes, freedom in marriage, open admission into university, equal employment opportunity, and the like. In Beijing as well, following the example of Tianjin, coeducational student organizations were formed.

The Tianjin Student Union published a *Journal of the Student Union*, edited by Zhou Enlai, which printed news about social re-form and the subjective transformation of consciousness, and advo-cated freedom and equality for women. Its impact on women was profound. The Academic Speech Department, which the Student Union oversaw, was also involved in the promotion of vernacular literature and in women's liberation. The Awakening Society, orga-nized by students, grew out of these activities and developed as a coeducational organization along the same lines, with the leadership of the organization's activities shared equally by men and women. (When Premier Zhou Enlai passed away in 1976, people were deeply touched by the eulogy displayed in front of his coffin. Written by his wife Deng Yingchao, it read: "Enlai, comrade-in-arms, your Yingchao laments deep within her heart." Their relationship dated back to the patriotic movement in Tianjin over fifty years before.)

Hardly unique to Tianjin, these developments were widespread in both Beijing and Shanghai. Even where men and women were not united in the same activist organizations, the ferocity of the struggles against traditional Chinese society and against imperialism forced young men who participated in these events into a confrontation with their families. As a result they were drawn to sympathize with the cause of women's liberation. Women too, as they joined these movements, became conscious for the first time of the traditional social constraints that bound them. As students at the Jinan Girl's Normal School lamented: "Before the May Fourth Movement, none of us had yet developed any awareness of the rigid, feudal poison that infected us. After May Fourth, our mental preparedness rose, and for the first time we gradually came to realize how deeply the feudal propaganda for ignorant people had penetrated into our own consciousness." [15]

In that atmosphere, magazines such as *New Youth*, *New Tide*, and *Shuguang* (Dawn) competed for readers. Women who took part in the May Fourth Movement experienced subjectively for the first time their own emancipation, and their thinking was radically transformed. For the first time, they were moved to cast off the chains of traditional morality that had encumbered their spirits, and they rose in mutiny against the old society. Conflicts over bobbed hair,[16] conflicts over coeducation, conflicts over freedom in love and marriage arose everywhere. More than 200 female students were expelled from the Tianjin Girls' Normal School for taking part in the National Humiliation Day demonstration on May 7, 1920, but they fought their sentences and were pardoned.

Thus, the May Fourth Movement drew women to the battle lines and broadened the struggle against imperialism and traditional Chinese society. In the process, sexual discrimination was gradually overcome, and women's liberation grew theoretically as well.

For ordinary women, who remained virtually untouched by the Revolution of 1911, these were critical experiences that broadened their horizons and made it possible for them to ask new questions —questions that grew out of the contradictions they encountered in their daily lives. Nonetheless, in the China of that time, a social base that could sustain their movement was still far from developing. The tangible results of their struggles were only seen in two areas: coeducational schools and women's suffrage.

At the time of the May Fourth Movement, only one Chinese university offered coeducation: the missionary school at Canton known as Lingnan University had been coeducational from the time of its founding in 1905. As the demand for coeducation grew stronger, Deng Chunlan, a student at Beijing Girls' Normal School who wanted to enter Beijing University in 1919 (the year of the May Fourth Incident), sent a letter requesting admission to Chancellor Cai Yuanpei. Cai Yuanpei had already taken an interest in the Patriotic Girls' School and had expressed considerable concern about women's education. He gave Deng permission to enroll as an auditor under the pretext that the regulations laid down by the government's Department of Education did not clearly stipulate that the student population would be limited to males. Beginning the following year, Beijing University and the Nanjing Higher Normal School both formally permitted female students to register, marking the first real opening of university doors to female students.[17]

Women had been admitted to one university in Japan six years before, when in 1913 Tōhoku University opened its classroom doors. But the establishment of coeducation in China, accomplished during the rise of the women's liberation movement, was not simply a formal change. On the contrary, what was most significant about it was that it came at a time when ideas about women's education were growing and when there was an actual demand for women's education to be on an equal footing with men's.[18] The Department of Education and the university authorities, in other words, did not open the door from above; instead, they were forced to do so by a movement that grew out of women's own self-awareness.

Finally, although women's suffrage was not necessarily a central theme in the May Fourth Movement, as calls for women's liberation grew louder, women in Hunan province acquired the right to vote, which had been their earnest desire ever since the 1911 Revolution.[19]

In Hunan after the May Fourth era, a movement developed that successfully drove out warlord Zhang Jingyao and established a provincial constitution. As part of that movement, the Hunan Women's Alliance lobbied at the constitutional convention for a six-point program that would (1) give women the right to vote and hold office; (2) create equal educational opportunities for men and women; (3) end job discrimination; (4) give women the right to make their own decisions in marriage; (5) guarantee women's inheritance rights; and (6) prohibit polygamy. Although the delegates to the convention were not united in their views on these issues, the representatives of the Women's Alliance kept the convention under siege day and night, and finally through the good offices of the Assistant Examining Officer Chou Ao, their demands were met. The provincial constitution promulgated in 1922 gave women the franchise. In the elections that soon followed, Wang Changguo, a woman activist in the suffrage movement since 1911, was elected to the provincial assembly, and a few women were elected to county assemblies.

Thus, the suffragists' goals were realized in Hunan. But ironically, at that point the limits of a bourgeois democratic revolution in a semicolonial country were already becoming apparent. Now they faced an era that witnessed the leap from the "old" Three Principles of the People to the "new" Three Principles of the People; and the framework of a simple women's rights movement had to be superseded.

We have seen how the May Fourth Movement developed out of the assault on the autocratic monarchy during the Revolution of 1911. In 1911 autocracy was overthrown, but the gloomy era of imperialism and warlordism followed it. To live in defiance of these forces required a violent clash with the oppressive power of a family system that had bolstered the servile morality undergirding the old autocratic order. The youth of the May Fourth Movement sharply denounced the family system for stifling human individuality and producing an endless supply of people who had gladly perpetuated the old structures. The subjugation of women, as they saw it, was the quintessential expression of that reality. These young people held that women's liberation lay at the heart of democracy, and they seized upon it as an urgent goal inextricably linked to their own emancipation from oppression. That is why this goal was so relentlessly pursued in the struggles against imperialism and traditional Chinese society that followed.

SIX

The Rise of Women Workers

Rapid industrialization in the early decades of the twentieth century transformed the conditions of life and labor in China's largest coastal cities. One of the major changes was the entry of women into the industrial labor force on a large scale. For women, the remarkable growth of both Chinese- and foreign-owned enterprises opened up an entirely new path of historical experience.[1]

"The Sad History of Women Workers" in China

Chinese-owned industry grew quickly in the period between 1914 and 1918, when the nations of Europe, preoccupied with the war, paid little attention to Asian affairs. Cotton spinning, silk reeling, and match making were the industries that did particularly well. The first column of Table 1 illustrates this development in textiles, expressed in terms of the number of spindles and looms in use. During the same period, Japanese-owned textile enterprises in China also made remarkable advances. This had much to do with Japan's own domestic economic circumstances, as well as the lack of customs autonomy in China. The prohibition in Japan against the use of female night-shift labor, as stipulated in the new factory laws of 1916, was also a significant element.[2]

The implementation of these reform laws caused a major shock within the Japanese cotton-spinning industry, whose profits depended on the day-and-night labor of young women workers. As the director of the Kanebō Spinning Company lamented: "If night shifts are prohibited, our production will decrease and our exports will dry up. *Should we value public health to the point of ruining our economy?*" Japanese textile capital accordingly began to search abroad for labor that could be engaged on a day-and-night basis, and its penetration of China was the result. Thus, while the reform laws granted some measure of protection to Japanese women workers—though they were not fully implemented until 1929, thirteen years later—the immediate result was the decision of the Japanese textile industry to transfer night-shift labor to the women workers of China.

The expansion of both Chinese- and foreign-owned enterprises led to the creation of a fairly large female working class. Though these figures come from a slightly later date, in 1927 there were 234,540 workers in the cotton-spinning industry. Of this national total, 59 percent (138,613) worked for Chinese-owned enterprises and 41 percent (95,927) were employed in foreign-owned factories.[3] The proportion of women in these numbers varied widely according to time and place. Place in particular made a marked difference (see Table 2): in Qingdao (Shandong province) women constituted a mere 6.4 percent of mill workers, whereas in Shanghai they accounted for fully 72.9 percent. The range in percentages is striking and reflects the considerable difference in the degree to which women participated in extradomestic labor in Central and South China as compared to North China.[4]

In the rice-growing region of the south, where agriculture was labor-intensive, women's labor power was essential; in the dry-field region of the north, this was not always the case. There, the notion that "a woman never leaves the three platforms" (well, mill, and stove) remained strong, and footbinding was almost universal. Looking beyond these differences to the national total, there were roughly 140,000 to 150,000 women working in cotton mills by the time of the May Thirtieth Movement in 1925. There were in addition a large number of women working in other industries. In Guangzhou and Shanghai alone, roughly 120,000 women were employed in silk filatures (silk-reeling factories), 40,000 in match-making factories, and 40,000 to 50,000 in the tobacco-processing industry.[5]

By what route did women enter the work force in such large

TABLE I

Size of Shanghai Cotton Industry by Nationality of Ownership, 1890–1936

Year	Chinese		Japanese		British		Total	
	Spindles	Looms	Spindles	Looms	Spindles	Looms	Spindles	Looms
1890	35,000	530	—	—	—	—	35,000	530
1895	174,564	1,800	—	—	—	—	174,564	1,800
1900	336,722	2,016	—	—	80,548	—	497,270[a]	2,016
1905	355,588	2,016	23,912	—	80,548	—	540,048[a]	2,016
1910	497,448	2,316	55,296	—	80,548	—	713,292[a]	2,316
1913	484,192	2,316	111,936	886	138,036	800	823,152[a]	4,002
1919	658,748	2,650	332,922	1,486	244,088	2,353	1,235,758	6,489
1925	1,866,232	11,121	1,268,176	7,205	105,320	2,348	3,339,728	20,674
1931	2,453,304	17,629	1,714,604	15,983	170,610	2,691	4,338,518	36,303
1936	2,746,392	25,503	2,135,068	28,915	221,336	4,021	5,102,796	58,539

SOURCE: Yan Zhongping, *Zhongguo mianfangzhi shigao, 1289–1937* [A draft history of Chinese cotton spinning and weaving, 1289–1937], 2d ed. (Beijing: Kexue chubanshe, 1963), pp. 354–55. Translator's note: Considerably lower figures for Chinese and Japanese mills in 1925, 1931, and 1936 are given in Emily Honig, *Sisters and Strangers: Women in the Shanghai Cotton Mills, 1919–1949* (Stanford, Calif.: Stanford University Press, 1986), pp. 30–31.

[a] Includes American and German mills.

TABLE 2
*Composition of Cotton Mill Work Force
in Selected Cities, 1930*
(percent)

City	Women	Men	Children
Shanghai	72.9%	21.4%	5.7%
Wuxi	68.0	22.8	9.2
Wujin	61.0	12.7	26.3
Wuchang	58.3	41.7	[a]
Nantong	56.3	30.7	12.8
Wuhan	42.4	53.0	4.6
Suzhou	40.1	49.7	10.2
Hankou	32.9	59.8	7.3
Qingdao	6.4	93.6	[a]

SOURCE: Fang Xianting, *Zhongguo zhi mianfang zhiye* [China's cotton spinning and weaving industry] (Nanjing: Guili bianyiguan, 1934), p. 176.
[a] Statistics for Wuchang and Qingdao do not distinguish child from adult labor.

numbers? In Shanghai, many came from the poor rural villages north of the Yangzi River and were sold by their families into a life of indentured labor. The men who recruited them in this way acted as their bosses and were known as "labor contractors." A woman called Sister Qian who had once been a worker in this position recalls what happened when the man who became her boss showed up at her parents' home:

At this time, Froggy Zhou, who was a boss in Shanghai, came back to the village. He had been a small-time hustler for a long time, and his persuasive style had enabled him to swindle many people. Seeing that my family was in difficult circumstances, he spoke to my parents about taking me to a textile mill in Shanghai. Once I got to Shanghai, he said, everything would work out fine. I would be happy, living in a foreign-style house along the Wusong River, eating good food, and wearing stylish clothes. On top of that, my parents would get three *dan* of rice after I had worked for three years.[6]

Yet what awaited these women was a life unfit for human beings. For the tiny contract advance of 20 or 30 *yuan*, they were in fact being sold into bondslavery.

A boss usually had 20 or 30 women workers in his employ, though some had well over 100. He provided them with housing and food and in return put them to work. The housing was minimal. Ten to twenty women would be crammed into one small rush-mat shed six by ten feet, furnished with a single wash basin, a chamber pot, and a few ragged quilts. Food amounted to one meal a day of watery gruel. They would rise at three or four o'clock in the morning and line up like convicts to walk in file to their factory under the watchful eye of the boss. Day after day they set off in starlight and returned in the evening by the light of the moon, never seeing the sun. The pay they earned was taken from them by the boss. A 1938 investigation by the Industry Bureau of Shanghai shows that the bosses profited enormously from this arrangement. A woman worker making 12 *yuan* a month would in theory earn 288 *yuan* over the period of a two-year contract, though with the reduced wage during the initial period of apprenticeship when she was learning the trade, plus deductions for days off, the actual amount would be 265 *yuan*. She had to pay for food, which might cost 5 *yuan* a month, and for rent, water, and utilities at 0.4 *yuan* a month, amounting to 129.6 *yuan* over two years. When the contract fee is added on top of these expenses, her total costs would come to 165 *yuan* at most. The difference of 100 *yuan* went to the boss.

Women working under a boss of this sort were known as contract laborers (*baoshengong*).[7] Contractual bondage—virtual debt slavery—was not new to the Chinese economy, but the imperialist enterprises used it as a means for securing all the labor they needed. The boss served the function of recruiting and housing workers at low cost for the foreigners, who were unfamiliar with local circumstances and did not speak the language. This system of recruitment and housing was the means through which Japanese textile capitalists could impose low wages and long working hours on their women workers. They did not have to build dormitories as they did in Japan because the contractors provided housing. In any case, there was a surplus of female labor being generated by impoverishment in the rural areas. As the saying went, "it is easier to find a hundred women workers than it is to find a hundred dogs." Surplus labor combined with the requirements of the imperialist enterprises to produce this system of contract labor.[8]

About 20 percent of women workers lived with their families. We can learn something of their situation through statistics for Shanghai that give average incomes and percentage breakdowns by member for workers' households, as well as several surveys of

TABLE 3
*Average Monthly Income and Expenses of
Working-Class Families in Shanghai, 1930*

Category	Yuan	Percent
INCOME		
Wage-earner:		
Husband	14.17	43.5%
Wife	5.05	15.5
Son	3.21	9.9
Daughter	3.33	10.2
Second son	2.42	7.4
Second daughter	2.92	9.0
Non-wage income	1.47	4.5
TOTAL	32.57	100.0%
EXPENSES		
Item:		
Food	18.21	56.0%
Clothing	3.06	9.4
Rent	2.09	6.4
Utilities	2.45	7.6
Other	6.70	20.6
TOTAL	32.51	100.0%

SOURCE: Yang Ximeng, *Shanghai gongren shenghuo chengdu de yige yanjiu*
[A study of the standard of living of workers in Shanghai] (Shanghai:
Shehui diaochasuo, 1930), p. 35, based on the family budgets of 230
cotton-mill workers. Translator's note: Comparable figures for Tianjin
may be found in Gail Hershatter, *The Workers of Tianjin, 1900–1949* (Stanford, Calif.: Stanford University Press, 1986), p. 68.

household budgets from about 1930. The figures given in Table
3 are for experienced workers. Even in such households, the husband's income met less than half the total expenses of the household. With household expenses kept to a barest minimum, it was
absolutely essential that the wife work. It is important to recognize
that selling her labor power cheaply was not just a way for the wife
to supplement her husband's low wages; the family wage economy
was part of what created the depressed wage structure characteristic
of a semi-colony.

This kind of wage depression accounted for the low cost of production in China. In 1929 the cost of producing one bale of twenty-
count cotton yarn in Japan was 42 yen; in China it was 22 yen (see
Table 4). The difference lies mainly in the cost of labor, which in
China was forced down to roughly half of what it was in Japan, and

TABLE 4
*Cost in Yen of Producing One Bale of Twenty-Count
Cotton Yarn in Japan and in China, 1929*

Cost component	Japan	China
Energy	5.50	5.00
Labor	20.00	9.20
Housing, welfare	3.50	0.60
Machinery	1.50	1.20
Raw material	2.30	2.00
Transport	1.00	0.20
Operating	1.00	0.80
Taxes	4.00	0.50
Salaries	1.50	1.20
Insurance	0.50	0.50
Travel, miscellaneous	1.20	0.80
TOTAL	42.00	22.00

SOURCE: *Shina bōsekigyō no hattatsu to sono shōrai* [The development of the Chinese textile industry and its future] (Tokyo: Tō-A keizai chōsakyoku, 1932), pp. 38–39.

also in the substantial reduction in China of such indirect labor costs as housing and welfare. This cost difference between Japanese- and Chinese-produced cotton became the source of enormous profit for the major Japanese companies like Naigai Wata (Neiwai Cotton)[9] operating in China. Even in 1920, during a time of domestic depression and financial panic, Naigai Wata actually distributed to shareholders unprecedented dividends of 162 percent of the original value of the stock, and the next five semiannual distributions continued to pay the high dividend of 60 percent. The exploitation of female labor in both China and Japan was thus generating large profits for Japanese textile capital.

A good place to begin looking at the lives of the women working in textile mills is the book *Jokō aishi* (The sad history of women workers) by Hosoi Wakizō (1897–1925).[10] Hosoi wrote this volume on the basis of material collected in Japan, first of all from Naigai Wata, the company where he himself worked, and also from Kanebō, Fujibō, and Dai Nippon Spinning Companies. Naigai Wata was the Japanese company most involved in textile production in China, though the other enterprises also made inroads there. When reading the descriptions of Japanese factories in *The*

Sad History, one cannot fail to notice the strong similarities with what went on in China. This is hardly coincidental since these enterprises took their methods of labor management with them when they went to China. Women workers both in Japan and in Japanese factories in China were subjected to the same forms of exploitation and control by the very same capitalists. Viewed in this way, Hosoi tells a story in *The Sad History* that applies equally to the women workers of both countries. Even so, Chinese women workers found themselves in circumstances that in some respects were as different as night and day—as different "as heaven and hell," as Xia Yan put it in his famous reportage on contract labor.[11] This is because, even more so than in Japan, these companies had in China the backing of state power to put into effect harsh labor practices and coercive forms of labor management.

As stated in an issue of *Xiangdao zhoubao* (Guide weekly), official organ of the Chinese Communist Party in those years: "All of the ingenious methods now being used in the factories for oppressing and exploiting workers were first started in the factories of Japan." For example, the Ta Kong (Da Kang) Cotton Mill revised the ratio of machine supervision from three workers per two looms to two workers per three looms, even one worker per two looms in some cases. Or again, Naigai Wata set up a training system for the purpose of inculcating among the workers a sense of loyalty to the company. Yet at the same time it removed the chairs from the work place, thereby taking away any place where women with bound feet could sit; the supervisors, known as "Number Ones," carried whips when they were on duty; and women were not free to go to the lavatory but had to ask for the key.

We can hear their complaints expressed in a 1925 strike manifesto from the workers at the Doko (Tong Xing) Cotton Mill:

Brothers and sisters! It is truly a bitter experience to labor in a Japanese factory.

1. The Japanese beat people without any reason whatsoever.
2. The Japanese cruelly impose fines and fire people on a whim.
3. The Japanese are immoral and rude. They make advances toward the women workers. The clever ones flirt with them; the less clever ones reject their advances and scorn them, so that sometimes they are forced to quit. This drives us to a violent anger that we cannot control.

4. In the past there used to be one paid day off every half a month, whereas now the Japanese violate this regulation and allow the day off but without pay.

5. There are two Japanese individuals, enemies of the employees, who beat and curse people and flirt with women workers. At the time the women enter the company, these Japanese men usually look them over and pick out the stylish ones with normal feet.

6. When the price of rice and fuel was cheap, we could get by on low wages. Now, even though everything has become very expensive, the wages have still not gone up. But this is not everything.

7. We bring lunch to the factory every day, but the Japanese make us work on empty bellies and keep the machines running right up to [the lunch break at] half past eleven, so that despite the fact that we need time to prepare our food, there is no time even to boil water. On many occasions some of us have become sick from eating cold food. Are we not truly wretched?

8. The Japanese constantly curse us, calling us slaves and outcasts and people without a country, saying that there is nothing we can do because we have no common purpose, like a tray of loose sand.

Brothers and sisters! These items are but the simplest crimes of the Japanese and touch on only a tiny fraction of all their villainies.[12]

Living under such conditions, the women used their ingenuity secretly to oppose the capitalists and their rationalization schemes. One method was to stick a dumpling from lunch onto the drive belt that powered the machines. This slowed the machines down and gave the workers a brief respite. We learn of this in the following two work songs sung by women in the Da Sheng Cotton Mill:[13]

> Vegetable Dumplings Hard as Rocks
> A whirring machine spitting sparks,
> Her face is pale with hunger pain;
> Two vegetable dumplings hard as rocks,
> She sticks them on the belt again.

When a Number One finally noticed what had happened, he would clean off the belt and in no time have the machines running at full speed.

> Even Ghosts Would Be Scared
> The machine runs fast once the belt is clear.
> The girl must work at a hectic pace.

The supervisor's shout grates in her ear,
Even ghosts would be scared of the boss's face.

The Da Sheng Mill was Chinese-owned, but the situation was largely the same in the Japanese-owned factories.

Another song tells of the life of a woman working in a silk filature (almost all of which were controlled by Chinese capital):

I've just noticed the eastern sky glowing red,
I pull on my clothes and jump out of bed.
I gaze intently at the face of my child:
Your mother goes off, and you look so pale.
I drop my gaze and rush out the door
To see the sun already up once more.
Today will I once again be too late?
Will the mill have already barred its gate?
But the doors of this prison are still open to me,
I hurry to enter the factory.
The hot steam rises and scalds my skin;
Were it not for the money, who would come in?
I reel off the silk until twelve o'clock,
Then fill my belly with the cold food I brought.
I pause to think of my husband's hard lot,
Sweating right now as he pulls his cart.
In boiling water, my hands never pause;
The afternoon passes, the day slowly dies.
By the time work is done, six has already passed,
Outside the factory the streets are pitch black.
Please, don't ask your mother to hold you, my son,
My body aches and I can't bear the pain.
Your father has not yet pulled his cart back,
Bringing home rice for your mother to cook.

Marriage Resistance

Although subjected to a life of hardship day after day, some women by their labor were able to achieve a measure of economic independence and build confidence in their own skills. Their work brought them the freedom to live on their own rather than having to rely on men, something that Chinese women had never been able to do before. The practice of learning the trade of silk reeling through one-to-one relationships with skilled older women led to the creation of spinsters' homes among Cantonese women, and it also fortified an older Cantonese custom, marriage resistance. Lesbianism among women workers in Guangzhou was an additional sign of this independence.[14]

A spinsters' home was a sort of women's hostel. It was an autonomous organization centering on one woman who was both skilled in her work and popular among her fellow workers. Anywhere from a dozen to 20 or 30 women would set up such a home by renting a house where they would cook their meals together and live communally. The discipline within these homes was rather strict, based on the subordination of the younger women to the older worker on whose skills they relied to learn their trade. The emotional bonds between these women were strong, such that even women who had fought against their parents were said to have never dared oppose the elder woman of the spinsters' home. There they lived in what was for them a new world, completely different from the world of the traditional Chinese family from which they had come.

Not surprisingly, lesbian relationships developed among some of these women. The term in local parlance was "golden orchid match." A woman would first declare her love for another by giving her a gift of peanuts or honey. If the second woman accepted the gift, it meant that she also accepted the offer of love; if she did not, it signified that she rejected the offer. A woman who was successful in her declaration of love, if she had saved some money, would invite her friends to a party to celebrate the match, just as one would celebrate a marriage. She and her beloved would then live together as a married couple. They might even adopt daughters to whom they could pass on an inheritance.

Marriage resistance was another aspect of the same larger phenomenon. A woman worker who simply refused on her own initiative to get married for fear that marriage would rob her of her freedom invariably found the oppression within her natal family so severe that such a relatively straightforward decision was impossible to carry through. Women workers accordingly came up with a new strategy called "not going down to the family." According to this strategy, a woman might still go ahead and get married, but she would not move in with her husband's family. When the day of the wedding had been chosen, a group of women who had jointly agreed to resist marriage would weep out loud together. Then, when the wedding day arrived, they would bind the bride with rope and sew her trouser legs together tightly. For the first three days in her husband's family, the bride would neither eat nor drink and would resolutely refuse to go near her husband. If he tried to exercise his prerogative as a husband, she would resist to the point of fending him off with a knife. On the customary visit home three days later, the other women checked the rope and trousers to make sure that the bride had not had intercourse with the husband, and then the bride would go back to work at the silk filature with her friends as though nothing had happened. In certain cases, brides of this sort used a portion of their salaries to engage a concubine for the spurned husband.

Such customs predated industrialization in the Guangzhou region, but as the silk industry flourished they spread among mill workers, specifically in Nanhai, Shunde, and Panyu counties. Every so often laws prohibiting such conduct were brought up for discussion, but prohibition was impossible. These customs eventually died away of their own accord in the late 1920's and early 1930's, however, when the silk-reeling industry went into decline.

Although marriage resistance could develop in the direction of lesbianism, in some cases it was successfully resolved through the free choice of a marriage partner. One story of this sort from Shunde county tells of a young woman who had her own boyfriend but could not escape the marriage that her parents had arranged. After the wedding, she resorted to violence to repel the husband that had been forced on her only to discover, when she heard his voice, that he was in fact the boyfriend she had hoped to marry. Marriage resistance thus did not necessarily amount to an outright denial of marriage.

Lesbianism and freedom in choosing a marriage partner should be recognized as two sides of the same coin since lesbianism was a way through which women could realize their erotic impulses, much expressed in women's love songs of the region, on their own terms. The economic independence and freedom from the family that these women achieved through industrial labor made them more conscious of their sexuality. To be a bride meant putting all this aside since neither a woman's independence nor her sexuality were acceptable within the traditional household. Caught between an awareness of their sexuality and the reality of having to deny it, some women workers turned to lesbianism. These women were struggling against sexual repression, and though lesbianism may seem like deviant behavior, it emerged naturally out of their longing for freedom and can best be understood as a sign of refusal to give up the struggle for liberation from the traditional family system.

Labor Activism

The development of consciousness and solidarity among some women workers led to their participation in the nascent labor movement. Women workers had begun their political activism in the May Fourth Movement, but it was the founding of the Chinese Communist Party (CCP) in 1921 that created new possibilities for the women's movement. At its first congress, the Party set as its primary task the building of the labor movement by organizing unions and leading strikes. Through its Labor Secretariat, the CCP convoked the first All-China Labor Congress in Guangzhou in May 1922, adopting the slogans "Down with imperialism" and "Down with the warlords," calling for an eight-hour workday, and setting up a strike fund. Under this impetus, the workers' movement in China entered a period of expansion. In the years 1922 and 1923, there were more than a hundred strikes reported in China, involving over 300,000 workers. Women were part of this surge of labor activism, joining the strikes in great numbers. In fact, at two series of strikes in Shanghai in 1922, first against the Sino-Japanese (Ri Hua) Cotton Manufacturing Company and later against Chinese-owned silk filatures, women constituted the overwhelming majority.

The main factory of Sino-Japanese Cotton was purchased in 1917, just prior to the May Fourth Movement, as a joint capital venture by Nippon Cotton, Fuji Cotton, and the Ito Shu Company.[15] Given the anti-Japanese climate of the time, efforts toward rationalization by Japanese capitalists, as one would expect, provoked a negative response from the workers. Indeed, by the beginning of 1918, there were recurring labor disputes at the factory, such as a strike against the system of imposing fines on workers and sabotage for the rebukes suffered by women workers for falling asleep on the job. Experiences of this sort eventually built up into a mass strike at the company's first and second mills on April 16, 1922. The strikers publicized the following four demands: (1) a 20 percent pay increase; (2) the payment of wages otherwise lost during the strike; (3) an annual pay increment; and (4) recognition by the company of the workers' right to collective bargaining. Of the 3,800 workers who went out at Mill Number Two, more than 3,000 were women.

This strike was led by the Pudong Textile Workers' Union. Right up until the final day of the strike, which lasted until April 25, the women workers "maintained good order and were extremely civilized in all their actions," according to one contemporary observer; "avoiding the violence to which men are prone is one of the things at which women excel." During the strike, the head of the Pudong Constabulary undertook to arbitrate the dispute. The strike was resolved when the company acquiesced to the first three of the strikers' demands. The company declined to reply to the fourth demand, though by entering into negotiations with the workers, Sino-Japanese Cotton was tacitly recognizing the right to collective bargaining. On April 26 the women workers set off firecrackers in celebration of their complete victory and returned to work. The strike had lasted ten days.

At the time of this strike, all the members of the Pudong Textile Workers' Union were men. After the strike, however, not only did the union admit women as members, but union membership became in effect compulsory. The power of the union was strengthened in the work place to such an extent that the employees would not comply without orders from the union, the authority of the supervisors diminished, the workers with power in the union wielded authority in the work place, and the employees all respected the instructions of the union. The workers were beginning to realize that they were no longer powerless against this giant imperialist enterprise.

On May 9, 1922, a woman working in the waste thread section of the Sino-Japanese mill was fired for improper conduct, probably for stealing some thread. It was a minor matter, but women had on occasion been unjustly accused of misdemeanors and fired arbitrarily. Given the tense atmosphere at this time, the factory became a scene of great agitation. As well as objecting to the firing, the workers also demanded the implementation of a system of piece-work pay for inexperienced workers. Some of the women even engaged in sabotage. In response the company refused to negotiate with the union, and on May 29 the workers at both mills went out on strike. The strike came at the time of the Dragon Boat Festival when the women needed their wages to meet holiday expenses, yet they were firm in their determination, and not a single worker drew her pay. As a result the company had to make some concessions. The strike was called off after seventeen days, and the workers went back on the job.

The leaders of the union lost their jobs because of this strike, but they went on to broaden their organization outside Sino-Japanese Cotton by setting up a school for workers and engaging in propaganda. The influence of the union thus spread from there to other foreign-owned enterprises in the area, such as the British-American Tobacco Company, which employed 8,000 people. For this reason, Japan and Great Britain pressured the Chinese police to shut down the Pudong Textile Workers' Union in September.

Deprived of their organization, the workers found themselves back where they had started. Removing the ban on the union thus became the central demand when the workers went out on strike again at the beginning of November 1922. Particularly significant among the six other demands made at this time, and one that came from the women workers themselves, was the call for recognition of the right to nurse children on the job. At Chinese-owned enterprises women were tacitly allowed to bring their children with them to work, but this was not the practice at Japanese-owned factories. Since milk at this time was an expensive commodity, completely beyond the means of women working in textile mills, the separation of mothers and infants during working hours was a serious problem. Inadequate nursing was in fact closely linked to infant mortality.

The company adopted violent measures in response to this last strike of 1922. Coordinating with the army through the military commander of the Shanghai region, the company arranged for warrants to be issued for the arrest of two union representatives and absolutely refused to enter into negotiations with this or any other labor collective. The union was outlawed, and none of the workers' demands was met. A strike of 25 days ended in complete failure. The women at Sino-Japanese Cotton in 1922 had thus in the space of barely a year mounted three strikes lasting a total of 52 days. The workers did not have their own strike fund, though several outside women's groups provided a certain amount of assistance. For women, this was an age when "one day without work and you worry, two days and you go to the pawnshop, three and you become a prostitute." It requires little imagination to see that 52 days was a long stretch for these women. But through this struggle, many women workers came to realize that the union was their only real protection.

In the same year, 1922, there was another massive strike in Shanghai which involved more than 10,000 women workers at 44 silk filatures in Xinzha and Zhabei.[16] This strike was set off by a trivial event. It was the height of summer, and a woman at the Da Lai Silk Filature was showing what appeared to be symptoms of cholera. When she asked her superior for permission to go to the doctor, she was turned down. Angered by this, her co-workers under the auspices of the Women Workers' Society for Moral Improvement (a management-organized friendly society) went out on strike on August 5. They put forward four demands: (1) formal recognition of their association as a bargaining unit; (2) a ten-hour work day; (3) some respite every two weeks as stipulated in the factory regulations; and (4) agreement not to extend arbitrarily the working day in winter or summer. By the second day of the strike, workers at the 44 factories had gone out in support. Were it not for the harsh conditions under which these women labored, a small spark such as this would not have flared up into so great a blaze.

Though we know that several members of the Provincial Assembly of Jiangsu offered their encouragement to the Society for Moral Improvement in organizing the strike, the concrete circumstances and the general attitudes from which the Society arose remain unclear. The word "improvement" (*jinde*) in their title, derived from the more general term for progress (*jinhua*), shows the main direction of thought behind the group and is perhaps suggestive of an anarchist orientation. This collectivity was not designed as a strike vehicle, however. Rather, its purpose was to encourage self-improvement among the women workers, changing their habits for the better and promoting a general respect for female virtue. This is clearly spelled out in its statement of principles, which includes several clauses that worked to the advantage of the capitalists: do not hinder your work by engaging in unjustified strikes; do not cause trouble in the work place or otherwise show disrespect for the rules of the factory; and do not do anything as shameful and immoral as stealing cocoons. It was an organization designed to encourage cooperation between labor and capital; more explicitly, the Society pursued the reactionary goal of seeking to improve the moral character of women workers in order to guarantee their exploitability as a labor force.

Despite the Society's amenability to industrial discipline, Da Lai Silk not only refused to extend its recognition, but proposed to lengthen the work day. At that point, the women had no choice but to go on strike. On the first day of the strike, nine leaders of the Society along with Mu Zhiying, a female supervisor who was the Society's vice president, went around to other factories with banners on which were emblazoned the slogans "A united world," "Equal rights for men and women," "Improve morality," and "Guarantee human rights," hoping to attract the support of workers there. Although the police were mobilized to suppress the strikers, the mass of women grew to the point that the police were unable to do anything. The demonstration moved from Zhabei, where most of the silk filatures were located, to Hongkou [Hongkew] in the International Settlement, and there the demonstrators were eventually dispersed by Settlement police.

By the second day of the strike, the movement had swollen to some 20,000 women from 44 factories. The Society for Moral Improvement, however, did not promote further organization among the women, and as a result, by the third day of the strike some of the workers began heading back to their jobs. On the fourth day, August 8, the police arrested six of the leaders, including Mu Zhiying. Four of them were released the following day, but the demand for the release of the other two caused the strike to build once again. When Mu and the other leader were finally let out, the women could hope for nothing more and ended the strike.[17] In the end, none of their original demands were met, although through the mediation of other labor groups in Shanghai, the goal of shortening the work day was eventually achieved.

It was the momentum of the labor movement that induced an

organization like the Women Workers' Society for Moral Improvement to step temporarily into a leadership position. Even though the character of the Society may have ultimately been responsible for the failure of the strike, the event does show that the aspirations of the workers could oblige a reactionary organization of this sort to put forward such demands as the recognition of unions and the shortening of the work day. The strike is also significant in that it was not restricted to one factory but spread beyond its bounds and forged a unity among women throughout the silk industry. Women workers recognized the need to carry on their struggle in concert with each other and in doing so matured from being a "class in itself" to becoming a "class for itself." They would no longer remain slaves of the old order.

Regardless of whether the enterprises were owned by Chinese or by foreigners, strikes became widespread throughout China. Table 5 presents tabulation by year of the number of strikes, strikers, and days on strike. In February of 1923, the warlord government in Beijing bloodily suppressed the massive strike of railway workers on the Beijing-Hankou line in the hope of stemming the tide of the labor movement. In the wake of the February Seventh Massacre, as it came to be known, many unions were outlawed, and the movement was temporarily diminished. But, as the table suggests, this was the calm before the storm.

Women in the May Thirtieth Movement

In January 1924, Sun Yat-sen convened the first national congress of the Nationalist Party or Guomindang (GMD) in conjunction with the Communists. At the congress, the GMD underwent a complete reorganization, and a three-point policy of alliance with the Soviet Union, cooperation with the CCP, and support for workers and peasants was enunciated. Significant for our purposes is this statement in the political program: "We recognize the principle of equality between men and women in legal, educational, economic, and social terms, and we will further the development of the rights of women." Liao Pingjun and He Xiangning[18] were installed as the heads of the Women's Department.

The formation of a united front between the GMD and the CCP caused the revolutionary movement to advance dramatically.

TABLE 5
Strike Activity in China, 1918–25

Year	Strikes	Strikes where no. of strikers is known	No. of strikers	Average no. of strikers per strike	Strikes where days struck is known	No. of days struck	Average no. of days on strike
1918	25	12	6,455	537.9	15	124	8.27
1919	66	26	91,520	3,520.0	52	294	5.65
1920	46	19	46,140	2,428.0	22	157	7.14
1921	49	22	108,025	4,910.2	21	155	7.38
1922	91	30	139,050	4,635.0	54	452	8.37
1923	47	17	35,835	2,107.9	21	134	6.38
1924	56	18	61,860	3,436.8	26	241	9.27
1925	183	103	403,334	3,915.9	95	505	5.32
1925[a]	318	198	784,821	3,963.7	120	2,266	18.88

SOURCE: Chen Da, "Jin ba nian lai guonei bagong de fenxi," *Qinghua xuebao* 3: 1 (June 1926), p. 810; English translation, "Analysis of Strikes in China, from 1918 to 1926," *Chinese Economic Journal* 1: 10 (Oct. 1927), p. 841.
[a]Including the strikes connected with the May Thirtieth Movement.

It also contributed to strengthening the CCP's leadership among the workers and peasants.[19] In Shanghai alone, party members set up a workers' school and organized such groups as the Workers' Society for Moral Improvement and the West Shanghai Workers' Club. As the CCP was penetrating workers' organizations, the February Strike, the forerunner of the May Thirtieth Movement, occurred.

In the early hours of the morning of February 2, 1925, a Japanese supervisor in the roving department of Naigai Wata's Mill Number Eight found a girl laborer not twelve years old sleeping on the job and beat her so brutally that she was unable to stand. Incensed, the male workers in her department got into a fierce argument with the supervisor. An hour later, the company announced that it was firing all 50 men in that workshop and that it would replace the rest of the male workers with women or apprentices, as it had long desired to do.

The male workers who showed up that morning for work immediately resolved to strike in protest.[20] Seven of the workers' representatives were arrested when they went to draw their pay, and they accordingly used this as an excuse to go out on strike on February 9. Their demands were that Japanese hereafter not beat employees, that wages be raised by 20 percent, and that the order to fire the workers be rescinded.[21] Some 10,000 workers gathered at a mass meeting, carrying placards which read: "We are resolutely opposed to the 'Asians' beating people."[22] Their pent-up fury broke forth, and they threw down the company-issued hats they were wearing and stamped on them, shouting, "We will no longer wear 'Asian' hats!" This marked the birth of the General Textile Union.

The strike immediately spread to other factories owned by Japanese. Just prior to this, an incident occurred at the Toyota (Feng Tian) Spinning and Weaving Company in which a woman worker had been kicked in the stomach by the factory director, a man by the name of Harada, and was off work for two weeks because of her injury. At once the male workers resolved to plan an attack on Harada. Such incidents involving Japanese brutality were not uncommon at other factories. For this reason, the strike that started at Naigai Wata came to involve altogether some 40,000 workers employed at 22 different mills and lasted until February 26. The February Strike constituted a major blow to the Japanese, for branches of the union were set up in the various enterprises whose workers were involved in the strike, and this greatly advanced the process of labor organization.

Two months later, in April, there was a large strike at a Japanese factory in the city of Qingdao in which eight workers were shot and killed. At this tense point in the upsurge of the labor movement, the CCP convoked the second All-China Labor Conference in Guangzhou from May 1 to 7. In addition to emphasizing the role that workers need to play in the revolutionary struggle against imperialism and feudalism, the congress identified tasks for the current economic struggles. These included demands for higher pay, an eight-hour work day, and a prohibition against all forms of brutality, as well as a call for improvements in the living conditions for women and child workers.[23]

The Japanese Textile Federation of Shanghai in turn decided on May 7 to extend no recognition whatsoever to labor unions, to respond to union-inspired strikes with lockouts, and to negotiate with the authorities of the International Settlement as well as with the Chinese police to bring the unions under control. Then, on May 15, a nineteen-year-old named Gu Zhenghong was killed in Naigai Wata's Number Five Mill. Workers angered by the unilateral lockout at Naigai had broken into the factory, Gu at their head, and thugs hired by the company opened fire. Gu was wounded and died two days later. He had been a member of the CCP.

The young man's death stirred the workers into action. All of the factories owned by Naigai Wata were hit with an indefinite strike. An Association to Avenge Wrongs was organized to protest the crime committed by the Japanese. On May 24 more than 10,000 workers and students gathered in the International Settlement at Gu Zhenghong's memorial and vowed to avenge his death. The foreign entrepreneurs' concern not only led to the quick arrest of a number of students but also resulted in new regulations to bring the students' propaganda activities under control.

May 30 was the day on which the students arrested by the Settlement police were to be tried. Students and workers—shouting "Release the accused immediately," "Return the foreign concessions," and "Shanghai belongs to the Chinese"—filled the streets of the Settlement. The Settlement police began arresting these students and workers, which caused such indignation among the crowd that they surrounded the police. The people were totally unarmed, but the police opened fire without warning. Several dozen workers and students were wounded, and eleven died. The Shanghai General Union was founded the following day. On June 1 the streets of Shanghai were filled with striking workers. For the first time since the May Fourth Movement, students, workers, and merchants all joined the struggle, quitting class, going out on strike, and closing their shops. By June 5 more than 170 unions had joined the Shanghai General Union, and the strike had grown to over 200,000 workers. Within a week it had spread to 39 Japanese-owned factories employing 65,000 workers and 26 British-owned mills employing 36,000 workers. As of June 13, 156,000 people were still on strike at 115 mills. The electricity was shut off, the streetcars did not budge, and the telephones were out.

Women working in the Japanese textile mills participated in the strike. By contrast, women in the silk industry, with the exception of a few of the factories owned by foreign capital, did not join the strike. They took the nationalistic view that striking would reduce China's silk output and give greater competitive advantage to Japan.

Other organizations outside labor circles sprang up in Shanghai at this time. Those specifically involving women included the Shanghai Women's Federation (founded June 5, 1925), the Women's Movement Committee of the GMD, the Women's Political Association, and the Women's Association for the Promotion of a National Assembly. There was in addition the Shanghai University Women Students' Federation and organizations at a number of schools, such as the Patriotic Girls' School.

In response to this activity, the United States, Great Britain, and Japan dispatched warships to the Shanghai region and landed marines, hoping to intimidate people through a show of force. If one includes a number of shootings in Wuhan and Guangzhou in addition to the deaths on May 30, altogether several dozen people were killed during the May Thirtieth Movement.

The response from the people of Shanghai was a mass rally on June 11 at the Public Recreation Ground. More than 100,000 people attended, and particularly noticeable among them were the large numbers of women textile workers and the ragged dockworkers —people who had never before made an appearance at a rally of this kind. Seventeen separate demands were ratified at this meeting, including the prosecution of those responsible for the killings, the enactment of legislation to protect workers, the abrogation of the power of the Mixed Court,[24] and the withdrawal of British and Japanese marines stationed in Shanghai. The rally was followed by a demonstration that stretched over five kilometers.

Another citizens' rally was held in Zhabei district on June 17 in which 2,000 women mill workers from Xiaoshadu and Yangshupu participated. Though some of them seemed barely six or seven years old, they shouted: "The fate of China hangs in the balance; carry on the struggle!" The strike against the Japanese textile mills dragged on until the end of August.

The Story of Sister Shi, Laborer

We can glimpse something of what life may have been like during this time through the reminiscences of a mill worker known as Sister Shi.[25] Sister Shi was only nine years old when her father led her by the hand through the front gate of the Shen Mao Cotton-Spinning Mill. As it happened, that was 1900, the year of the Boxer Rebellion. When she reached marriageable age, Shi was married into a family that could not support her, so she brought her husband into her natal family and went on working. She gave birth in due course to a son, named Cailiang, but within ten days of giving birth she had to return to work. Having no nursery to which she could entrust the baby, she hid him among the sacks in a storeroom in the corner of her work place and hoped that the supervisor would not notice him.

By the age of two, Cailiang was toddling about near his mother and had become the darling of her women co-workers. Whenever they heard the supervisor approaching, they put him in the storeroom and threw an empty sack over him so that he would not be discovered. Imported silk drove the factory into bankruptcy during the First World War, when it was bought by the Sino-Japanese Cotton Manufacturing Company. Chinese-owned enterprises unofficially allowed women like Sister Shi to bring their children with them to work, but the Japanese did not. Cailiang simply could no longer come with his mother to the factory. Separation from his mother made young Cailiang resentful of the Japanese, and he would make threatening gestures at Japanese whom he met in the street. Shi constantly reprimanded her son, saying: "You do that, and there'll be trouble."

Shi recalled the day in April 1922 when, without warning, the strike began.

While I was at work, the women workers suddenly flooded out of the factory and all the machines stopped. What was going on? I wanted to go out and see for myself, so my friend Wenjuan and I headed out together. As the women crowded forward, Wenjuan and I got separated. All alone, I was carried along by the crowd and ended up outside. I still wasn't very clear about what was happening, though this kind of thing had occurred the previous month: the workers had decided to go on strike, and we had dropped our work and gone outside. At the time I only knew that I worked to make money. I didn't understand much about anything else. But since we workers were like members of a family, when it came time to strike, everybody went, and so did I.

Hobbling along in great pain on bound feet, Shi and her friends learned that the strike the previous month had been to demand a raise in wages and that this strike was to oppose the outlawing of the Pudong Textile Workers' Union.

During the strike, the workers received help from students, among them her son Cailiang, who had been able to attend a Christian mission school. Cailiang in fact was injured in a skirmish with a guard in front of his mother's mill. On another occasion he distributed desperately needed strike support money, which was something that had never been available to the women before.

"This is money collected from the workers of the Soviet Union," he told his mother.[26] She had never heard the term "Soviet Union" before and asked him who these "workers of the Soviet Union" were. Cailiang told her about the Russian Revolution and the new state that it had brought to power.

"They overthrew the capitalists, the large landlords, and the emperor. Now they run things by themselves," he said. Five years passed before news of the Russian Revolution of 1917 had finally reached the ears of women working in the mills of Shanghai in 1922; and it was the young people reared in the May Fourth era who conveyed the news.

In the hope of breaking the strike, the company hired thugs to intercept the support money, which was, as a result, slow in reaching the hands of the women workers. Sister Shi volunteered to do the work of distributing it, and through this activity she became a member of the CCP. In 1924, after working at the Sino-Japanese mill for over twenty years, she was fired. She went on to run a night school for workers and was involved in the underground organization of women workers leading up to the May Thirtieth Movement. Cailiang died in the White Terror of 1928.

The White Terror and the Story of Xiang Jingyu

The great revolutionary upsurge of the period was not limited to the cities. As I shall discuss more fully in Chapter 7, the revolutionary storm swept through the countryside as well. It was under such conditions that the GMD government made its preparations for a national revolution. When in July 1926 the National Revolutionary Army of the GMD set out from Guangdong on its quest to overthrow the warlord regimes to the north, the revolution began.

Along its path, the army was greeted by sympathetic uprisings of workers and peasants. In Shanghai as well, the workers responded to the national revolution by staging three armed uprisings, and a provisional government was established by workers, students, and others in March 1927. The women workers of Shanghai were deeply involved in these uprisings, making bandages from old clothing sterilized in boiling water, organizing first-aid teams to care for the wounded, and transporting weapons and ammunition.

Sister Shi, under Party orders, also took part in this work, smuggling weapons across the Huangpu River. To hide what she was doing, she carried a baby. While waiting to be searched at the ferry dock, she would pinch the baby's bottom, and the child would begin to cry frantically. In the general hubbub Sister Shi was able to avoid inspection by the soldiers guarding the pier and smuggle her weapons to the other side. This episode shows how women made good use of their creative resources during the struggle.

The GMD was deeply ambivalent about the sudden development of a revolutionary situation in the wake of its Northern Expedition. Accordingly, Jiang Jieshi (Chiang Kai-shek), with the help of foreign interests, launched a counterrevolutionary coup d'état on

April 12, 1927. Troops under Jiang's orders disarmed the workers, took over the General Labor Union, and began a relentless hunt for Communists. During the rest of 1927 and on into 1928, when Jiang Jieshi replaced the first united front with the White Terror, 330,000 revolutionaries inside and outside the CCP were illegally executed. A thousand of them were women.

Among the women executed in this bloodbath was Xiang Jingyu (1895–1928).[27] Xiang, a native of Xupu county, Hunan, first came into contact with the new trends of thought in her youth by reading Liang Qichao's two serial publications, *Qingyi bao* (Journal of moralistic criticism) and *Xinmin congbao* (New citizen's journal), which her brother passed on to her. In 1912 in the wake of the Revolution, Xiang went to Changsha and entered the Third Hunan Women's Normal College, transferring later to the First Women's Normal College and then to Zhounan Women's College. The principal of Zhounan was a progressive thinker named Zhu Jianfan. From this school the revolutionary Cai Chang,[28] who would later become Xiang's sister-in-law, also graduated.

Xiang joined the movement in Changsha to oppose Yuan Shikai's capitulation to Japan's Twenty-One Demands, participating in demonstrations with her fellow students. As Cai Chang later recalled: "At that time she made many public speeches, during which she became so emotional that she nearly collapsed and fainted."[29] In these speeches she called for opposition to Yuan and the boycott of Japanese goods, quoting Gu Yanwu's (1613–1682) phrase, "the survival of the realm is everyone's responsibility." She graduated from Zhounan and then returned home to Xupu to become the principal of the county primary school, which was the first coeducational school in the province. There she launched attacks on the old ways of thought by advocating the equality of men and women and opposing footbinding.

At this time, France was accepting Chinese laborers in large numbers to compensate for a labor shortage. Through the Sino-French Educational Association and the Work-Study Association, the anarchist Li Shizeng and others were sending students to France to study as well as to work.[30] This was in the immediate aftermath of the Russian Revolution when there was great interest in socialism and belief in "the sacredness of labor." The movement struck a responsive chord among Chinese students then seeking a new path, and it expanded quickly. After fellow Hunanese Mao Zedong and others had gone to Beijing to promote the movement there, students in Hunan responded in the summer of 1918 by popularizing the work-study program through the New People's Study Association. This Association had been founded earlier that year by Mao Zedong, Cai Hesen (Cai Chang's brother and Xiang Jingyu's future husband), and others under the influence of the New Culture Movement, and many later members of the Communist Party emerged from the Association. Cai Chang was initially the only female member. As soon as news of the work-study movement reached Xupu, Xiang returned to Changsha. First she helped organize the Hunan Women's Association for Work-Study in France; then she herself set off for France together with Cai Chang and Cai's mother, Ge Jianhao.[31]

In France, the women engaged in both labor and study. Working in such places as light bulb factories, they put in ten-hour days on the job and then, despite their exhaustion, returned home to study French and, dictionary in hand, plow their way through *Humanité*, the official organ of the French Communist Party. They lived on a daily fare of beancakes and potatoes. Down and out in Paris, they got a personal taste of the lives of the workers at the bottom of society, an experience that propelled them further in the direction of socialism. The students organized "work-study cooperatives" to discuss the situation in China and what should be done. In the debates that arose with the anarchists in France, Xiang Jingyu and Cai Hesen played leading roles. In response, the Sino-French Educational Association cut off the students' support in 1921. In anger the students surrounded the Chinese embassy on February 28 to demand their rights to livelihood, study, and work. In the ensuing struggle, later known as the Twenty-Eighth Movement, the ambassador was assaulted. Xiang played a leading role in the event, for which she was arrested by the French police. Even among those who did not share her Communist viewpoint, Xiang was greatly admired and vividly remembered in later years for all she had done.[32]

Xiang married Cai Hesen, Cai Chang's brother, in France, but shortly after their marriage he was deported back to China, and she followed him. She joined the CCP in 1922, was elected to the Central Committee at the Second Party Congress, and was involved in working with women's organizations as the chief of the Central Women's Department of the Party. Xiang advocated building ties with women workers and was active in organizing workers in cotton-spinning and silk-reeling factories, where she was involved in leading strikes.[33] In 1926, she went to Moscow for a year to study at the University of the Toilers of the East. Upon her return she worked in the Propaganda Department of the Wuhan General Labor Union until the spring of 1928, when she was apprehended in the French Concession of Hankou and handed over to the GMD. On May 1 at the age of 33, she was executed. Many years later, Cai Chang recalled Xiang's heroism to Helen Foster Snow:

The workers prepared an uprising to try to capture her, so the [GMD] government hurried the execution. Martial law was declared in the city on the day of her public execution. . . . As she went through the streets she made speeches to the people and shouted slogans. The gendarmes beat her cruelly to try to stop this but she continued. Many people on the streets were crying.

In our Chinese Party I have never seen another member to compare with Hsiang Chin-yü [Xiang Jingyu]. Her death was an incalculable loss. She was a good, brave, loyal, active member from the earliest days of our Party. . . . She was an intellectual and liked to think and use her brain and could estimate political situations accurately.[34]

Her husband and fellow Communist leader Cai Hesen was captured in Hong Kong in 1931 and secretly put to death. Their two surviving children were raised by Ge Jianhao.

The White Terror continued, halting for a time both the labor movement and the women's struggle. But these movements could not be held back for long.

The Transformation of Rural Women

Infanticide, Adopted Daughters-in-Law, Rented Wives

The 1927 counterrevolutionary coup of Jiang Jieshi forced a temporary setback in the urban anti-imperialist movement centered in Shanghai. In China's vast countryside surrounding the cities, however, there was a force steadily growing in opposition to imperialism and the traditional landlord system. Soon the day for the land revolution would come. Before discussing this development, let me lay out a brief sketch of rural life and peasant women in China.

Although the 1911 Revolution overthrew the Qing dynasty, warlord dominance and imperialist aggression brought on the swift decline of the countryside. There were a number of reasons for this. First of all, the rural self-sufficiency which had existed until then was abruptly destroyed. As agricultural goods were transformed into commercial products, foreign commodities, protected by tariff privileges, came pouring into China. And as the prices of native agricultural products dropped sharply, peasant income steadily declined.

Second, warlord fighting devastated the countryside. Fields and rice paddies were laid to waste, and homes were burned to the ground. With every round of fighting, losses ran into the hundreds of millions of *yuan*. Furthermore, excessive issuance of paper money and military scrip by warlords to pay for war expenditures served only to fuel inflation. Prices skyrocketed.

Third, local governments levied heavy taxes. Additional taxes multiplied annually until the total sum was often more than 25 times the basic tax. On top of that, peasants were forced to pay future taxes years in advance. In 1926, for example, taxes in Henan province were levied through the year 1929, while in Shanxi province they were assessed through 1931.

The fourth factor was control by cruel landlords. Farm rent was generally at least 50 percent of the harvest, sometimes as much as 70–80 percent. What remained was never sufficient for peasants to survive on for a year. They therefore had no choice but to borrow rice and money to live through the slack season, and that led to formidably high interest payments. Peasants were strangled by the monthly interest rates of 5–10 percent, which amounted to more than the principal almost immediately. No matter how hard peasants worked, their income could never meet their expenditures. As one saying had it, "The poor man faces two swords—heavy farm rent and high interest. The poor man has three roads before him— to run away at night, to hang himself, or to go to jail."

For women in these villages, birth was only the beginning of their troubles. Baby girls had to be fed precious food even though they were not useful in the work force and played no role in carrying on the family line. In addition, when they grew up, they had to be married off. Because girls were considered utterly superfluous, infanticide by drowning developed into a common practice. Also, baby girls always received less food during periods of famine and were thus the first to die from starvation. As a result, the ratio between male and female children was markedly unbalanced. A look at the sex ratios—the number of males for every 100 females —shown in Table 6 will bear this out.[1]

In a general population, the sex ratio at the time of birth is approximately 105. Thus male births normally outnumber female, but the number of males to females usually balances out because the mortality rate of male infants is higher. In China's case, however, there were fewer female infants than average from the start, and as their age increased, this imbalance tended to become larger and larger. Moreover, when women reached childbearing age, their death in childbirth became another cause of mortality. The ratio of men to women eventually evens out when the male death rate surpasses that of women after the ages of 45 to 49. Although infanticide was not the sole cause of this imbalance between men and

TABLE 6
Sex Ratio by Age, Eleven Regions, 1924

Data	7 provinces, 2,640 rural families	Wuhan, 625 laborer families	Wuxi, 332 laborer families	Qinghezhen, 371 families	Dingxian, 515 rural families
Population	14,925	3,621	2,239	18,117	3,571
Age					
0–4	106.0	120.0	119.5	142.3	84.9
5–9	143.0	113.6	139.0	142.1	111.1
10–14	119.5	114.5	104.0	119.0	126.1
15–19	117.1	133.2	97.0	124.0	135.5
20–24	93.8	146.1	93.8	111.9	124.0
25–29	90.1	140.0	88.7	140.0	108.2
30–34	102.5	133.0	104.5	118.0	125.1
35–39	97.7	101.5	98.0	100.0	114.6
40–44	114.1	93.1	119.0	106.0	101.9
45–49	90.0	105.0	115.0	100.0	101.0
50–54	124.2	67.2	107.2	71.1	88.1
55–59	73.8	71.0	55.6	68.4	98.4
60–64	86.8	54.6	77.0	72.5	104.0
65–69	59.8	75.0	33.3	92.3	66.6
70–74	60.7	22.2	63.7	83.3	77.8
75–79	51.9	63.7	33.3	40.0	114.1
80 +	43.8	0.0	16.7	33.3	33.3
Average	105.7	112.2	100.1	111.5	105.7

SOURCE: Rural Village Economic Research Institute of Beijing University, *Zhongguo jingji niankan* [China economic yearbook], (1924).

women, it and its companion, neglect, were obviously major factors in the deaths of infant girls.

There were also cases in which women were not included in the family registers: a product, needless to say, of the perception that women were something less than human. These population statistics provide clear proof of male dominance over women.

This imbalance of men and women in the population naturally made marriage difficult for young men. According to Mac Zedong's "Investigation of Xingguo County," the landlords and rich farmers had both a wife and any number of concubines; however, 10 percent of middle peasants, 30 percent of poor peasants and craftsmen, 90 percent of unemployed itinerants, and 99 percent of hired farmhands did not have wives. Poor peasants accounted for approximately 70 percent of the rural population, and calculations show that, in fact, one quarter of all rural men were without wives.

Cruel exploitation even deprived poor peasant men of the freedom to have a family. In order to marry, a man needed on the order of 200 *yuan* for expenses, an amount nearly equal to the entire assets of a middle peasant; and poor peasants could not possibly afford such an expense.

One solution for the shortage of women was the custom of adopting a daughter-in-law.[2] At a low cost, a bride could be provided for a son by adopting a future daughter-in-law while she was still a child. In Shanxi province the price was set according to the girl's age: the older she was, the higher the market price. Adoption of a daughter-in-law served two purposes at once. The girl's parents were spared the expense of her board, plus they received a small sum from her sale. Meanwhile, the groom's parents could ensure that their son would have a bride as well as cut down on the marriage expenses.

The daughters-in-law so purchased were frequently older than the boys for whom they were intended. This was done so the family could get at least some useful labor from the girl early on. There were cases throughout China in which a girl carried her future husband on her back and washed his diapers, a laughable situation had it not been so tragic. Many songs, such as the following, were sung about the sorrows of being sold as an adopted daughter-in-law.[3]

Blooming Peaches

Peach blossoms bloom, peach blossoms wither.
Regrettably my parents sold me for money so they could eat.
They don't know the hardships I endure in my husband's home.
Grinding the handmill until noon, spinning thread till dawn,
Gathering firewood on the snow-covered mountain.
I meet my brother and tears roll down my face.
Brother, brother, sit for a while and listen to me.
The stone *kang*, the thin bed quilt,
It's so cold I can't sleep at night.
I hear the cock crow as I wait for the light of day.
If I open the window, the whole sky would be twinkling with
  stars.
I jump out of bed at my mother's voice,
Tie my hair in a scarf and scoop ashes from under the stove.
The well is far away and the road is slippery,

Two pails weigh heavily on my shoulders.
The sky is cold, the firewood damp,
And I've already gone through half the matches.
My uncle calls me a fool, my aunt beats me,
My husband's little sister pinches my ear.
My husband just stands by and frets.
When everyone has finished eating,
All that is left for me is an empty bowl.
Brother, brother, what on earth shall I do?

Thus, purchased daughters-in-law worked hard, endured the torment of their mothers-in-law, and were often nursemaids to their infant husbands. It was marriage in name only.

Do I Really Have a Husband?
The bride is eighteen, the groom is three.
I take the lamp and go to the bedroom.
When my husband grows up, my beauty will have already faded.
When the flower blooms, the leaves have already withered.
The bride is eighteen, the groom is three.
Every night I carry him to bed.
My eyes open in the dead of night and I wonder,
Is he my child or my husband?
Do I really have a husband?
Every night I sleep in a cold bed.
If I could only talk to my pillow,
It would feel sorry for me.

Research conducted in 1936 by Fei Xiaotong in Kaixiangong, a village south of Lake Tai in Jiangsu province, showed that 17 percent of married women and 39 percent of unmarried women were adopted daughters-in-law; there was on average one adopted daughter-in-law for every 2.7 households. The high proportion of adopted daughters-in-law among unmarried women reflects the economic depression of the 1930's. The more difficult the times, the greater the likelihood that girls would be sold into adoption in this way. Of course, some adopted daughters-in-law had less objectionable marital relationships than others; if a young woman was lucky, she might have a kind husband or mother-in-law.

Many men in Chinese villages, though, could not even afford to buy an adopted daughter-in-law for a wife. One way for men in this position to obtain a conjugal partner was for two or three of them to purchase one jointly (a practice called *huoqi*); another method was to rent another man's wife for a period of time (known as *dianqi* or *zuqi*).[4] Aside from these inhuman means, there was no other way to acquire a spouse. These forms of "marriage" through purchase or rental were tragic not only for the women involved, but for the men as well.

Conditions were more or less the same for women who were not sold as adopted daughters-in-law. Love was taboo in a system in which marriage was always contracted by the parents. One's property and family line constituted one's material base, and these considerations were accompanied by the barbaric intrusion of divination and fortune-telling under the traditional authority of religion. In such marriages women were treated not as human beings but as things, as private property. Whether bought as a sex object, as labor power, or as a machine for producing sons, a woman was regarded as a thing, not a person. Two sayings of the time ran, "You can ride or whip the wife you married and the horse you bought —it's up to you"; and "A demon is not a god, a woman is not a person." Although society recognized that marriage need not be based on love, was this "marriage" any different than prostitution by long-term contract?

Friedrich Engels once pointed out that while the bourgeoisie practiced monogamy, the proletariat actually had no families and thus resorted by necessity to overt forms of prostitution. It was inescapable that a peasantry without families as well as both overt and covert prostitution would develop as a result of the cruel exploitation inherent in the traditional order.

Men practiced unrestricted freedom in divorce. The following seven conditions in traditional lore became only too infamous as grounds for divorce: "If she disobeys her parents-in-law, divorce her. If she has no children, divorce her. If she's licentious, divorce her. If she talks too much, divorce her. If she becomes seriously ill, divorce her. If she's jealous, divorce her. If she steals, divorce her." And there was no recourse from male arbitrariness in divorce.

Women, however, had no freedom to choose divorce. Escape from marriage for a woman came either by being kicked out of the home or by death. "If a woman marries a chicken, she should obey the chicken; if she marries a dog, she should obey the dog." A woman was fundamentally unable to plead for divorce.

A woman who lost her husband, even if she had only been engaged, was not permitted to remarry. It was said, "It is better to die of starvation than to lose one's honor." No matter what, a widow had to remain single.[5] Many songs described the sorrows of widowhood.

The Twelve Lunar Months of a Widow's Grief

The New Year comes in the first month,
I'll pay a new year's call on the usurer.
Other people's calls are greeted with hospitality.
A widow is greeted with ice.

Flowers blossom in the second month.
I haven't enough food to eat twice a day.
Like a mute person tasting bitter herbs,
A widow can tell her pain to no one.

The Qingming Festival comes in the third month.
I carry a basket and visit the grave.
I see the mound of earth over there,
And nearly cry myself to death before I can calm down.

The nights are long in the fourth month.
I lie in bed and think about a lover.
Bound as I am by family law,
I yearn for an independence that I'll never see.

The Dragon Boat Festival arrives in the fifth month.
Dragon boats compete on the lake.
People who've come to watch are dressed in gay colors,
A widow wears ragged clothes.

The hot weather peaks in the sixth month.
I fan myself on my bed under a torn mosquito net,
There's no husband under the netting,
Only a pillow.

Autumn begins in the seventh month.
Without a husband I sink into gloom.
Like clothes hung out on a pole with no one to mind them,
I'm exposed to the rain and the sun.

The eighth month is the time to harvest rice.
A scythe in hand and a basket weighing on my back.
Don't laugh at me when you pass by,
With my husband dead, there is no other way.

The Double Nine Festival comes in the ninth month.
Being a farmhand isn't permanent, being a widow lasts forever.
A farmhand's term ends after three years,
A widow is alone for her whole bitter life.

Winter begins in the tenth month.
My quilt is torn with no patch to mend it.
If I stretch out my legs, I'll be cold,
If I curl them up, the chill will seep in the sides.

Snow dances about in the eleventh month.
My husband is already a person of the next world.
It doesn't matter that my clothes are ragged,
If there's no rice to eat, I can't go on living.

The year comes to an end in the twelfth month.
Families everywhere celebrate New Year's Eve,
Both rich and poor gather in circles in the evening.
The poor widow all alone,
Oh, God, the poor widow is all alone.

It has already been mentioned that such sexual discrimination was one link in the patrilineal structure of family control that supported the autocratic order under the Qing dynasty, but nothing in this regard changed after China became a republic in 1912. Rather, the more acutely the family system was felt to be threatened, the more the chastity of widowhood was commended. The peasant uprisings in the 1920's, however, greatly changed this situation.

Emancipation from the Husband's Control

The early cooperation between the GMD and the CCP unleashed a new era in peasant uprisings. A Peasant Department was organized at the GMD center, and a Peasant Movement Training Institute was established in Guangdong to train leaders for the movement (there were about thirty women among its graduates).[6] And a system of peasant associations begun in South China spread throughout the country.

The remarkable work accomplished by the women of Guangdong in the peasant uprisings prompted Zhu De to call them the most "heroic" women in China. In Guangdong most women shouldered the burden of agricultural production because the men worked away from home. For this reason, those who robbed the women of the literal fruits of their labor earned their hatred. These women voluntarily threw themselves into the peasant uprisings.[7]

For example, a peasant association was formed in 1924 in Guangning, Guangdong province, and began a struggle for the lowering of rents. The peasants involved in the uprising armed themselves and destroyed the landlord's gun towers. These were turrets built by landlords for self-defense, with guns aimed at the peasants. As the peasants burned down these towers, they shouted such slogans as, "Peasants and gun towers can never coexist," and "We can't live a single day in peace until we knock down the gun towers." Nor were peasant women afraid of the landlord's gunfire; they joined in the attack and carried the kerosene.

After the gun towers were destroyed and the landlords' arms confiscated, the peasant association spread rapidly. Publicity by peasant women was largely responsible for the expansion of this organization. More than a hundred peasant women themselves were said to have enrolled. In another case, women organized a Powder Spear Corps, and Hakka women as well participated in armed combat in regions to the northwest. As a result of these uprisings, some reductions in rent were attained, and the first Chinese soviet formed in Hai-Lufeng in 1927. In a short time, this regime enacted revolutionary policies under the dictatorship of the proletariat.

How did rural villages and the position of women change after the peasants rose and crushed the landlords' authority? Mao Zedong's "Report on an Investigation of the Peasant Movement in Hunan" addresses these issues most clearly for the case of Hunan province.[8]

The first major rural revolution erupted in 1926 in the southern and central parts of Hunan.[9] With two million people in the peasant associations, and the number of people over whom they exercised direct control at ten million, the peasant associations seized power. The old order fell into disarray, and the authority of the landlords collapsed. The peasants taunted the landlords with abusive questions, thronged to the landlords' houses and consumed their food, and on occasion publicly paraded them about in dunce caps. They campaigned for reductions in rent, tenancy deposits, and interest, and prevented the landlords from repossessing the land. Armed landlord associations were dismantled and replaced by armed peasant associations. Officials at the county level of government could no longer conduct business as they pleased since everything was decided by conferences between the county heads and mass organizations. Once the offending landlords were stripped of authority, litigation in the county courts simply disappeared. In the midst of these developments, the position of peasant women changed remarkably.

According to Mao Zedong, Chinese men were ordinarily controlled by three systems of authority. The first of these, political power, formed the state structure extending from the national, provincial, and county levels, down to the village. The second, the authority of the clan, evolved a structure ranging from the central ancestral temple of the main family and branch temples down to the heads of each household. The third form of authority was that of religion, which encompassed the realm of the gods, from the King of Hell and the guardian deities of the nether world at the county and village levels to the Great Jade Emperor and all the myriad deities and spirits of the celestial heavens. For women there was a fourth form of control, that of their husbands. These sources of authority—political, clan, religious, and male—embodied the entire ideology and institutions of the traditional familial system. These "four thick ropes," as Mao Zedong called them, bound the Chinese people, especially Chinese women.

The political authority of landlords constituted the backbone of these four types of dominance. Once their authority was overturned, the other forms of control began to weaken. First—clan authority. Where the peasant association assumed power, the clan heads could no longer oppress their descendants. Cruel corporal and capital punishments carried out in ancestral halls under the cloak of the ancestors' name were abolished as was the customary practice of barring women and the poor from joining in banquets at ancestral temples. In the town of Baiguo in Hengshan county, women broke into the ancestral temple, planted themselves down, and joined in the celebrations. And no one dared say a thing about it. Such an event would previously have been beyond anyone's imagination.

Religious authority also began to waver. Like the character of Xiang Lin's Wife in Lu Xun's short story "The New Year's Sacrifice" the deities themselves shackled women spiritually with an invisible rope.[10] Statues of Buddhist deities were smashed everywhere. The ancestral temples, which until that time had been used for worship, became offices for the peasant associations. Images of the deities were shoved into piles in the corners, and nobody complained.

The dominance of husbands had not been that strong among poor peasants. Poor peasant women were compelled to work in order to eat. For this reason, they had greater power to speak and make decisions in the family. Women formed associations and took an active part wherever peasant movements developed, weakening the dominance of men all the more. Mao Zedong noted the following:

In a word, the whole feudal-patriarchal system and ideology is tottering with the growth of the peasants' power. . . . Where it [the landlords' political authority] has been wholly destroyed, [the peasants] are beginning to press their attack in the three other spheres of the clan, the gods, and male domination. But such attacks have only just begun, and there can be no thorough overthrow of all three until the peasants have won complete victory in the economic struggle. Therefore, our present task is to lead the peasants to put their greatest efforts into the political struggle, so that the landlords' authority is entirely overthrown. The economic struggle should follow immediately. . . . As for the clan system, superstition, and inequality between men and women, their abolition will follow as a natural consequence of victory in the political and economic struggles.[11]

Mao vividly portrayed how, in the destruction of the old order, peasants, who had once been "a group of slaves," unleashed their limitless energies, and in the process women began to gain their freedom. He also sharply confronted the fact that oppression of women was actually rooted in landlord control, and only by destroying the landlords' authority (namely, political control) would it be possible to destroy clan, religious, and male dominance. Mao once accused Chinese society of having "murdered" the bride Zhao Wuzhen,[12] and he made it exceedingly clear that society was controlled by landlords. Thinking of women's liberation not in terms of the relationship between the sexes, but rather as being connected to the reform of the whole of society, particularly the elimination of landlord authority, was the concept that would illuminate the route to women's emancipation in China's future.

Two Marriage Laws

After the GMD's coup of April 12, 1927, the CCP organized a peasant insurrection in the city of Nanchang in Jiangxi province. Armed with guns, they moved the battlefield from the city to the countryside. The encirclement of the counterrevolutionary cities with revolutionary villages marked the strategic beginning of the Communist revolution.

During this period Mao Zedong led the peasant army insurgents on a march to Jinggangshan. He used this natural stronghold in the mountains to establish a soviet-style regime. By 1930 a total of fifteen liberated areas had expanded into provincial border zones centered around Jiangxi province. Delegates from each of the liberated areas met to establish the Chinese Soviet Republic (chaired by Mao) in 1931.[13]

The soviet regime was set up in these liberated areas, where landlord power had been crushed. Representatives were naturally elected *without discrimination between the sexes*. The Constitution of the Jiangxi Soviet stipulated that under the revolutionary administration everyone was equal in the eyes of the law regardless of sex, race, religion, or status as worker, peasant, Red Army soldier, or ordinary person. Anyone over the age of sixteen had the right to vote and was eligible for election. Elections on the basis of these regulations brought the total number of women representatives in the Soviet government to as high as 25 percent in certain places. Indeed, one might say that the Chinese Soviet Republic inaugurated women's suffrage at the "national" level.

In these areas a thoroughgoing land reform was also carried out. The Chinese Soviet Land Law declared that all land be confiscated from landlords (including rich peasants) and distributed to poor and middle peasants with no discrimination by sex among the able-bodied. With the slogan "Down with local bullies, divide up the land," peasants moved forward in the land revolution. In the midst of the movement, the peasants' consciousness underwent a major change. In order to protect their new political rights, participation in the Red Army and the people's militia increased. Women's activities in the people's militia were spectacular.

Amid the collapse of landlord rule and shortly after the establishment of the Chinese Soviet Republic, marriage regulations were promulgated on December 1, 1931. Even before this, the Xinjiang "provincial" government at the Min-Zhe-Gan base area under the leadership of Fang Zhimin was said to have announced provisional land and labor laws together with a marriage ordinance, but the actual content of these laws remains unclear.[14] The Marriage Regulations of 1931 were framed on the basis of Soviet Russia's Legal Code of 1926, with actual Chinese circumstances taken into account. It was China's first modern marriage law.[15] The Marriage Regulations proclaimed clearly that marriage was to be based on the volition of the man and woman involved, that the traditional system of marriage was to be entirely abandoned, and that the institution of monogamy was to be firmly established. It also declared that the rights of children should be protected.

We need to pay particular attention to the bylaws concerning divorce. Whereas in the old society, as mentioned above, women did not have freedom of divorce, the new law granted wives this freedom. Considering the diversity of cases that arose during the course of implementing the Marriage Law of 1950, it is readily imaginable how radical a step granting freedom of divorce was in the early 1930's. Moreover, thorough protection was provided for divorced women just emancipated from traditional restraints. There were also extremely concrete stipulations for a divorced man, such as assuming responsibility for his former wife's support and cultivating the farm land in her stead until such time as she remarried. As concerned responsibility for the upbringing of the children, men had to provide two-thirds of the living expenses in cases in which women raised the children. In addition, all property from the marriage was to be divided equally between the former couple, but all debts jointly incurred were to be shouldered by the man.

The Marriage Regulations ultimately developed into the Chinese Soviet Marriage Law, promulgated on April 8, 1934. The law was adopted in the bases of resistance during the war against Japan, and finally evolved into the Marriage Law of the People's Republic of China.[16]

Approximately six months before the Marriage Regulations

were enacted by the Chinese Soviet Republic in December 1931, the Nationalist government of Jiang Jieshi also proclaimed as part of the new Civil Code of the Republic of China a section on family law.[17] It was part of the GMD regime's modernization policies, but, insofar as it was actually instituted, one would be hard-pressed to say that it denied the traditional Chinese system of marriage. For women in particular, it failed to so much as acknowledge adequately the rights of the individual.

With respect to freedom of marriage in the GMD's Family Law, if a marriage was formally arranged through a go-between, it was regarded as legal even if the parties concerned had not initially agreed to it. If it had not been formally arranged, however, it was deemed illegal even if the persons involved had consented to it. The law stated, for example, that if a boy and girl had reached seven years of age and were willing to be married, the wedding ceremony could be conducted by legal proxy, providing it was in concurrence with Article 982 of the Civil Code, which required the presence of two or more witnesses. A marriage was considered legitimate even if the couple did not actually cohabitate. In addition, there were strict regulations regarding extramarital affairs; whether both parties to the affair loved each other was irrelevant. If either the man or the woman was already married, the case was naturally judged to be adultery. Even in the case of a formal divorce, such lovers were forbidden to then marry. Bigamy was prohibited, but a husband who kept a concubine was not regarded as a bigamist, and a woman could not demand a divorce on such grounds.

Although freedom of divorce was officially recognized for both men and women, it was strictly limited by a clause consisting of ten parts that caused women in particular considerable difficulty in filing for divorce. For example, a divorce could be approved if either the man or the woman had been so abused that cohabitation was no longer tolerable. According to the legal interpretation of the Supreme Court under the Nationalist regime, however, as long as a mother-in-law did not abuse her daughter-in-law to the point of breaking her limbs or inflicting upon her a serious handicap, the woman could not demand a divorce. Even in such cases, if the husband had not been complicit in his mother's conduct, the law stated that there were insufficient grounds for divorce. This meant that freedom of divorce effectively did not exist.

Thus, not only did the Family Law not truly recognize freedom of marriage, but in addition the Nationalist government lacked both the will and the capacity to implement this law honestly. The Marriage Regulations of the Chinese Soviet Republic included concrete protective provisions aimed at guaranteeing women's freedom of divorce, whereas the Family Law section of the Civil Code of the Republic of China recognized freedom of divorce while adding a clause of strict limitation that actually denied women this freedom. The difference between the CCP's and the GMD's policies concerning women is vividly reflected in the difference between these two marriage laws.

Portraits of Women Who Participated in the Long March

Jiang Jieshi was reinstated as Supreme Commander of the National Revolutionary Army in 1928, at which time he recommenced the Northern Expedition. Although the Nationalist government achieved unity for a time, in reality this was only domination by the new warlords of the GMD under the name of the Nationalist government. Chiefly as a means of strengthening its dictatorship, the GMD publicized economic construction with much fanfare under a series of modernization policies. Every year the imbalance between trade revenues and expenditures grew, and the demise of the countryside became more and more imminent. Meanwhile, Jiang Jieshi and the four big families[18] accumulated enormous fortunes in bureaucratic capital.

By contrast the revolutionary base areas under CCP control were expanding steadily. At even the lowest estimate, in 1934 the Communists controlled an area of 100,000 square miles with a population of roughly 36 million. In order to crush the Communists, Jiang Jieshi, who continued to receive aid from imperialist sources, laid siege to the revolutionary base areas in a series of encirclement campaigns. The campaign of October 1933 proved especially threatening. With a force of one million troops and 200 planes,[19] he launched a full-scale attack, deploying 500,000 troops to execute the main thrust of the assault against the central base area in Jiangxi. The Chinese Soviet Republic fought to repulse this attack with 100,000 regular troops and 200,000 of the people's militia. The leadership made errors, and the Red Army not only failed to repel the attack but suffered serious casualties as well.

Taking advantage of this civil war, the Japanese military had begun an open invasion of China from the Manchurian Incident of September 18, 1931. In the spring of 1933, the Japanese captured Rehe and concluded the Tanggu Accord with the Nationalist regime; this rendered the Jidong region a demilitarized zone and put all of North China under Japan's supervision. In response, the Chinese Soviet government formally declared war on Japan in 1932 and appealed for an immediate end to the civil war and for a nationwide armed resistance against the Japanese imperialists.

In the face of this unprecedented national crisis, the CCP finally decided to abandon its revolutionary base and send the main force of the Red Army north. This was the Long March of some 6,000 miles, a grand revolutionary epic as never before seen in world history. On October 16, 1934, the Red Army's First Front Army began a great strategic migration from western Fujian to southern Jiangxi. It then proceeded to cross western China's eighteen precipitous mountain ranges and ford the rough waters of fourteen rivers before arriving in northern Shaanxi in October of 1935. The total distance of the Long March is approximately five times the length of the entire Japanese archipelago. While 300,000 members of the Red Army began the march, only 30,000 remained when they reached northern Shaanxi. In the words of Mao Zedong, the Long March was the revolution's manifesto, its propaganda team, and its machine for planting the seeds of revolution. It demonstrated the Red Army's indomitable spirit and spread the revolutionary word to the Chinese people. In a short time the revolutionary seeds that had been sown would ripen and bear abundant fruit.

At this time the Red Army comprised the First, Second, and Fourth Front Armies. Thirty women cadres belonged to the First Front Army. Through the recollections of one of them, Deng Yingchao, we can retrace the steps of such women who made the 6000-mile journey on foot.[20] In October of 1934 the First Front Army departed from Ruijin, Jiangxi province, broke through Jiang Jieshi's encirclement, and repeatedly fought battles with large armies numbering in the tens of thousands as well as with local warlords. The 30 women cadres worked in the middle echelons in charge of operations, and they were frequently threatened by enemy attack. When they entered Guangxi province from Hunan, they came under enemy fire while crossing Laoshanjie Mountain. This crossing was extremely steep, though it did not compare with the dangerous places they would encounter at a later date. The worst of these were Dadu River, Great Snow Mountain, and the Grasslands.[21]

The Dadu River flows in western Sichuan. At the fording point it rages through a deep gorge spanned by Luding Bridge, an iron chain suspension bridge. When the Red Army arrived there, nearly half of the bridge's planking had been dismantled, making a full-scale crossing impossible. Select Red Army troops crossed the bridge under a shower of gunfire from the other side of the river. The first, second, and third soldiers to attempt a crossing were gunned down, but the soldiers who followed were not afraid. When at last they reached the opposite side, they pursued the enemy army and rebuilt the bridge. The whole army then crossed the bridge, victorious in its battle for the Dadu River.

Great Snow Mountain awaited them next. This remote, unexplored mountain commanding a view of Tibet measures 4,000 meters in altitude. The higher they climbed, the thinner the air became, making it increasingly difficult to breathe. A cold fog covered the dark sky, and snow lay several feet deep under foot. The weather was unbelievably frigid in July. The Red Army had to complete the hike over the mountain by four o'clock in the afternoon, before night fell—up and down for thirty kilometers, with no rest permitted along the way. Weakened, sick comrades were unable to keep up. Many died atop Great Snow Mountain, buried in snow storms or unable to stand up again after a short rest. As they made the crossing at Maheba, it was as if the four seasons of an entire year passed in a single hour. At the foot of the mountain was the blazing June heat. Halfway up the mountain they were met with the beautiful foliage of a glorious spring. When they climbed further up, the weather suddenly turned cold, and the trees were all colored in autumnal yellows and reds. They advanced a little higher, and as far as the eye could see there was nothing but snow as in the dead of winter.

They then arrived at the Grasslands, which from the distance looked like a natural green carpet spread over the entire area. When they looked closely, though, they saw that there was mud beneath the grass and no way to go around it. The whole area was like a giant sponge. One misstep off firmer ground meant sinking into a bottomless quagmire; the more one struggled, the deeper one sank. Anyone who tried to help would be sucked into the muddy swamp as well. Those comrades who tried to help others often died after becoming hopelessly mired themselves. Also, changes of weather in this area were severe. If at one moment the sky was clear, it might cloud up the next and pour down torrents of rain. Since there were no shelters, they camped out in the open, not even able to boil rice. The emergency food they carried just barely held off starvation. The march across the Grasslands lasted seven days and nights. Deng Yingchao was suffering from tuberculosis at the time, and she contracted a high fever on the second day of the march. By the last day, after seven days without a single grain of rice to eat, she could not even walk. She spent the last day atop one of the horses, apparently stopping every five minutes to rest. When they finally arrived at Banyou, she found an old barn, full of cow and horse manure, and she at last felt hopeful about the future.

Thus, the Long March was both a battle against Jiang Jieshi's forces and a battle with nature. What sort of women were the 30 cadres who limped into Yan'an after having miraculously endured so much daily suffering? Let me first commemorate these sturdy women who took part in the Long March by naming each one of them: Liu Qunxian, Chen Huiqing, Wei Gongzhi, Liu Ying, Li Bozhao, Qian Xijun, Zhou Yuehua, Wu Zhonglian, Xie Xiaomei, Li Jianhua, Qiu Yihan, Li Jianzhen, Wei Xiuying, Liao Yuehua, Wu Hulian, Wang Ganzhi, Dong Yulin, Liu Caixiang, Li Xiaohong, Kang Keqing, Zheng Yu, Yang Houzeng, Jin Weiying, He Zizhen, Cai Chang, Deng Yingchao, A Qing, Liao Shiguang, Han Shi-ying, Deng Liujin. Nearly all of these women were married, most being wives of Communist Party leaders. Another 30 non-cadre women reportedly also participated in the Long March. Included in that group were pregnant women, women who had given birth scarcely a month before departing, and astonishingly one woman with bound feet.[22]

Nym Wales (Helen Foster Snow), who acquired an excellent understanding of the Chinese revolution, smuggled herself into Yan'an in 1937 where she was able to meet with some of these women. What follows are some profiles of these women based in part on her report *Inside Red China*.[23]

Cai Chang (born in 1900) had been active since the May Fourth Movement.[24] She helped organize the work-study group with which she traveled to France, and she later also studied at the University of the Toilers of the East in Moscow, before returning to China in 1925 to engage in revolutionary work. She was the first woman appointed to the GMD's General Political Department at the time of the Northern Expedition. In 1928 she participated in the Sixth Congress of the Comintern as a representative from Jiangxi province. In 1931 she entered the Chinese Soviet area. Although she suffered from tuberculosis during the Long March, Cai frequently cared for other soldiers. Her fellow troops affectionately called her "Big Sister Cai," and they often cajoled her into singing the Marseillaise in French.

During her long revolutionary experiences, Cai lost many of her friends. At the time of Jiang Jieshi's coup of April 12, 1927, she watched more than 100 women comrades die shouting, "Long live the Chinese Communist Party" and "Long live the proletarian revolution." Three of her close family members also lost their lives in the revolution: her older brothers, Cai Hesen and Cai Linzhen, and her sister-in-law Xiang Jingyu. The death of Xiang Jingyu made the deepest impression on her. Watching Cai Chang recall these events while struggling to keep her grief under control, Nym Wales felt it was indeed a wonder that a woman who possessed such richly subtle emotions as Cai had not been spiritually destroyed by the brutality she had encountered during her long revolutionary service. While studying in France she married Li Fuchun. Later in Yan'an she was the only woman among the leaders of the CCP. In addition, she served as Chief of the Women's Department in the Shaan-Gan-Ning base area, and after 1949 as a member of the Central Committee of the CCP and as head of the Chinese Women's Association.

Unlike Cai Chang, Liu Qunxian (born in 1907) came from a poor proletarian background. In her youth she made a living by plaiting and selling hairnets and by raising silkworms. At age eleven she was sold as an adopted daughter-in-law. Not able to endure the abuse from her husband's family, she returned to her own home and became a factory worker in a textile mill in Wuxi. There she worked a fourteen-hour day starting at 4:30 in the morning. It was during this period of harsh working conditions that she began to question capitalist exploitation: "Why do they curse at us if we are gone too long at the toilet? Why do they have to search inside the pants of women after work?" Consequently, she moved toward accepting Communist ideas, and at the time of the Northern Expedition she sprang into action together with 20,000 other workers. Afterward, the Party sent her to study in Moscow, where she married Bo Gu. Upon returning to China, she became involved in the labor movement and shortly thereafter moved to the Soviet area.

She made the trek of the Long March in great pain, having just given birth. Although she was said to have argued with Cai Chang about food, she was apparently satisfied to eat wild plants all day, as long as they were cooked; one can only imagine what a strong stomach she must have had. Tragically, she had to bear the responsibility of bringing her twelve-year-old child on the Long March only to watch her freeze to death on the Grasslands; the child, although young, had been working as an army nurse.

Kang Keqing (born in 1912) was of Jiangxi peasant stock. At the age of sixteen she joined the Red Army, and the following year she married Zhu De at Jinggangshan. In 1931, in the midst of the GMD's five extermination campaigns, she joined the Communist Party, received military training at the Red Army University in Ruijin, and graduated with honors. At times she commanded as many as 300 soldiers in battle against the enemy. She was feared even by Red Army troops—"Zhu De's wife is ferocious," they said, and they nicknamed her the "Woman Commander."

She referred to the Long March as a long stroll. Although she occasionally rode a horse, she walked almost the entire way, carrying her belongings on her back. At times she even carried the bags of weaker people as well. In Yan'an she entered the Anti-Japanese Military and Political Academy where she studied how best to become a commander of military field operations. As she remarked to Nym Wales: "I don't care much about the women's problem; I always work with men, not with women."[25] In order to remain active in the military, she kept herself in perfect physical condition and had no children.

Li Jianzhen (born in 1907) came from a poor peasant background in Guangdong. She was sold as an adopted daughter-in-law shortly after birth, and she was married at age seventeen. Unable to love her husband, who was ten years her senior, she soon became attracted by the slogan of "equality between the sexes," and she participated in the peasant movement in Hai-Lufeng. In 1927 she joined the CCP. Several members of her husband's family also sympathized with the revolutionary cause, and four of them were killed by enemy troops, one of them being her husband. After the Hai-Lufeng uprising, she fought in eastern Guangdong, distributed land, and publicized the revolutionary movement. Moreover, she took charge of women's operations in Dapu, and there she organized a thousand women coolies into a Coolies' Union of which she became the leader. She too found the Long March not so difficult an experience. While women were permitted to ride horses, only a very few actually did, so that the horses could be reserved for comrades wounded or injured along the way.

The women cadres who marched with the First Front Army were mentally and physically tough. After the year-long march, these 30 women reached Yan'an safely and found a new place to work. The 2,000 women with the Fourth Front Army, however, fared less well, because the leader of the Fourth Front Army, Zhang Guotao, split up his troops and abandoned the plan to go north to fight the Japanese. These women took the reverse route south, and with the Fourth Front Army they ended up crossing the Grasslands and Great Snow Mountain three times and spent eight months wandering over the Tibetan plateau. Later, they once again headed north, with one group taking the Silk Road and continuing the dreadful march across the Gobi Desert with no clear destination in sight. The women in this group either died of illness or deserted the ranks. Only two returned safely from the desert.

Huang Liangcheng was with the Fourth Front Army and left the following story in his memoirs of the Long March.[26] Once while being transferred as a captured prisoner, he ran into a woman comrade who had deserted. She was all alone, a ghostly figure walking in great pain along the road. At the time Huang was planning to escape and flee to Yan'an, but without revealing the details of his plans, he asked this woman to join him. She refused to believe that Huang had served in the ranks of the Red Army. She surveyed him dubiously—hadn't he been tricked and captured?—and refused his invitation. Wearing a smile of victory, she continued on her way. As he watched her figure retreating in the distance, Huang marveled at how steadfast and brave a soldier she must have been. Whether they reached Yan'an or not, all the women on the Long March lived dauntless lives as revolutionaries.

The War Against Japan and the Liberation of China

The Japanese invasion of China escalated from the early 1930's. In 1935 the He-Umezu Accord was signed, and a Japanese puppet regime—the Eastern Hebei (Jidong) Anti-Communist Autonomous Government—was established. The Japanese were trying to turn North China into a second Manchuria. During the Long March, the CCP issued a proclamation on August 1, 1935, appealing to their fellow countrymen to cease the civil war and join together in a movement to resist Japanese aggression and save the country. They resolved that the establishment of a united front against Japan was to be their immediate new policy.

The student movement in Beijing erupted on December 9, 1935, leading to a mass anti-Japanese movement which spread throughout the country. The famous Xi'an Incident took place around this time. The GMD's Northwest and Northeast Armies, inflamed with anti-Japanese feelings, imprisoned Jiang Jieshi who had come on a visit to encourage them. They demanded an end to the civil war and his cooperation in resisting Japan. Jiang Jieshi was forced to accept their demands.

The movement to resist Japan continued to grow stronger. Then, on July 7, 1937, came the Marco Polo Bridge Incident. Claiming that soldiers who had left their posts to relieve themselves during night maneuvers had never returned, the Japanese sent three army divisions into North China. Fighting spread at once. Beijing and Tianjin fell to the Japanese, and Shanghai capitulated soon thereafter. On August 14 the GMD government at last formally declared war on Japan and accepted the CCP's proposal to establish a national united front against Japan. It was the second GMD-CCP collaboration in ten years.

For more than a year after the start of the Sino-Japanese War, the Japanese army seemed to have gained an overwhelmingly superior position. It occupied North China, East China, and part of

South China—an area extending over ten provinces. All China's major cities—Shanghai, Nanjing, Hankou, and the like—fell into Japanese hands.

When Nanjing surrendered, the Imperial Army of Japan murdered an estimated 200,000 people,[27] including not only soldiers but unarmed civilians as well. So many dead bodies were thrown into the Yangzi River that it looked as if it had been dyed red. Every day mountains of corpses were doused with gasoline and burned. Later a trial before the International Military Tribunal of the Far East examined this massacre and poignantly expressed the dreadful suffering brought about by the war.[28] For as long as the war continued, pillaging, burning, rape, and slaughter became everyday affairs all over China.

A soldier in the Japanese army at the time recounted the assault on women during the rape of Nanjing in the following manner.

In any case, the women suffered the most. All the women were raped, from the youngest to the oldest. We rode on a charcoal truck from Xiaguan to a village, rounded up the women and divided them among the soldiers. Fifteen to twenty soldiers shared each woman, you know. They'd choose a nice sunny place near a warehouse or some building like that and lean tree branches up against it. Soldiers who got their sergeant's chop mark on a slip of paper—it was called a red ticket—took off their breechcloth and lined up to wait their turn. There wasn't a soldier who missed this chance to commit rape. Usually we killed the girl after we finished. We'd jump off her, then shoot her in the back. If we didn't kill 'em, they'd cause trouble for us later. If the military police found out, we'd get court-martialed. We didn't want to kill 'em, but we had to.[29]

The rape victims ranged in age from helpless nine-year-olds to women as old as 76. According to testimony at the International Military Tribunal of the Far East, raped women numbered in the thousands to the tens of thousands. Moreover, as this former soldier explained, nearly all these women were killed because the act of rape itself violated military regulations.

Even though a state of war existed, the outrageous atrocities committed by these soldiers cannot be condemned enough. By the same token, it must have been a tragedy of a different order for the Japanese men ignorant of the fact that sex was something to be cherished, and it certainly must have been a tragedy for those

Japanese women who had sexual relations with these men. All reports of these events in Nanjing were painstakingly covered up by
the Japanese. It was said that the troops of the Japanese Imperial
Army had risked their lives in a "holy war" to bring a realm of
peace and prosperity to war-ravaged China. However, the Eighth
Route Army in North China and the New Fourth Army in Central China blocked the advance of the Japanese forces. These armies
attacked the Japanese in the rear and established anti-Japanese bases
of resistance throughout the country. Mobile and guerrilla warfare
were their strengths, and they exhausted the Japanese troops.

During the anti-Japanese war, upon which hinged China's national fate, women did not end up only as victims. Both the anticipation and the experience that war brought humiliation to women
drove many to rise up and play an active role.[30] Following the Marco
Polo Bridge Incident, women in Beijing immediately organized
into rescue teams, first-aid teams, and political propaganda teams,
and some joined Song Zheyuan's Twenty-Ninth Army. When the
Twenty-Ninth Army was annihilated, many of these women proceeded to Qingdao by boat or to Nanjing by land. Some women
broke through the Japanese blockade and joined the regular Chinese
army along the Beijing-Hankou rail line or along the Grand Canal.
Others joined the guerrillas in the mountains around Beijing, and
some joined the Eighth Route Army.

Some of the women who remained in Beijing published underground newspapers in towns that had fallen into enemy hands,
appealed to people to resist Japan, and served as lines of commu-
nication to the guerrillas. The struggle in Shanghai reached a peak
of violence; and women there formed a volunteer corps, carrying wounded soldiers back from the front to give them medical
aid. Women also took it upon themselves to write letters for the
wounded and to organize entertainment to rouse their spirits. They
hurriedly established a nurses' training school, trained 2,000 nurses
in two months, and sent them to hospital facilities at the front lines.

During the next year, 1938, the War of Resistance and the
women's movement rose in unison. The older YMCA, the new
Women's Wartime Relief Association (with over one hundred
branches at the time), the National War Orphans Shelter Association, and other groups all merged to form a Women's Steering

Committee. In July 1938, just one year after the Marco Polo Bridge Incident, this Committee held a meeting in Hankou at which CCP leaders, who had been hiding underground during the civil war, also took part. The new political climate resulting from the second GMD-CCP united front for the first time enabled GMD women, CCP women, and unaffiliated women to combine forces in the resistance against Japan. The Committee planned to aid orphans and wounded soldiers, to comfort the troops at the front lines, to educate peasant women, and to publish magazines. It also planned to revive handicraft production and develop agricultural production in the countryside under wartime conditions. Thus, the Women's Steering Committee grew rapidly as a united front organization of women.

Many groups were active under the umbrella of the united front, each retaining its individual character. The Hunan War Zone Service Corps accompanied the fighting troops from Shanghai to Hankou. The Yunnan Women's War Zone Service Corps marched 6,000 *li* (3,000 kilometers) from the remote southwest to the battle lines of Central China. And, the Guangxi Women's Fighting Corps walked 4,000 *li* (2,000 kilometers) from Guilin to their destination, the Fifth War Zone, north of the Yangzi River. Each group joined the fight against Japan in its respective theater of battle.

The liberated areas or border regions under CCP control became the bases of the anti-Japanese resistance. Besides the Shaan-Gan-Ning border region centered in Yan'an, the Jin-Cha-Ji border region (at the vortex of Shanxi, Chahar, and Hebei provinces), the Jin-Ji-Lu-Yu border region at the frontiers of Henan, Hebei, Shandong, and Shanxi provinces (centering around the Taihang Mountains), and the Jin-Sui border region in the Shanxi-Suiyuan area were all built as bases of resistance for fighting the Japanese. The New Fourth Army also constructed a number of anti-Japanese bases in Central China. Extensive areas of guerrilla activity, in which the armed populace conducted guerrilla warfare, surrounded the liberated areas.

The border regions functioned as giant strongholds in the war against Japan. Because these regions had a regular army plus a militia that was several times larger, even if the Japanese army penetrated the liberated areas, it eventually had to retreat. But there was another reason as well. Although the democratic regimes in

TABLE 7
*Number of Women Serving as
County-Level Representatives from Thirteen Counties
of the Shaan-Gan-Ning Border Region, 1941*

County	Number	Percent of all representatives
Yan'an	18	22%
Chishui	8	14
Fuxian	9	14
Tongguanyao	3	13
Yanchi	4	10
Gulin	3	9
Chunyao	4	9
Jingbian	6	7
Qingyang	5	6
Ansai	4	5
Suide	9	4
Zhenyuan	2	4
Ganquan	1	4

SOURCE: "Zhongguo funü" [Chinese women], no. 2, *Jiefang ribao* [Liberation daily], Oct. 2, 1941.

the base areas were recognized by the GMD government as border governments according to the united front agreement, an altogether new society was emerging there under the leadership of the CCP.

The administration of these liberated areas was carried out in conjunction with the will of the people. Representatives to regional assemblies were chosen by election, and these assemblies then formed governments. Men and women over the age of eighteen enjoyed equal voting rights and were eligible for election without discrimination by sex. Nearly 95 percent of the people in these border areas were illiterate, and it was not easy for them to exercise the franchise. At election time beans were dropped into tea bowls of different colors distinguishing the candidates, or the beans themselves were colored to indicate the candidates and then dropped into a bowl. The rate of women voters was fairly high: from 22.5 percent to 47.5 percent of all voters in many areas.

For the ratio of female to male representatives elected in 1941, see Table 7; for a more detailed look at the backgrounds of the eighteen women from Yan'an, see Table 8. Inasmuch as Yan'an was the seat of the border region's government, it may have been a somewhat special case, but we can still discern general tendencies.

TABLE 8
*Backgrounds and Social Positions of the Eighteen
Women Representatives from Yan'an, 1941*

Background	Number	Social position	Number
Worker	1	Elementary school teacher	3
Poor peasant	12	Women's movement activist	9
Middle peasant	3	Public servant	2
Petty bourgeoisie	2	Peasant	4

SOURCE: "Zhongguo funü," no. 4, *Jiefang ribao*, Nov. 9, 1941.

As Table 8 shows, a significant majority of the women came from poor peasant families, and many had been activists in the women's movement. Eight women were between the ages of 18 and 23; ten were between ages 24 and 44; one was a university graduate; and three were normal school graduates. Half of the group of eighteen were completely illiterate, and five others could just barely read. When illiterate women took part in such an important affair of state through participation in this region's elections, they were doing something unprecedented in China.

Each of the liberated areas had a provisional constitution made up of general principles of administration. For example, the provisional constitution of the Shaan-Gan-Ning border region declared its support for "Raising women's political, economic, and cultural position in society on the basis of the fundamental principle of equality between the sexes; giving full play to the positive economic contributions of women; protecting women workers, pregnant women, and children; and adhering to monogamy based on free will."

The women in these areas, however, unlike the "formidable" women of South China, did not as a rule venture beyond the gates of their homes all day and in general did not engage in fieldwork. In addition, the severe cold of the winter climate served to make society even more closed, and discrimination against women was extremely severe. To call for equality between the sexes was too radical in such a place. When the local women heard such slogans as "Freedom in marriage," "Economic independence," and "Oppose the four oppressions," they refused to accept them. Support for the wife in a marital quarrel or siding with a daughter-in-law who was having trouble with her mother-in-law only led to social ostracism.

At this juncture petty bourgeois feminism ran into an immense wall. Cai Chang realized, "Today the slogans of our women's work movement can no longer be 'Freedom in marriage' and 'Sexual equality.' They must be 'Save the children' and 'Prosperity for the family.' "[31] This practical realization gave rise to the four pillars of the women's movement at this time: production, literacy, hygiene, and democratic harmony in the family. Needless to say, the most important of these four pillars was production.

In 1943 the Central Committee of the CCP issued a "Resolution on Women's Work at Present in the Anti-Japanese Base Areas."[32] Mao Zedong was said to have gone over it meticulously. The following excerpt comes from that report.

We have three major tasks in the anti-Japanese bases: combat, production, and education. What all peasant women can most easily and most appropriately participate in is production. It is just as combative and glorious for all women to work hard in production as for men to go to battle at the front. To enhance women's political position and cultural level, to improve women's standard of living, and to achieve liberation, we must start with economic improvement and independence. Raising production, increasing savings, and realizing a comfortable standard of living for women and the family will exert enormous influences on economic construction in the base areas. Furthermore, by achieving these material improvements, women will be able to escape from feudal oppression. These are the central problems in working with the masses, which are also of particular interest to peasant women, and they point to a new direction for women's work in the anti-Japanese bases of resistance.

Indeed, the move for production changed women's status and played an important role in raising their consciousness. For example, no one in Liulin (Yan'an county) had known how to spin cotton. The Women's Association tried without success to form a cotton-spinning group. A cotton-spinning factory was built and people were invited to work in it, but this approach had equally little success. Nevertheless, the head of the local cooperative demonstrated attentive concern in planning for women's experiences and feelings, and this tenacity proved persuasive. In the end, each family did their cotton-spinning at home, and as a result families prospered financially and domestic quarrels decreased. Later, women ventured over to the cooperative in groups because the men were unable to discriminate between good and bad cotton. There they took raw cotton, spun it into thread, and made it into cloth. This activity rapidly freed women who until then had been confined inside their homes. Women were happy to do their part, as was needed, in both cotton-spinning and the cooperative. And they became interested in politics.

Furthermore, in attempting to spin cotton, they found that bound feet proved to be a disability in every respect. Until this period women in this area of China had had bound feet, and although the custom of binding the feet of young girls did not disappear, women gradually came to oppose it. Since some ability in reading and arithmetic was helpful in the delivery of thread and raw cotton, women's cultural aspirations rose as well. Thus, women's participation in production raised the economic capacity of the base areas and became an important force supporting the war of resistance against Japan.

The main issues involved in the second "pillar"—hygiene—were the dissemination of new techniques in child delivery and the improvement of child care. A variety of superstitions about the delivery of newborns as well as methods of delivery that contradicted common medical science made the mortality rate both for mothers and newborns extraordinarily high. Of course, every mother was interested in whatever concerned her own life and that of her baby, and this helped to destroy religious superstitions and to spread a common knowledge of medicine. We should also note that women were taught the physiology of pregnancy and methods of birth control.[33] By contrast, in Japan during the war, women were regarded as baby-producing machines and were encouraged—with the slogan "Have more babies!"—to deliver as many children as possible.

As for the third "pillar"—the literacy movement—small literacy classes were set up in many villages. The campaign was directed at illiterate women, who made up 90 percent of the pupils. In addition, a literacy class called "winter school" was held during the slack season in farming. Results of the literacy movement in the Jin-Ji-Lu-Yu border region, for example, can be seen in Table 9. After only six months, 20–25 percent of the students learned to read at the rudimentary level of 50–200 characters. Of course, these women were not satisfied to remain at this elementary stage. With the distribution of land under land reform, some groups formed

TABLE 9
Results of the Literacy Program for
Women in the Jin-Ji-Lu-Yu Border Region,
First Six Months of 1941

Illiterate women over age 15	8 villages in Liaoxian	4 villages in Licheng
Total (in early 1941)	1,568	1,165
Learned 50–200 characters (in 6 months)		
Number	389	233
Percent	24%	20%

SOURCE: "Zhongguo funü," no. 8, *Jiefang ribao*, Jan. 16, 1942.

for the study of agriculture and others for the study of Marxism. Women even started to play sports. That the Communist Party instilled a desire for knowledge among peasant women who until then had scarcely left their houses and who had had virtually no chance for education is truly remarkable.

At a different level, a women's college (headed by Meng Qishu) was established in Yan'an.[34] Not an institution for local women, its main purpose was instead to educate a variety of young women from outside Yan'an. Characteristic of the Yan'an landscape, the college "buildings" were a row of consecutive caves resembling a harmonica. Nearly a thousand young women, divided into three classes, took courses there. The first class included all those unable to read or write; they studied Chinese, social issues, hygiene, politics, military affairs, and introductory CCP history. The next class studied social history, political economy, various issues confronting the CCP, Sun Yat-sen's "Three Principles of the People," military affairs, introductory philosophy, and public hygiene. The third class was more advanced; the curriculum at this level included political economy, Marxism-Leninism, philosophy, the history of the world revolution, and foreign languages. Surprisingly, study of the women's movement was the only course in the required curriculum that reminded one that it was a women's college; all three classes examined the subject within the context of Chinese social issues.

Except for uniforms and bedding, the women's college was free of charge. As was the case at other Communist universities, the students were self-supporting. They cleared the land on the hillside and planted their own food. More than half of the graduates went into local educational work or returned to their home villages in guerrilla areas to become leaders in mass organizations. Only a few graduates went on to receive further military training at the Anti-Japanese Military and Political Academy.

In Yan'an, the famous writer Ding Ling wrote her "Thoughts on March 8" (International Women's Day),[35] a sarcastic account of the traditional view of womanhood still prevalent in Yan'an, for which she was roundly criticized. This was a time when it was necessary to promote women's work while actually living with the peasant women of North China and simultaneously pursuing the war against Japan. Thus, bourgeois feminism in the style of a Miss Sophie (the heroine of Ding Ling's novel *The Diary of Miss Sophie*) was regarded as useless.[36]

In the meantime, sustained by the anti-Japanese base areas and the fighting of the Eighth Route and New Fourth Armies, the war gradually reached a stalemate, with neither side yielding to the other or making a decisive attack. Eventually the Eighth Route and New Fourth Armies launched a full-scale counterattack, and the Soviet Union entered the war. In August 1945 final victory over Japan was won. Property damage in China caused by the war amounted to some fifty billion dollars, and ten million Chinese lives were lost.

Land Reform and the Transformation of Women

Although China won the War of Resistance against Japan, the land was devastated, and the people were weary of fighting. The CCP pushed strenuously to avoid a return to civil war, but Jiang Jieshi betrayed the peoples' hopes once again. With an enormous quantity of military aid from the United States, the Nationalist Army began a full-fledged civil war in July 1946. Aiming for control over Chinese markets, the United States poured countless dollars into the Nationalist Army, which at that time totaled 4.3 million troops, including more than two million regular troops, most of whom were armed with American weapons. The 1.2 million troops of the People's Liberation Army (PLA) were poorly equipped by comparison. Jiang Jieshi openly boasted that with his military force he could attack the liberated areas and conquer them within three to six months.

At the beginning of the civil war, it certainly seemed as though the Nationalists had a tremendous advantage. They launched a major assault against the liberated areas, penetrated deeply into them, and even occupied Yan'an. They repeated the raping, burning, and pillaging of the Japanese before them throughout China. Moreover, wherever the Nationalists went, they returned power to the landlords, took land from the peasantry, and killed peasants indiscriminately. In Anyang, Henan province, it was reported that four hundred elderly men and women were killed or buried alive. The Nationalists completely alienated the population inside and outside the liberated areas.[37]

Just prior to the beginning of the civil war, the CCP issued its May Fourth Directive (1946); in October of 1947, the Outline Land Law was promulgated, in which a clear policy was enunciated for the confiscation of land from landlords and its redistribution to the peasants. On the basis of the May Fourth Directive, work teams were dispatched, and a land reform movement began in various parts of the country. This land reform was never simply a matter of work teams seizing land from landlords and parceling it out to the local peasantry. The work teams were strictly forbidden to make deals or bestow favors. Although it was not easy for peasants, who had for so long worked as slaves of the landlords, to rise up, the work teams found that by living, eating, and working together with the peasants they were able through persistent persuasion to help the peasants locate the root of their sufferings. The work teams then guided the peasants in establishing their own authority and redistributing the land.

Land reform was a big step in the direction of emancipation, but women did not initially recognize its significance. For example, in the case of Gaozhuangzi, Chang county, in the Jin-Cha-Ji border region, the assigned work team organized a poor peasant group, but not one woman joined it.[38] When the work team explained the need for women to be organized, the peasants turned away and said, "I don't know about other men's wives, but that's not for mine. She can't even talk right." Then the work teams gathered the poor peasant women together and held meetings at which they explained in depth such subjects as the causes of female poverty in poor families and the necessity for women in the liberated areas to be liberated along with men. Although eighteen poor peasant wives and three daughters attended, they kept their mouths clamped shut and did not say a word. One woman finally opened her mouth, but merely said: "Poverty's bitter, but it's not so bitter we can't stand it."

When the work team then explained clearly how landlords had been exploiting the poor, the women continued to listen in silence, but the work team did notice that their eyes were filled with tears. The work team talked about how their own mothers had suffered from the time of their youth and about how hard the landlords had driven them when they grew up. They used bitterness to draw out bitterness; by talking about their own mothers' pain, they tried to draw out the pain of the peasant women. Their hardships may have taken different forms, but each of them had experienced hardship in her own way. The work team's stories provoked sympathy from the women, and at last one wife stood up and said:

It was the same for me. Ever since I was a child, all my mother and I knew was suffering. I came here as a bride when I was nine years old, and my husband's family was poor too. My husband became the landlord's hired hand, and I worked in the landlord's house for more than a year, I can't tell you how much we suffered. At one point, we went without eating for two days. I helped with the landlord's laundry for half-days, and I thought we could eat somehow. But they complained about my washing and turned me out.

She cried bitterly as she spoke. Everyone cried. Finally, each of fourteen women told stories of her own suffering, leaving nothing unsaid.

This process was called *suku*, or indictments of bitterness. The rural women had never talked about their own experiences in front of others, so this was their first opportunity for self-expression. The "self" that they described was not an isolated or abstract entity. For peasant women the "self" did not exist apart from the family, the village, and daily life. While talking about themselves, these women became keenly aware of the meaning of landlord domination, and their hatred was directed at the landlord. At the same time, *suku* deepened their consciousness of class solidarity with other poor peasant women as well as poor peasant men. Unlike liberal individualism, this form of self-awakening marked the beginning of a consciousness that society worked against the individual self. According to Deng Yingchao, the women's *suku* played a leading role in the struggle against landlords.

The enlightened women joined the poor peasant corps and the poor peasant association. In the land reform movement, they shouldered a variety of responsibilities, such as investigating numerous crimes committed by landlords, examining landlords' property holdings, and surveying the land. Not a bit of landlord property escaped the notice of these women who had spent their entire lives attentive to every grain of rice. During the civil war when the men were often needed at the front lines, women became the main promoters of land reform under the slogan, "Men support the front lines, women distribute the land."

Thus, land reform contributed to the emancipation of women in a number of ways. First, it brought down two thousand years of landlord control and destroyed the economic foundation of the traditional family system. By the same token, the sexual discrimination embedded in the traditional family system began to give way. Men lost the bases by which they were able to control women.

Second, through land reform women too gained their fair share of land, which enabled them to live independently insofar as they wanted to work. The fact that petitions for divorce came pouring in during land reform indicates that economic independence was the minimal requirement for women to free themselves from their husband's control.

Third, the land that women obtained did not fall from the sky or spring from the earth. The consciousness of these peasant women, who had once prostrated themselves before the landlord, had undergone extraordinary change because the women themselves had joined the fight against the landlords, built up peasant power, and earned their own plots of land. Enormous energy burst forth from these women once they gained the conviction that they were changing their world.

In this way the women who took part in land reform retrieved the land from the landlords and fought desperately to protect their land, just as peasant men did. Considering all the peasants who died from starvation because they had no land, land was literally life itself for them. Under no circumstances would they allow an invasion by the Nationalist forces aimed at restoring landlordism. Many peasants willingly joined the PLA or the people's militia and fought bravely. The women's militia acted in concert with the PLA to help implement military strategy.[39] For example, the women's militia in Yi county, Shandong province, numbered 3,000. Sixty of these women were charged with escorting 240 enemy prisoners of war, and not a single prisoner escaped. In the Beihai region, 1,995 members of the women's militia enthusiastically studied demolition techniques, and the Jizhenlan Young Women's Corps buried land mines, causing serious damage to the enemy's transportation. Militiawoman Sun Yumin was said to have killed seventeen enemy soldiers single-handedly.

Women also became the mainstay in agricultural production while the men were fighting at the front. They learned techniques for rice planting, plowing, and harvesting; and one source claims that 70 percent of all women began to work outside the home. Textiles had always been women's work; during the three years of the civil war, all the cloth for the 170 million people in the liberated areas and three million PLA soldiers was supplied by women's hands.

Nursing wounded and sick soldiers was also important women's work. Some women went to the front lines and others worked in the rear areas. They washed the blood and the mud from PLA soldiers at the front and cared for them with maternal affection. These devoted, self-sacrificing women were praised as "Chinese [Florence] Nightingales."[40]

One heroine of the civil war was fifteen-year-old Liu Hulan.[41] She joined the CCP in Wenshui county, Shanxi province. While engaged in revolutionary work, she was captured by Nationalist troops, who tried to force her to reveal secrets of the CCP's organization. Though they threatened to "cut off her head with a straw-cutter," she revealed nothing. With her secret information intact, she boldly placed her head in the straw-cutter and pulled the handle with her own hand. The heroism of this fifteen-year-old girl was said to have made the enemy tremble and crushed their morale. Mao Zedong immortalized her: "Great Life, Glorious Death."

At this time conflict in the areas under GMD control was growing more intense. Opposition to the civil war and protests against hunger broke out throughout the country, and women students and workers joined the fight. The Nationalist Army could not continue the offensive for another year in the liberated areas where peasants were staking their lives to defend themselves. In the fall of 1947 the PLA first won a victory in a counterattack in the northeast, and in the same period created the Central Plains Liberated Area between the Yellow and the Yangzi Rivers. They took the Northeast in 1948 and entered Beijing the following year, January 1949. After crossing the Yangzi in April, they captured Nanjing and Shanghai in succession, and there was rapid expansion of liberated areas. In the end Jiang Jieshi led 500,000 soldiers in an escape to Taiwan. Twenty-eight years after the founding of the Chinese Communist Party, the long battle against enemies inside and outside China finally came to an end.

EIGHT

The Impact of the Marriage Law of 1950

On October 1, 1949, from atop Beijing's Gate of Heavenly Peace, Mao Zedong proclaimed the establishment of the People's Republic of China (PRC). It was the victory, in his words, of the New Democratic Revolution that had begun with the May Fourth Movement, and the start of a new Long March toward a socialist China. Kang Keqing, a revolutionary from the age of thirteen in 1926, reminisced about the events that fall day:

I was carried away by indescribable emotion. Gazing down, I saw the figure of so many gallant women among the hundreds of thousands of workers, peasants, and soldiers filling the wide square before the Gate of Heavenly Peace. Joyfully, with thumping hearts, they stood before Chairman Mao's inspection. Was this not truly the symbol of the Chinese people and her women having risen up? Did not the wave of red flags, like the sea, and the fireworks that burned in the night sky symbolize new China's brilliant future?

Earlier, on March 24, shortly after Beijing came under Communist control, the First Chinese National Women's Congress convened,[1] and the formation of the All-China Federation of Democratic Women was announced. In September the Chinese People's Political Consultative Conference met, and its Common Program, containing the basic principles for the "people's democracy" of the new nation, was adopted. The sixth article addressed the emancipation of women: "The People's Republic of China shall abolish the feudal system that holds women in bondage. Women shall enjoy equal rights with men in political, economic, cultural, educational, and social life. Freedom of marriage for men and women shall be put into effect."[2]

This new idea of equality described by the Common Program was to be realized in three stages following the establishment of the People's Republic: the enactment and promulgation of the Marriage Law of 1950; the Great Leap Forward and People's Communes of 1959; and the Cultural Revolution, lasting about ten years from 1966. We will examine the first of these three here.

The "Marriage Law of the People's Republic of China" was issued on May 1, 1950, in accordance with the "Executive Order Concerning the Enactment and Promulgation of the Marriage Law of the Central People's Government of the People's Republic of China" (April 30, 1950) under the name of Chairman Mao Zedong.[3] In its first paragraph, the law proclaimed the abolition of the traditional ("feudal") Chinese system of marriage and the establishment of a "new democratic" marriage system. This new system legislated freedom of choice in marriage, monogamy, equal rights for men and women, prohibition of bigamy, concubinage, and child-bride marriages, freedom of remarriage for widows, and the like.

Formerly, marriages were usually based on "parental orders" or "matchmakers' arrangements," as well as a family's material wealth and pedigree, and with the interference of the "religious authority" of diviners. The foundation of the new Marriage Law, however, was that marriage had to accord with the free will of the man and woman involved and had to be decided upon as an individual act by both parties. No interference by third parties or spirits was to be permitted, and no property or family qualifications could serve as a substitute for mutual love. "Husband and wife are companions living together and shall enjoy equal status in the home." People were to aspire to such principles as "Husband and wife are duty bound to love, respect, assist and look after each other, to live in harmony, to engage in production, to care for the children, and to strive jointly for the welfare of the family and for the building up of the new society."[4] Divorce also became a matter of choice, and in such cases the interests of women and children just emancipated from traditional restraints were to be fully protected.

The enactment itself of such a marriage law, with its rejection of traditional marriages and its concurrent democratic transformation of the family, was of epochal significance, to say the least. As

Edgar Snow wrote of the Marriage Regulations of the Shaan-Gan-Ning border area: "Changes in marriage, divorce, and inheritance were in themselves radical against the background of semi-feudal law and practice elsewhere in China."[5] Beyond this, though, the implementation of the law aimed consistently at the ideal of gender equality. The main incentive for its promulgation was the registration of marriages and divorces, although registration was not intended merely as the perfunctory reporting of a marriage.

In the first place, the government took the position that marriage was not a private matter unrelated to state or society; rather, it united public and private interests in men and women as constituent members of that state and society. In the process of marriage registration, the government carried out an investigation to verify whether the marriage was one of free will, whether the minimum age prescriptions of the law (twenty for males, eighteen for females) had been satisfied, whether it was a "purchase" marriage or some other form of marriage violating the spirit of the Marriage Law. In the case of divorce registration, a similar investigation would be undertaken, with special attention given to the problems of divorced women and their children. In addition, registration played a role in the propaganda work for the ideal of gender equality contained in the new Marriage Law. In clear distinction from the formal rationalism of conjugal bourgeois marriage laws, it was the aim of the new Marriage Law that the government of the PRC actively participate in the lives of the individual members of Chinese society.

This Marriage Law certainly brought much hope to young men and women. By freedom of marriage, we tend immediately to think of the freedom to choose a partner in marriage. Prior to this time in China, though, poverty often made even marriage itself extremely difficult. As we have seen in earlier chapters, poor people might purchase a young girl to raise as a future bride for a son, rent another man's wife for a fixed period of time, or form a group of two or three men to share a single wife.

In opposition to such practices, the Marriage Law prohibited anyone from using problems related to marriage as a pretext for extorting goods or money. Marriage was to be based on the couple's mutual love and free will, with no need for wealth or property. In this way poor peasants for the first time gained genuine freedom of marriage. For men as well as for women, the Marriage Law constituted, after land reform, the "second transformation."

Equally important, freedom of marriage not only meant freedom to marry but also included freedom in cases of divorce. Formerly, the latter freedom had simply not existed as far as women were concerned. The Marriage Law recognized women's right to divorce, and Edgar Snow's reference to the "radical" quality of the earlier Chinese Communist reform in this area clearly had this point in mind. That the Marriage Law was often called the "Divorce Law" speaks directly to the epochal significance that freedom of divorce had in contemporary China.

As a result of the legislative enactment of this freedom of divorce in the new Marriage Law, the number of divorces in China rose dramatically. The breakdown by year of divorce cases brought before the People's Courts is given in the following tabulation:[6]

Year		Number of cases
1950		186,167
1951		409,500
1952	(first half)	398,243

The overwhelming majority of those applying for divorce were women, nearly 75 percent of the total, a fact attributable directly to the formerly superior status of husbands. The Marriage Law clearly had a profound impact in this regard. Behind these statistics, furthermore, were many women who desired divorce but, because of diverse constraints and restrictions, did not apply for it. These numbers reflect only those who managed to overcome those constraints—a drop in the bucket. The Marriage Law became an influential weapon for the emancipation of such women from traditional marriages.

Women who opted for divorce, however, faced an enormously difficult future. Customs and habits fostered for so long could not possibly be altered overnight, and the traditional Chinese conception of all these things persisted tenaciously among the populace. In pre-Communist Chinese society, a woman was not considered a human being, but a thing, a piece of private property—indeed, something on the order of a domestic animal. For poverty-stricken peasants, the loss by divorce of a wife for whom one had long saved money was tantamount to the loss of a cow, a sheep, or some land. They certainly were not about to acquiesce in so serious a matter as divorce. A bride was expected to behave in such a way that the issue of divorce would never arise. For a woman to pursue divorce was virtually high treason against a natural order. As two sayings put it, "If marriage is free, the world will fall into chaos," and "A good woman hangs herself, while a wicked woman gets a divorce."

Another crucial element of the Marriage Law was the freedom for widows to remarry. Shi Guo's novella, *Fengpo* (Storm), deals specifically with this issue in precisely the period of the enactment of the Marriage Law.[7] In the story, there stands in the ancestral hall of the Yang family a stele upon which is inscribed: "All women of the clan will cleave to one husband for life. If there are instances of illicit intercourse or remarriage, her fate will be left in the hands of the clan members." If a widow fell in love with someone, she might be tied to a millstone and thrown into the river, or she might be beaten half-dead with a whip. The head of the clan, Old Man Yang, has the following thoughts about the new Marriage Law: "Without widows preserving their chastity, parents won't be able to decide on their children's marriages. What sort of a world would that be? . . . I'm just a pathetic old clan head, but I've got to write a letter to Chairman Mao. He can't have seen this Marriage Law yet!" Old Man Yang's perspective probably represents the average consciousness of China's peasant masses; namely, the CCP may be great, but the Marriage Law is not only bad, it goes against the interests of poor peasants and hired farmhands.

This sort of erroneous class consciousness among the peasantry and the sense of patriarchy fostered within the clan structure remained well entrenched even among Party cadres. When a wife sought a divorce on the basis of the Marriage Law, the district government required a letter of introduction from the village government, and cadres abused this system, being in no hurry to issue such letters. Furthermore, some cadres secretly put together "supplementary marriage laws" (in violation of the actual Marriage Law) which allegedly included such illegal regulations as "After divorce, if the man is not yet married, the woman may not remarry." These were occasionally committed to writing and discovered, but for the most part each cadre retained his own version of a "supplementary marriage law" inside his head. And these became the criteria surrounding the implementation of the Marriage Law. In more extreme cases, some cadres set up their own courts and even executed people. For this reason, the peasant women came to fear Party cadres: "If you're thinking of divorce," the saying of the time went, "you've got to go through three barriers: the husband barrier, the mother-in-law barrier, and the cadre barrier. And the cadre barrier is the toughest!"

Curiously enough, it was the same story with women cadres. When one village teacher proposed publicizing the Marriage Law, the head of the village women's association cut him off and said: "Things like the Marriage Law aren't for propaganda! Poor people won't ever be able to marry!" Women who for so many years were subject to the dominance of men came to adopt beliefs that fit within that structure of power. Whatever "woman's point of view" she might possess would be little more than the flip side of patriarchy. And cadres, especially women cadres, who should have represented the women's perspective in this regard, did not find it easy to cast off this fallacious "women's point of view." This was the most difficult obstacle to the work of publicizing the new Marriage Law.

Thus, filing a divorce claim required tremendous determination. Women had to fight their battles all alone, even under the threat of possible bloodshed. Many women were killed by their husbands or mothers-in-law, and many women chose to struggle to their deaths. During the year following the promulgation of the Marriage Law, more than 10,000 women were killed in South-Central China; in East China in 1950-52 the figure reached 11,500. During the two or three years following the Law's enactment some 70,000–80,000 people per year were killed over marriage-related issues throughout the country.

The majority of the dead were young women who had boldly resisted traditional conventions. Clearly, many of them had received land during land reform and had decided on divorce once their livelihood was assured. No sooner had they ceased being their husbands' slaves and decided to live as individual human beings then their lives were cut off. Ironically, their sad deaths bespeak a personal drive toward self-reliance upon which these women had staked their lives in pursuit of personal freedom. In each one of the great number of divorce suits, one senses that remarkable resolution on the part of those women who often paid the ultimate price.

In July 1951 in East China and in August in South-Central China, guidelines for the thorough implementation of the Marriage Law were issued. Then, on September 26, the Government Administrative Council issued, in the name of Premier Zhou Enlai, "Directive on Investigation into the Circumstances of the Application of the Marriage Law." This document recognized the need to reform the old family system through the Marriage Law, so that the masses of women might participate in the construction of a new society. It also accepted the fact that this change could only be completed through a tenacious, systematic ideological and legal struggle to overcome traditional Chinese practices. It thus ordered a strengthening of educational and judicial work. Presented seriatim in Zhou's directive were concrete methods for promoting a mass legal struggle, simplifying of marriage procedures, and the like.

On October 23 the government dispatched a team of investigators (led by Shi Liang, China's Minister of Justice)[8] to observe the implementation of the Marriage Law. The team visited places in North, Southeast, Northwest and East China, at the same time organizing a network of investigative teams at the subprovincial level. Thus, propaganda for the Marriage Law was linked to a wide-ranging investigation into its enforcement. In small gatherings and discussion groups organized throughout the country, women complained of their sufferings under the old marriage system. They used posters, cultural work teams, and a host of other means to mobilize for propaganda. In addition, mass meetings were held at which judicial officials offered explanations and judgments on model divorce cases. *Renmin ribao* (People's daily) even published an editorial under the title, "Resolutely Protect the Safety of the Lives of Women."

Although these measures alleviated the situation somewhat, the penetration throughout Chinese society of the Marriage Law would take considerably longer. Apart from areas liberated by the Chinese Communists during the anti-Japanese war, arranged marriages, early marriage, and even the child-bride system persisted. Nor had suicide and the murder of women disappeared. During the early years of the PRC, Party cadres focused their energies on land reform; work for the Marriage Law was not seen as equally crucial. Once land reform was completed, late in 1952, they began to concentrate their efforts on the implementation of the Marriage Law. On January 14, 1953, a committee to lead the campaign on the implementation of the Marriage Law was formed. On February 1 Zhou Enlai released the "Directive of the Government Administrative Council Concerning the Thorough Enforcement of the Marriage Law"; and on February 18 the Central Committee of the CCP announced "Supplementary Instructions Regarding the Campaign for the Implementation of Marriage Law Month," which began nationwide in March.

This campaign was the first broad, systematic propaganda effort of this sort since the proclamation of the Marriage Law. In villages and cities alike, propaganda activities spread. Mass meetings were held, and many adults underwent "propaganda education" two or three times, some as many as ten or even more times. More than 20 million pamphlets were distributed nationally. On March 18 the vice-chair of the committee for the campaign to steer the implementation of the Marriage Law, Liu Jingfan, made a broadcast to the entire nation entitled "Implementation of the Marriage Law is an Important Duty of Every Level of the People's Government and of the People." By early April the campaign was on schedule in roughly 70 percent of the country.

The campaign aimed at systematically criticizing the ideology and vices of the traditional Chinese marriage system, creating a new family, and restructuring human relations. Most important, the implementation of the Marriage Law reached those cadres in the field who had to enforce it; and the long-term, complex, and difficult problems facing work on behalf of the Marriage Law were confronted. With this foundation, propaganda for the Marriage Law then became part of the regular duties of every level of government, every organization, and every school.

This concentrated effort for the implementation of the Marriage Law was undertaken at this time because it was seen as necessary in social construction. One month after the Marriage Law was announced, the Land Reform Law of the People's Republic of China went into effect, and land reform commenced. At that time, 700 million *mu* (about 117 million acres) of land were distributed to 300 million peasants without regard to their sex, and the old land-holding system was abolished. Then the First Five-Year Plan began in 1953. At this stage, the government used the force of the mass movement that had emerged during land reform to commence a full-fledged assault on the traditional Chinese marriage system.

The transformation of the traditional family into a democratic, harmonious one and the emergence of genuine individuality were needed for the enhancement of productivity. For example, in Lu-shan county, Henan province, there was a proverb: "The Marriage Law will cure a lazy man's disease and increase the food supply." One story tells of a certain Feng Zongyi who lived in this area and who had such a bad marriage that for many years he and his wife had not slept in the same bed. Unable to apply himself to work, he passed his time idly, and all day long the sounds of insult and argument could be heard from his house. In this village there also lived a child bride by the name of Zheng Guixiang who spent her days weeping over her maltreatment. When the Marriage Law went into effect, they were both encouraged to petition for divorce. They later fell in love and married. Having now obtained a wife he loved, Feng Zongyi began to exert himself in production as if re-born. Combining their energies, they not only harvested over 500 pounds of corn and about 9,000 pounds of sweet potatoes but also stored away 25 cartloads of fertilizer. In this story, the Marriage Law truly "cured a lazy man's disease and increased production."

The case of women was even more remarkable. As the Marriage Law transformed the family and fostered basic equality, women actually participated in the work of mutual-aid teams. In 1952, for example, when a water control project needed for the control of drought was begun along the Huai River, the conservancy work required the labor of virtually all of the men in the area. The women therefore took charge of the bulk of spring plowing. The old folks, sensing a change in the world around them, would apparently re-mark, "In the old days women and men weren't equal and women didn't go out into the fields. Nowadays, women can go work in the fields and get more work points." The Marriage Law served to draw women, whose whole lives had revolved "around the stove," into the work outside the home.

Factory workers had similar experiences. Although there were many married women workers, most of them gave all of their pay to their husbands' families, split it between their natal and marital families, or had it collected for them by their husbands. In any event, they rarely saw the money they had earned. And, when they returned home from the factory, they were still "slaves." They performed burdensome household chores for their in-laws and husbands, which markedly sapped their desire to work. Marriage Law propaganda provided an initial solution for this problem. There were more than a few examples of women's on-the-job attendance rising and output rapidly increasing when the problem of salary was solved through negotiations with the marital family or when household injustices were ironed out. New family relationships and the establishment of a place for the individual among them stimulated the desire to work and raised production remarkably.

Thus, the new Marriage Law emancipated women who had been at the very bottom of the traditional family system. For the first time women gained the freedom to choose their husbands and to obtain divorces of their own free will. In other words, they gained the right to live as they wished. They ceased being chattel, being animals, being machines for the generation of sons, and they thus obtained for the first time the freedom to live as individual human beings. The new slogan was, "Men and women are equal; to each his/her own." "Women's unequal treaty with men" had been abrogated. Although the Marriage Law was frequently criticized as the "Women's Law," it clearly was a law for women.

The Marriage Law did not bring about only the liberation of women. By bringing the genuinely "radical" ideas of freedom of marriage and gender equality into the family, it propelled the cleansing of all familial relations—husband and wife, bride and mother-in-law, parents and children. For the Chinese, this was tantamount to transforming the traditional family into a democratic and harmonious one and thus strengthening the foundation of all family relations. As the Communist slogan went, "The Marriage Law is good for men, good for women, good for the old, good for the young, and good for production!"—the Five Goods.

It has often been said that at this time the Marriage Law together with land reform overturned the long-standing landlord control and removed the existing authority of the traditional clan and marriage systems. The ideological apparatus of landlord control, though, certainly did not self-destruct as a result. A forceful struggle against this ideology was required, and the campaign to implement the

Marriage Law provided just such a struggle. As land reform aimed at destroying the economic basis of the traditional landlord-tenant system, so the Marriage Law sought to destroy it from its super-structural aspect in the clan system. Socialist construction required transformation from two directions—a change in the economy and a change in consciousness.

Appendix

Appendix

Chronology for the History of Women in
Modern China, 1840–1953

1840

June. The Opium War breaks out.

1841

May. Several thousand men and women in the village of San-
yuanli (Guangdong province) organize an anti-British militia and
contest English troops in armed conflict.

1843

Hong Xiuquan organizes the Society of God-Worshippers.

1844

Mary Ann Aldersey of the British Society for Promoting Female
Education in the East establishes the first school for girls in Ningbo.

1851

January. The Taiping Rebellion erupts in Guangxi province.
Hong Xiuquan orders the men and women to live in separate
"camps."
September. The Taipings occupy Yongan and set up 36 "camps."

1852

April. Hong Xiuquan orders his male and female generals to prepare to break out of the besieged Yongan.

1853

March. The Taipings occupy Nanjing. Men and women in the occupied territory are housed in "male halls" and "female halls."

The Taipings promulgate their "Land System of the Heavenly Dynasty," which calls for the distribution of land to all, regardless of gender.

1854

September. Food shortages bring an end to the allotment of food for the "female halls," and the women are sent outside Nanjing.

1855

February–March. The Taipings open up the female halls and allow men and women to live together.

1864

July. The Taipings are defeated.

1875

November. Qiu Jin is born in Xiamen (Amoy).

1877

He Xiangning is born in Hong Kong.

1878

Paul Brunat manages the Shanghai Silk Filature.

1883

In Guangdong, Kang Youwei proposes China's first Anti-Foot-binding Society.

1890

In Shanghai, China's first textile mill, the Shanghai Mechanized Cotton Company, begins operations.
Song Qingling is born.

1894

August. The Sino-Japanese War breaks out.

1895

July. Xiang Jingyu is born in Xupu, Hunan province.

1896

Liang Qichao begins publishing serially his article "General Discussion of Reform" in *Shiwubao*. Tan Sitong sets to work on his *Renxue* (continues through 1897).

1897

May. Liang Qichao publishes "Concise Rules for the Experimental Anti-Footbinding Society" in *Shiwubao*.
June. The Anti-Footbinding Society is founded in Shanghai.
November. Liang Qichao publishes "Proposal Calling for the Building of Women's Schools" in *Shiwubao*.

1898

June. Jing Yuanshan's school for women is founded in Shanghai. The Hundred Days Reform begins.
August. Kang Youwei memorializes the throne for a prohibition on footbinding and for support for the Anti-Footbinding Society.
Tan Sitong is executed, and Li Run follows him in death.

1900

The Boxer Uprising erupts. Red Lanterns, Blue Lanterns, and Black Lanterns become active.
Cai Chang is born in Xiangxiang, Hunan province.

1901

Autumn. The first Chinese women students overseas enter the Girls' Practical School in Tokyo.

In India, Kang Youwei nears completion of the *Datong shu* (continues through 1902).

1902

August. The Qing government promulgates "Imperial Regulations for Establishing Schools," but there is no mention of women's education.

Winter. The Patriotic Girls' School is founded in Shanghai.

China's first periodical for women, *Nübao*, begins publication in Shanghai.

Herbert Spencer's "The Rights of Women" [a chapter in his *Social Statics*] is translated into Chinese by Ma Junwu.

Deng Yingchao is born.

1903

April. The Mutual Love Association is founded in Tokyo. At an emergency general session called by the Mutual Love Society, Chinese women students overseas resolve to join the military in order to resist Russia.

December. The women's magazine *Nüzi shijie* begins publication in Shanghai.

Jin Tiange publishes *Nüjie zhong*.

1904

The Qing court announces its "Imperial Regulations on Education" and expects that women's education will be domestic education.

Hattori Shigeko organizes a women's conversation group in Beijing.

February. The Russo-Japanese War breaks out.

July. The Girls' Practical School graduates its first class of overseas Chinese women students.

1905

July. With the establishment of a department for overseas students, the Qing government sets up a separate facility of the Girls' Practical School in Hinoki-chō, Akasaka, Tokyo.

August. The Revolutionary Alliance is founded in Tokyo. Qiu Jin and others join.

Lingnan University, a private institution, is founded in Guangzhou and admits women students.

1906

February. The Empress Dowager issues orders to the Ministry of Education concerning the promotion of women's education.

August. The Ministry of Education lays down "Regulations on the Education of Women."

The Beiyang First Girls' Normal School is established in Tianjin.

1907

January. Qiu Jin inaugurates publication of *Zhongguo nübao.*

March. The Chinese Ministry of Education issues "Regulations of the Ministry of Education on Elementary Schools for Girls" and "Regulations of the Ministry of Education for Women's Normal Schools."

June. He Zhen organizes the Society for the Reinstatement of Women's Rights in Tokyo and begins publishing *Tianyi.* In Paris, Wu Jingheng and others begin publishing the journal *Xin shiji.*

July. Qiu Jin is executed in Shaoxing, Zhejiang province.

1908

April. Construction of the "Chinese department" of the Girls' Practical School is completed.

1910

Rice riots erupt in Changsha and other places, with many women participating.

1911

October. The 1911 Revolution breaks out. Efforts to organize a Women's Army begin in Shanghai and elsewhere.

November. The Women's Suffrage Alliance is founded in Shanghai.

December. The abridged regulations for the provisional assembly of Guangdong recognize women's right to vote.

1912

January. Lin Zongsu, representative of the Women's Suffrage Alliance, visits Sun Yat-sen and reaffirms women's right to the franchise.

March. The provisional constitution is promulgated without a clear indication of gender equality. The provisional government abolishes footbinding. The Shenzhou Women's Assistance Society is founded in Shanghai. Members of the Women's Suffrage Alliance take up arms and force their way into the Nanjing parliament.

April. To secure the right to vote for women, various women's rights groups come together to reorganize the Women's Suffrage Alliance in Nanjing.

August. At the inaugural meeting of the Guomindang (GMD), a platform that fails to include the idea of gender equality is passed.

September. Mrs. Carrie Chapman Catt of the International Women's Suffrage Alliance visits China; a reception is held in Shanghai.

November. Women delegates to the Guangdong Provincial Assembly petition to have women's suffrage ratified by the assembled body, but they are voted down.

Kang Keqing is born in Jiangxi.

1913

February. Tang Qunying and others in Changsha, writing in *Changsha ribao*, call for direct action and the use of force.

November. The Women's Suffrage Alliance is ordered dissolved.

1914

March. "Police Regulations on Public Order" ban women from joining political associations and from participating in political campaign meetings.

August. Qinghua University for the first time sends women students to the United States.

1915

January. *Funü zazhi* begins publication in Shanghai.

September. *Xin qingnian* begins publication.

1917

February. Wu Yu's essay "The Family System Is the Foundation of Authoritarianism" appears in *Xin qingnian.*

1918

May. Yosano Akiko's essay "On Chastity" is published in Chinese translation in *Xin qingnian.*
June. *Xin qingnian* runs a special issue on Ibsen.
August. Lu Xun's "My Views on Chastity" is published in *Xin qingnian.* Women workers at the Sino-Japanese Cotton Manufacturing Company go on strike.

1919

February. Women workers at the Sino-Japanese Cotton Manufacturing Company again go out on strike.
April. Deng Chunlan asks Chancellor Cai Yuanpei of Beijing University for permission, as a woman, to enter the university.
May. The May Fourth Incident takes place. The Women's National Salvation Society is founded.
June. The Women's Student Union is formed in Shanghai. Women laborers in the textile mills of Naigai Wata, Sino-Japanese Cotton, and Shanghai Cotton go on strike.
July. *Funü jiuguo ribao* commences publication.
November. The young bride Zhao Wuzhen commits suicide, and a number of articles appear in succession in the Changsha newspaper *Dagongbao,* decrying the conditions that lead to such deaths.
December. The Hunan Women's Association for Work-Study in France is formed.

1920

January. *Xin funü* begins publication. Workers at Sino-Japanese Cotton go on strike.
May. *Funü pinglun* begins publication in Suzhou.
September. Beijing University and Nanjing Higher Normal School officially permit women students to enroll.

1921

February. The Qunbaoshe in Guangdong begins publishing *Laodong yu funü* [Labor and women].

July. The Department of Education of the Beijing Government orders the rapid establishment of middle schools for girls throughout the provinces of China.

August. *Funü pinglun* (a different journal from the one of the same name that began publishing in Suzhou in 1920) begins to appear as a supplement to *Minguo ribao*.

December. *Funü sheng* commences publication.

1922

January. The constitution of Hunan province recognizes women's right to vote. Provincial and county assemblies emerge.

April. Women workers at Sino-Japanese Cotton go out on the first of three strikes this year.

July. At the second congress of the Chinese Communist Party, a "Resolution on the Women's Movement" is put forth.

August. Women workers in Shanghai spinning mills go out on a mass strike. The Society for the Advancement of Women's Suffrage is organized in Beijing. The Women's Rights Alliance is formed in Beijing, with branches established in Zhejiang, Shanghai, Nanjing, Shandong, Zhili, and Hubei.

1923

May. The Women's Department of the Third International (Comintern) sends its "Letter to Chinese Women Students," which is published in *Xiangdao zhoubao*.

August. *Funü zhoubao* commences publication.

1924

January. The GMD undergoes reorganization, and the first United Front between the Chinese Communists and the GMD goes into effect. The First Congress of the GMD recognizes the principle of gender equality.

March. International Women's Day (March 8) is celebrated for the first time, in Guangdong.

June. Women workers in Shanghai silk-reeling factories go out on strike.

1925

February–April. A strike of workers at Japanese-owned enterprises in Shanghai and Qingdao spreads.

April. The Women's Rights Alliance demands gender equality of delegates to the National Assembly. They convene a Women's National Assembly in Shanghai.

May. The May Thirtieth Movement explodes. The Association of Chinese Women is formed and demands that the National Assembly give women full civil rights.

June. The Shanghai Women's Federation is formed in the midst of the May Thirtieth Movement. Heated discussions arise over educational issues at Beijing Women's Normal University. Some 8,000 women workers participate in the Guangzhou–Hong Kong strike.

Peng Pai creates the Women's Liberation Association in Guangdong.

1926

January. The CCP's "Resolution on the Women's Movement" is adopted.

March. Liu Hezhen and Yang Dequn, students at Women's Normal University, are killed among others in the March 18th Incident.

December. The First Peasant Assembly of Hunan province adopts a "Resolution on the Question of Rural Women."

He Xiangning and others create the Women's Movement Training School in Guangdong.

1927

February. The Women's Political Training Institute is organized in preparation for the Women's National Revolutionary Army. Roughly 200,000 women workers take part in the Shanghai General Strike.

March. Women participate in armed risings in Shanghai; they are in charge of relief work. Mao Zedong's "Report on an Investigation of the Peasant Movement in Hunan" is published.

April. Jiang Jieshi carries out the April 12 coup d'état.

June. The Fourth National Labor Congress adopts a "Resolution on Child and Female Labor." Women silk workers in Hongkou (Shanghai) go on strike.

November. The North Shanghai Women Silk Factory Workers hold a founding meeting at which the building collapses, causing many casualties.

December. The Canton (Guangzhou) Commune fails. Chen Tiejun and others are executed.

1928

May. Xiang Jingyu is captured in Wuhan and executed.

July. The Sixth Congress of the CCP adopts a "Resolution on the Women's Movement" and defines concrete policies on women workers, peasant women, and female youth.

1930

November. Mao Zedong's wife, Yang Kaihui, is executed.

1931

May. The GMD government promulgates and implements the "Family Law" section of the Civil Code of the Republic of China.

November. The constitution of the Chinese Soviet Republic provides for gender equality.

December. The Marriage Regulations of the Chinese Soviet Republic are promulgated and implemented.

1932

April. Mao Zedong affixes his signature to the "Essential Program for the Organization of a Committee to Reform the Lives of Women."

June. Mao signs the "Instructions Concerning Organization and Work for the Protection of Women's Rights and the Establishment of a Committee to Reform the Lives of Women."

1934

April. The Marriage Law of the Chinese Soviet Republic is enacted.

October. The Long March begins. Some 30 women cadres participate.

1935

December. The December Ninth Movement takes place, with women students participating. The Shanghai Women's National Salvation Society is founded in Shanghai.

1936

November. Some 15,000 Chinese laborers at Japanese-owned cotton enterprises go on strike.

1937

March. Women workers in Shanghai silk-reeling factories go out on strike.

July. The Sino-Japanese War begins, leading to formation of the anti-Japanese national united front between the GMD and the CCP. Song Qingling, He Xiangning, and others organize a group of women to aid in the anti-Japanese resistance.

December. Thousands of Chinese women are raped and murdered in the Nanjing massacre.

1938

July. A Women's Steering Committee is formed in Hankou.

1939

January. The Consultative Assembly of the Shaan-Gan-Ning Border Area enacts gender equality and freedom of marriage in its administrative program.

March. The Women's Movement Committee of the Central Committee of the CCP issues a "Directive of the Direction and Responsibilities of the Women's Movement at Present."

April. The Marriage Regulations of the Shaan-Gan-Ning Border Area are promulgated.

1940

Summer. The GMD government issues a proclamation against the hiring of married women in the Bureau of the Post Office. The rural education plans of the women's youth association are suspended.

1941

Spring. The GMD calls a conference of women activitists and condemns political participation by women.

July. The Administrative Committee of the Jin-Cha-Ji Border Area issues a directive, "On Our Marriage Regulations."

September. *Jiefang ribao* begins publishing a special section on Chinese women.

1942

March. Ding Ling publishes "Thoughts on March 8" in *Jiefang ribao.*

1943

January. The Consultative Assembly of the Jin-Cha-Ji Border Area enacts care for mothers and identical wage scales for men and women as part of its administrative program.

February. The Marriage Regulations of the Jin-Cha-Ji Border Area are promulgated. The Central Committee of the CCP issues a "Resolution on Women's Work at Present in the Anti-Japanese Base Areas."

May. The Administrative Council of the Jin-Cha-Ji Border Area issues a "Notice on Problems of Marriage Registration."

1944

March. The Revised Provisional Marriage Regulations of the Shaan-Gan-Ning Border Area are promulgated.

1945

February. Women in Chongqing demand the establishment of a united government.

April. The Jin-Cha-Ji Border Area government issues a "Directive on the Protection of Mothers and Infants by Women Cadres."

August. China is victorious in the war against Japan.

December. In opposition to a civil war, Bang Yan demands democracy and peace, and dies in the December 1 massacre.

1946

March. A large number of women workers launch a campaign

opposing continued civil war and demanding the withdrawal of United States troops.

April. The Marriage Regulations of the Shaan-Gan-Ning Border Area are promulgated.

December. Women workers participate in demonstrations against continued civil war.

1947

January. Protests widen in the 1946 rape case of a Beijing University coed by a soldier of the United States. Liu Hulan meets her untimely death heroically.

October. An Outline Land Law to distribute land regardless of gender is promulgated.

1948

February. A massacre takes place at the Shenjiu Silk-Reeling Factory in Shanghai. Women workers arise in the struggle.

March. The Jin-Cha-Ji Border Area issues a "Provisional Law on Care for Infants and Hygiene for Pregnant Mothers."

December. The Central Committee of the CCP issues a "Resolution on the Direction of Women's Work in the Villages of the Liberated Areas at Present."

1949

March. The First All-China Congress of Women convenes.

April. The All-China Federation of Democratic Women is formed.

July. *Xin Zhongguo funü* begins publication (in 1956, renamed *Zhongguo funü*).

September. The Chinese People's Political Consultative Conference adopts the "Common Program."

October. The People's Republic of China is established.

1950

May. The Marriage Law of the People's Republic of China goes into effect.

August. The All-China General Labor Federation convenes a conference of women laborers in the Labor Federation.

1951

February. Regulations on labor insurance and the care of mothers are enacted.

September. The Government Administrative Council issues a "Directive on Investigation into the Circumstances of the Application of the Marriage Law."

October. The first meeting convenes of the Women and Children Welfare Work Association. The government sends investigative teams to numerous sites to survey conditions surrounding implementation of the Marriage Law.

December. *Renmin ribao* carries the editorial "Resolutely Protect the Safety of the Lives of Women" as part of the implementation of the Marriage Law.

1952

November. The All-China Conference on Women's Work convenes.

1953

January. The committee for the campaign on the Implementation of the Marriage Law Campaign is formed.

February. Premier Zhou Enlai issues "Directive of the Government Administrative Council Concerning the Thorough Enforcement of the Marriage Law." The Central Committee of the CCP issues "Supplementary Instructions Regarding the Campaign for the Implementation of Marriage Law Month."

March. Campaign Month for the Implementation of the Marriage Law goes into effect.

April. The Second All-China Congress of Women convenes.

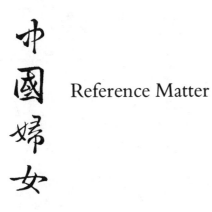

Reference Matter

Notes

1. Luo Xianglin's *Yuedong zhi feng* [Ballads of Eastern Guangdong] (Beixin shuju, 1936; Taibei reprint, Dongfang wenhua shuju, 1974), includes a selection of Hakka songs as well as essays about them. During the 1920's and 1930's, Chinese scholars actively gathered folk songs under the sponsorship of Beijing University's Society for the Study of Folk Songs, which came into being during the May Fourth Movement. Gu Jiegang, ed., *Wu ge jiaji* [Songs from Jiangsu, I] (Beijing: Beijing daxue geyao yanjiuhui, 1926; Taibei reprint, Dongfang wenhua gongyingshe, 1970) and Wang Yizhi, ed., *Wu ge yiji* [Songs from Jiangsu, II], (Taibei: Fulu tushu gongsi, 1969), are representative examples of these efforts. After 1949, great importance was naturally attached to collecting folk songs, resulting in the publication of the four-volume *Zhongguo geyao ziliao* [Materials on Chinese folk songs], comp. Materials Division of the Society for the Study of Chinese Folk Literature (Beijing: Zuojia chubanshe, 1959). Appended to this last work is a catalog of materials pertaining to folk songs. In addition, for a collection of popular songs about the Taipings, see *Taiping Tianguo geyao* [Folk songs of the Taiping Heavenly Kingdom], ed. Taiping Historical Museum (Shanghai: Shanghai wenyi chubanshe, 1962). Some songs about the Taipings are also recorded in Cheng Ying, comp., *Zhongguo jindai fandi fanfengjian lishi geyao xuan* [A selection of modern Chinese anti-imperialist, antifeudal historical songs] (Beijing: Zhonghua shuju, 1962). The nature of folk songs makes them difficult to translate, but they are of immense value as source materials for women's history.

2. Research in China to date has denied the existence of uninhibited relationships between the sexes in Hakka society. The general consensus has been that the love songs represented attempts to give vent to feelings

that had been held in check by the strong Confucian tradition and the repression of sexual love in Hakka society. For examples of this point of view, see the work by Luo Xianglin cited in the note above, and Zhang Tengfa, "Kejia shan'ge zhi shehui beijing (xu)" [The social background of Hakka mountain songs, part 2], *Minsu* 1: 2 (Jan. 1937), pp. 241–56. However, the existence of numerous love songs could also indicate that gender discrimination was not particularly strong among the extremely poor Hakka peasants and that spontaneous love relationships could occur with relative impunity in the remote places where they labored. As can be seen in Luo Xianglin, *Kejia yanjiu daolun* [An introduction to research on the Hakka] (Xingning: Xishan shucang, 1933), those scholars who emphasized the strength of traditional morality among the Hakka may have sought to depict these people as orthodox bearers of Han civilization in order to counter the prejudice against them so evident in the field of Hakka studies. We must await future research for clarification of this point.

3. Translator's note. The English translation for the quotation from Confucius in this passage follows Vincent Y. C. Shih, *The Taiping Ideology: Its Sources, Interpretations, and Influences* (Seattle: University of Washington Press, 1967), pp. 48–49.

4. A Japanese translation by Nishikawa Kikuko of "Land System of the Heavenly Dynasty" can be found in *Shinmatsu Minkokusho seiji hyōron shū* [Political commentaries from the late Qing and early Republican periods], vol. 58 of *Chūgoku koten bungaku taikei* [Compendium of classical Chinese literature], ed. Nishi Junzō and Shimada Kenji (Tokyo: Heibonsha, 1974), pp. 41–45.

Translator's note. The English translation used here follows Franz Michael, *The Taiping Rebellion: History and Documents*, vol. 2: *Documents and Comments* (Seattle: University of Washington Press, 1971), p. 314.

5. A collection of popular oral history concerning the Taiping Rebellion, as in this instance, can be found in *Taiping Tianguo geming zai Guangxi diaocha ziliao huibian* [A compilation of research materials from an investigation of the Taiping Revolution in Guangxi], comp. Guangxi Zhuangzu zizhiqu tongzhiguan (Nanning: Guangxi Zhuangzu zizhiqu renmin chubanshe, 1962).

6. Translator's note. Zhang Dejian, *Zeiqing huizuan* [Intelligence handbook on the Taipings], in Xiang Da et al., eds., *Zhongguo jindai shi ziliao congkan II: Taiping Tianguo* [A collection of historical materials on modern Chinese history, Part II: The Taiping Rebellion], 8 vols. (Shanghai: Shenzhou guoguangshe, 1952), vol. 3, p. 111.

7. Of the Taiping heroines, the one that should be mentioned first is Hong Xuanjiao, the younger sister of the Heavenly King Hong Xiuquan and the wife of the Western King Xiao Chaogui. Biographical materials

concerning this woman are extremely scarce, and there has been virtually no research done on her. A Ying's article, "Hong Xuanjiao," *Zhongguo funü* 9 (1956), p. 24, pulls together fragmentary pieces of evidence to provide a general outline of Hong's activities.

8. Translator's note. Long Qirui, *Huanyueshan fang shi* [Collected poems of Huanyueshan Cottage], 5 *juan*, in *Lingxi wujia shiwenji* [Poetry and literary collections of five authors from Lingxi] (Guilin: Dianya gongsi, 1935).

9. Translator's note. Quoted in Luo Ergang, "Nüying kao" [An examination of the female camps], *Xiandai shixue* 1 (Jan. 1933), p. 77.

10. This argument about the female camps and halls is advanced by Li Chun in "Nüguan nüying nü xiumian ying he tongzi bing" [Women officials, women's camps, women's embroidery camps, and child soldiers], the third section of the second chapter of his *Taiping Tianguo guanzhi junzhi tanlue* [A brief exploration of the Taiping civil service and military service systems] (Shanghai: Shanghai renmin chubanshe, 1958), pp. 68–81. In general, his argument on this score is convincing.

11. This description is based on Ma Shouling, *Jinling guijia xin yuefu* [A collection of new musical poems about Jinling (Nanjing) in the years 1853 and 1854], reproduced in *Taiping Tianguo* [The Taiping Rebellion], ed. Wang Zhongmin et al., (Shanghai: Shenzhou guoguangshe, 1953), vol. 4, pp. 723–46. The author was antagonistic toward the Taipings.

12. Translator's note. According to John Withers, "The rebels made an attempt to match work with physical capabilities. They established two categories which were designed to meet the problem: the *paimian* ('tag faces') were people between the ages of sixteen and fifty in good condition who were assigned the heavier jobs; and the *paiwei* ('tag tails'), people below fifteen and above fifty, who handled lighter duties." John L. Withers II, *The Heavenly Capital: Nanjing under the Taiping, 1853–1864*, Ph.D. diss., Yale University, 1983, p. 111.

13. Wang Shiduo, the author of *Yibing riji* [A diary of the years 1855 and 1856], ed. Deng Zhicheng (Beiping: Mingzhai congge, 1936), had three daughters. The eldest, who worked as a clerk in the office of the Eastern King (Yang Xiuqing), eventually did commit suicide. The second daughter starved to death. This diary is a fascinating account of the vicissitudes endured by a scholar during the Taiping Rebellion. A Japanese translation of the diary by Imamura Yoshio was published in *Chūgoku koten bungaku zenshū* [Complete collection of classical Chinese literature], vol. 32: *Rekidai zuihitsu shū* [Collection of literary jottings of successive dynasties] (Tokyo: Heibonsha, 1959), pp. 453–81.

14. Zhang Dejian, p. 159.

15. Translator's note. Augustus Lindley, *Ti-ping Tien-Kwoh: The History of the Ti-Ping Revolution, Including a Narrative of the Author's Personal Adven-*

tures, 2 vols. (London: Day and Son, 1966), vol. 1, p. 302. Japanese translation by Masui Tsuneo and Imamura Yoshio, *Taihei tengoku: Ri Shūsei no bakka ni arite* [The Taiping Rebellion, in the camp of Li Xiucheng] (Tokyo: Heibonsha, 1973).

16. A photograph and description of this marriage certificate can be found in Luo Ergang, *Taiping Tianguo wenwu tushi* [An explanation of Taiping historical relics] (Beijing: Sanlian shudian, 1956), p. 225. In 1954, a plasterer discovered the document embedded in the wall of the Sanxiu Buddhist Nunnery in Shaoxing, Zhejiang.

Translator's note: The phrase *longfeng,* "dragon and phoenix," denotes a betrothed or newly married couple, with dragon representing the man and phoenix the woman.

17. Frederick Engels, *The Origins of the Family, Private Property and the State* (New York: International Publishers, 1972), p. 146.

18. See Shang Yanliu, "Nü zhuangyuan Fu Shanxiang kaowei" [An examination of the bogus Number One Woman Scholar Fu Shanxiang], in his *Taiping Tianguo keju kaoshi jilue* [An account of the Taiping civil service examination system] (Beijing: Zhonghua shuju, 1962), pp. 74–81; Luo Ergang, "Taiping Tianguo shiliao li de diyibu da weishu *Jiangnan Chunmengyan biji*" [*Diary from spring dream hut in Jiangnan,* the primary forgery among the historical materials of the Taiping Rebellion], in his *Taiping Tianguo shiliao bianwei ji* [Distinguishing falsehoods in the historical materials on the Taiping Rebellion] (Beijing: Sanlian shudian, 1955), pp. 5–37; and Jian Youwen (Jen Yu-wen), "Nüwei kao" [An examination of the position of women], in his *Taiping Tianguo dianzhi tongkao* [A comprehensive study of Taiping institutions] (Hong Kong: Jianshi mengjin shuwu, 1958), vol. 2, pp. 1187–1276. (A fragment of this last piece appears in English in Jen Yu-wen, "Status of Women," in his *The Taiping Revolutionary Movement,* [New Haven, Conn.: Yale University Press, 1973], pp. 150–51).

19. Translator's note. Zhang Dejian, pp. 109–10.

20. Translator's note. Li Chun, *Taiping Tianguo zhidu chutan* [Preliminary study of Taiping institutions], rev. ed. (Beijing: Zhonghua shuju, 1963), p. 201.

21. Translator's note. The first through fourth Heavenly Commandments were as follows: "Thou shalt honor and worship the Sovereign God on High; thou shalt not worship false gods; thou shalt not take the name of the Sovereign God on High in vain; and on the seventh day, the day of worship, thou shalt praise the Sovereign God on High for his grace and virtue" (Shih, p. 18).

22. Translator's note. In Shih, p. 18.

23. Editor's note. The phrase generally translated as "virtuous women" (*lienü*) was reserved in late imperial times for women who had demon-

strated an unshakable commitment to preserving their chastity. Some *lienü* were simple, celibate widows who refused to remarry after their husbands died. However, demonstrating one's virtue often demanded violent martyrdom, since some women were expected to commit suicide in defense of their honor when threatened with rape. Still another form of "virtuous" behavior was a custom called *xunsi* ("following the husband in death"), in which a widow killed herself upon the death of her husband to demonstrate her fidelity to him and to avoid a forced remarriage. Because of the close relationship between female "virtue" and suicide, the phrase *lienü* is sometimes translated as "women martyrs."

24. Zeng Guofan, *Zeng Wenzheng gong quanji* [Complete works of Zeng Guofan] (Taibei: Shijie shuju, 1952), vol. 8, "Wenji," 3: 1b.

25. Fan Wenlan, *Zhongguo jindai shi* [Modern Chinese history] (Beijing: Renmin chubanshe, 1952), vol. 1, p. 135.

CHAPTER TWO

1. On the emergence and early history of women laborers in the cotton textile and silk-reeling industries, see Sanshigyō dōgyō kumiai chūōkai (Central Association of the Cooperative Union of the Silk Industry), comp., *Shina sanshigyō taikan* [General survey of the silk industry in China], (Tokyo: Okada nichieidō, 1929); Tō-A kenkyūjo (East Asian Research Institute), comp., *Shina sanshigyō kenkyū* [Studies of the Chinese silk industry] (Osaka: Ōsaka yagō shoten, 1943); Yan Zhongping, *Zhongguo mianfangzhi shigao* [Draft history of cotton spinning in China] (Beijing: Kexue chubanshe, 1955); and Sun Yutang and Wang Jingyu, *Zhongguo jindai gongye shi ziliao* [Historical materials on modern industry in China] (Beijing: Kexue chubanshe, 1957).

2. On mechanized silk-reeling in Guangdong, see Suzuki Tomoo, "Shinmatsu Minsho ni okeru minzoku shihon no tenkai katei, Kanton no seishigyō ni tsuite" [The process of the development of native capital in the late Qing and early Republican periods, on the silk industry in Guangdong], in *Chūgoku kindaika no shakai kōzō* [The social structure of the modernization of China] (Tokyo: Kyōiku shoseki, 1960), pp. 45–70.

3. Zhang Zhidong himself wrote an essay entitled "Jiechanzu hui zhangcheng xu" [Discussion of the rules of the Anti-Footbinding Society], *Shiwubao* 38 (Aug. 11, 1897), appended pp. 1a–2b. He explained as one of the reasons for his opposition to footbinding that it was not properly suited for women workers in the silk and cotton textile industries. The essay indicates that his opposition did not derive solely from his interest in increasing the wealth and strength of the state.

4. Among these study groups was a women's study association said to have been set up on the suggestion of Huang Jinyu, the wife of Kang You-

wei's younger brother, Kang Guangren. However, concrete details about the activities of this women's study group are unknown.

5. For Liang Qichao's views on women, see *Shiwubao* 23 (Mar. 11, 1897), pp. 1a–4a; and 25 (Apr. 11, 1897), pp. 2b–4a. His "Bianfa tongyi" has been reprinted in Liang Qichao, *Yinbingshi wenji* [Writings from an ice-drinker's studio] (Taibei: Taiwan Zhonghua shuju, 1960), vol. 1, pp. 1–93.

6. After writing this article, Liang escaped to Japan and began to publish periodicals such as *Xinmin congbao* in which he advocated reform. In 1902 he raised the issue again in his essay "Xinmin shuo" [On the new citizen] in the pages of *Xinmin congbao*. At this point, he somewhat revised his earlier view that regarded women solely as "consumers," and here he classified domestic labor as partially productive labor. However, insofar as he was trying to transform nonproductive labor, in which he saw 60–70 percent of women engaged, into productive labor, his perspective remained unchanged.

7. On women's education, the most detailed account is Cheng Zhefan, *Zhongguo xiandai nüzi jiaoyu shi* [A history of contemporary women's education in China] (Shanghai: Zhonghua shuju, 1936). On girls' schools established by missionaries, there is the excellent work of Hiratsuka Masunori, *Kindai Shina kyōiku bunka shi* [A history of modern Chinese education and culture] (Tokyo: Meguro shoten, 1942). My subsequent discussion is based on these two books. In addition, there are several good essays on women's education: Yu Qingtang, "Sanshiwu nian lai Zhongguo zhi nüzi jiaoyu" [Women's education in China over the past 35 years], in *Zuijin sanshiwu nian zhi Zhongguo jiaoyu* [Chinese education over the past 35 years] (Shanghai: Shangwu yinshuguan, 1931), pp. 175–214; Chu Jineng, "Nüxue xiansheng" [Preliminary announcement of women's education], *Dongfang zazhi* 31: 7 (Apr. 1, 1934), appended section on women and the family, pp. 23–27; and Chu Jineng, "Jiawu zhan qian siwei nü liuxuesheng" [Four overseas women students before the first Sino-Japanese War], *Dongfang zazhi* 31: 11 (June 1, 1934), pp. 10–15.

Translator's note. In English, see Ida Belle Lewis, *The Education of Girls in China* (New York: Teachers College, Columbia University, 1919).

8. Liang Qichao, "Chang she nüxuetang qi" [Proposal for the building of women's schools], *Shiwubao* 45 (Oct. 21, 1897), pp. 3a–4a; reprinted in his *Yinbingshi wenji*, vol. 2, pp. 19–20. "Shanghai xinshe Zhongguo nü xuetang zhangcheng" [Rules of the newly established Chinese women's school in Shanghai], *Shiwubao* 47 (Nov. 11, 1897), pp. 7b–10a.

9. See Chu Jineng, "Diyici ziban nüxuetang" [The first self-managed women's school], *Dongfang zazhi* 32: 3 (Feb. 1, 1935), pp. 127–31. According to this source, prior to the establishment of this women's school

by Liang Qichao and others, there was another girls' school set up by a woman in Suzhou.

10. Lin Qinnan, "Xin yuefu" [New *yuefu*], *Shiwubao* 49 (Dec. 1, 1897) and 50 (Dec. 11, 1897), separately paginated at the end of each issue. Translator's note. I would like to thank Kwok Pui-lan for help in translating this poetic song. A small part of it is translated in Virginia Chi-tin Chau, "The Anti-Footbinding Movement in China (1850–1912)," M.A. thesis, Columbia University, 1966, pp. 110–12 and was also brought to my attention by Ms. Kwok. A translation of three poems denouncing footbinding by Lin Qinnan also appears in Howard S. Levy, *Chinese Footbinding: The History of a Curious Erotic Custom* (New York: Walton Rawls, 1966), pp. 82–85.

11. On the anti-footbinding movement, see Kikuchi Takaharu, "Futensoku undō ni tsuite, hempō no haikei to shite no" [On the anti-footbinding movement, background to the 1898 Reforms], *Rekishi kyōiku* 5: 12 (Dec. 1957), pp. 31–40; and Kang Tongbi, "Qingmo de buchanzu hui" [The Anti-Footbinding Society of the late Qing], *Zhongguo funü* (May 1957), p. 12.

12. Liang Qichao, "Jiechanzu hui xu" [Discussion of the Anti-Footbinding Society], *Shiwubao* 16 (Dec. 1, 1896), pp. 12a–14b; reprinted in his *Yinbingshi wenji*, vol. 1, pp. 120–22.

13. Liang Qichao, "Shibian buchanzu hui jianming zhangcheng" [Concise rules of the experimental Anti-Footbinding Society], *Shiwubao* 25 (Apr. 11, 1897), pp. 2b–4a; reprinted in his *Yinbingshi wenji*, vol. 2, pp. 20–23.

14. Kang Youwei, "Qing jin funü chanzu zou" [Memorial requesting a ban on the binding of women's feet], dated June 1898, in *Wuxu bianfa* [The 1898 Reform Movement], ed. Zhongguo shixuehui (Chinese historical association) (Shanghai: Shenzhou guoguangshe, 1953), vol. 2, pp. 242–44.

15. Translator's note. For other materials on the anti-footbinding movement, see Levy, *Chinese Footbinding*, pp. 71–87.

16. *Renxue*, in *Tan Sitong quanji* [The collected works of Tan Sitong] (Beijing: Sanlian shudian, 1954), pp. 1–90. The first part of *Renxue* is translated by Shimada Kenji, in *Shinmatsu Minkokusho seiji hyōronshū* [Political commentaries from the late Qing and early Republican periods], vol. 58 of *Chūgoku koten bungaku taikei* [Compendium of classical Chinese literature], ed. Nishi Junzō and Shimada Kenji (Tokyo: Heibonsha, 1971), pp. 86–136; I have followed Shimada's translation. There is as well a complete translation by Nishi Junzō, in *Genten kindai Chūgoku shisō shi* [An intellectual history of modern China with original texts] (Tokyo: Iwanami shoten, 1977). In addition, on the ideas contained in the *Renxue*, see Shimada Kenji, "Chūgoku kinsei no shukan yuishinron ni tsuite" [On subjective idealism in modern China], *Tōhō gakuhō* 28 (Mar. 1958), pp. 1–80.

Translator's note. I have consulted the complete English translation of the *Renxue* by Chan Sin-wai, *An Exposition of Benevolence: The Jen-hsüeh of T'an Ssu-t'ung* (Hong Kong: The Chinese University Press, 1984), esp. pp. 46–47, 85–87, 178.

17. "Tan liefu zhuan" was published as one part of the essay "Wuxu bianfa ji" [Notes on the 1898 Reform], in issue 10 of *Qingyi bao*, the journal Liang Qichao published in Yokohama.

18. Kang Youwei claimed to have written *Datong shu* in 1884, but this is clearly untrue. The generally accepted theory is that Kang's basic conception of the book took shape around the time of the 1898 Reform Movement and saw rough completion while he was in India in 1901–2. However, the book was not immediately published. The first piece of it to appear was in the journal *Buren zazhi* in 1913, and the whole work was eventually published in 1935. We have no complete Japanese translation of the *Datong shu*, but Sakade Yoshinobu has published a partial Japanese translation, *Daidō sho* (Tokyo: Meitoku shuppansha, 1976). One work that discusses the ideas of the *Datong shu* in its relation to comparative women's liberation is Li Zehou, *Kang Youwei Tan Sitong sixiang yanjiu* [Studies in the thought of Kang Youwei and Tan Sitong] (Shanghai: Renmin chubanshe, 1958).

Translator's note. I have generally followed the partial English translation by Laurence G. Thompson, *Ta T'ung Shu: The One-World Philosophy of K'ang Yu-wei* (London, Allen & Unwin, 1958), though I have not always adopted his translations for the names of Kang's Utopian institutions.

19. Liang Qichao, *Qingdai xueshu gailun* (Shanghai: Shangwu yinshuguan, 1927); Japanese translation by Ono Kazuko (Tokyo: Heibonsha, 1974), p. 260.

Translator's note. My rendering of this passage from Liang Qichao is based on the original, although I did consult the English translation by Immanuel C. Y. Hsü, *Intellectual Trends in the Ch'ing Period* (Cambridge, Mass.: Harvard University Press, 1959), p. 96.

20. The examples of the inequality of women which Kang Youwei raised are as follows: they could not become officials; they could not sit for the official examinations; they could not become members of the assembly; they could not become citizens; they could not participate in public affairs; they could not become scholars; they could not be independent; and they were not free. Thus, Kang argued, women were no different from prisoners or convicts, slaves, personal possessions, or playthings.

21. As conditions for women's liberation in the age of ascending peace, Kang offered the following: (1) the establishment of girls' schools; (2) the franchise and the right to sit for the state examinations to gain bureaucratic posts; (3) participation in government; (4) equality under the law; (5) the right not to use the husband's name; (6) freedom of marriage for those

twenty years or older; (7) the institution of a marriage register and an official to handle marriages; (8) the freedoms of movement, social intercourse, travel, and entertainment for women with education who are twenty or older; (9) abolition of footbinding, corsets, and the like; (10) sexually integrated seating; and (11) abolition of clothing differences between men and women.

22. Mao Zedong, "On the People's Democratic Dictatorship" (June 30, 1949), in *Selected Works of Mao Tse-tung* (Beijing: Foreign Languages Press, 1967), vol. 4, p. 414.

CHAPTER THREE

1. Editor's note. The following account of the Red Lanterns is based mostly on hearsay, folk songs, and legendary materials, as indicated in the notes, primarily because almost no reliable information on the Red Lanterns exists. In his recent book *The Origins of the Boxer Uprising* (Berkeley, Calif.: University of California Press, 1987), Joseph W. Esherik notes (pp. 227, 235, 297–98) that the Red Lanterns were apparently organized separately from the Boxers because the latter saw women as pollutants. In addition, the Boxers were hesitant about attacking female missionaries for fear of pollution, and such tasks naturally devolved upon the Red Lanterns, who, by virtue of already being filthy, "did not fear dirty things."

2. Translator's note. These rather awkward English translations are meant to convey the sense of the Chinese terms, which are common to most martial arts groups in China. The key connotation is that the members are all "brothers" (*xiong*), being disciples of the same boxing master (*shi*). Thus, all Boxers were "brother-disciples" (*shixiong*), and the most accomplished of them were "senior brother-disciples."

3. Songs about the Boxers are collected in Liu Chongfeng et al., *Yihetuan geyao* [Boxer folk songs] (Shanghai: Shanghai wenyi chubanshe, 1960). See also Cheng Ying, comp., *Zhongguo jindai fandi fanfengjian lishi geyao xuan* [A selection of modern Chinese anti-imperialist, anti-feudal historical songs], (Beijing: Zhonghua shuju, 1962).

4. A collection of stories about the Boxers can be found in *Yihetuan gushi* [Stories of the Boxers], ed. Zhongguo minjian wenyi yanjiuhui (Chinese Folk Art and Literature Association) (Beijing: Renmin wenxue chubanshe, 1960). Some of these have been translated into Japanese by Makida Eiji and Katō Sendai, *Giwadan minka shū: Chūgoku no kōshō bungei* [Collection of Boxer folklore: Chinese oral literature] (Tokyo: Heibonsha, Tōyō bunko, 1973), vol. 1. I have followed the latter.

5. On the Holy Mother of the Yellow Lotus, see Geming lishi yanjiusuo, Jindai geming shi yanjiusuo nongmin zhanzheng shi zu (The Institute on the History of the Revolution and the Peasant War History Group

of the Institute of Modern Revolutionary History), " 'Hongdengzhao' de geming zaofan jingshen wansui" [Long live the revolutionary spirit of the "Red Lanterns Shining"], *Guangming ribao*, Apr. 27, 1967; and Tianjin shi lishi bowuguan (Tianjin Municipal History Museum) and Tianjin wenwu guanlichu (Tianjin Cultural Relics Management Office), "Tianjin Yihetuan fandi douzheng shiji diaocha jilue" [An investigation of relics of the Boxers' anti-imperialist struggle in Tianjin], *Wenwu* 240 (May 1976), pp. 11–17.

6. On Azure Cloud, see Di Pingzi, "Gengzi jishi" [A record of 1900], in A Ying, *Yihetuan shibian wenxue ji* [Literary collection from the Boxer Incident] (Beijing: Zhonghua shuju, 1956), p. 1002. Li Henian's "Hongdengzhao yuefu" [Song of the Red Lanterns Shining] is included in this same volume.

CHAPTER FOUR

1. On the topic of overseas students in Japan, see Sanetō Keishū, *Chūgokujin Nihon ryūgaku shi* [A history of overseas Chinese students in Japan] (Tokyo: Kuroshio shuppan), 1970.

2. On Shimoda Utako, see Ko Shimoda kōchō sensei denki hensansho (under the guidance of Fujimura Zenkichi), ed., *Shimoda Utako sensei den* [Biography of Professor Shimoda Utako] (Tokyo: Ko Shimoda kōchō sensei denki hensansho, 1943); Ono Kazuko, "Shimoda Utako to Hattori Unokichi" [Shimoda Utako and Hattori Unokichi], in *Kindai Nihon to Chūgoku* [Modern Japan and China], ed. Takeuchi Yoshimi and Hashikawa Bunzō (Tokyo: Asahi shimbunsha, 1974), vol. 1, pp. 201–21.

3. The formal name of the Gongaihui was the "Riben liuxue nüxuesheng gongaihui" (the Mutual Love Association of Overseas Students in Japan). According to its tenets, it aimed at "rescuing [China's] 200 million women and recovering their innate rights; then, by instilling in them the sense of nation, they would be able to fulfill their divine obligations as women citizens of the nation." The association was organized in Tokyo in April 1903. Its bylaws were published in the second issue of the journal *Jiangsu*, put out by overseas Chinese students in Japan. The conditions surrounding the emergency meeting of the Gongaihui are described in detail in the article on overseas students in the fourth issue of the journal *Zhejiang chao* and in the notice on overseas student activities in the fourth issue of the journal *Hubei xuesheng jie*. Women in Shanghai at this time were organizing the Dui-E tongzhi nühui (Women's Association Opposed to Russia), which centered around women in the Chong-Meng School for Women, a school established on the basis of Mencius's principle of reverence for the people ("Chong-Meng" meaning "honor Mencius"). The school principal, Chen Wanyan, and the headmaster, Tong Dongxue, preached democracy. As a

result this was a pioneer institution in which teachers and students alike all treated each other equally. When the Dui-E tongzhi nühui changed its name to Zhengcunhui (Struggle for Existence Society) in February 1904, the Gongaihui changed its name to Cihangshe (Barge of Compassion Society). For details on the Zhengcunhui, see *Jingzhong ribao*, a newspaper of the time.

4. During the reign of the Empress Dowager, educational reforms, involving primarily sending students abroad and establishing a new school system, were put into place. The "Imperial Regulations for Establishing Schools" (promulgated in 1902) provided for China's modern school system. However, it proved enormously difficult to eradicate the prejudicial notion current in women's education that "it was virtuous to be lacking in talent." While these "Regulations" stipulated detailed rules for the educational system, they never mentioned the content of women's education. With the "Imperial Regulations for Education" announced in 1904, women's education began to emerge as an issue, but even here women's education did not mean education in schools, for it was anticipated this would be exclusively domestic education. Thus, women's education became a genuine issue for the first time in the "Regulations of the Ministry of Education on Elementary Schools for Girls" and the "Regulations of the Ministry of Education for Women's Normal Schools" of 1907. On women's education in the late Qing, see the detailed account in Cheng Zhefan, *Zhongguo xiandai nüzi jiaoyu shi* [A history of contemporary women's education in China] (Shanghai: Zhonghua shuju, 1936). Also, the various "Regulations" are collected in Shu Xincheng, *Zhongguo jindai jiaoyu shi ziliao* [Materials on the history of modern Chinese education] (Beijing: Renmin jiaoyu chubanshe, 1962).

5. On Shimoda's educational thought, see Ono Kazuko, "Shimoda Utako."

6. Chen Xiefen, editor of *Nübao*, was the daughter of Chen Fan, owner of *Jiangbao*. Initially, *Nübao* was either issued together with *Jiangbao* or perhaps as the women's edition of *Jiangbao*. Later *Nübao* became an independent journal with the name *Nüxuebao*. The original is not to be found in Japan, and the text for "Duli pian" [On independence] below is taken from its republication in *Jiangbao*. On the journal *Nüxuebao*, see the short article by Zhang Jinglu, "Guanyu Zhongguo jindai diyifen nübao, *Nüxuebao*" [On the first modern women's newspaper in China, *Nüxuebao*], *Guangming ribao*, Aug. 18, 1962.

7. See Zhang Jinglu.

Translator's note. On Fukuda Hideko and Shimoda Utako as representatives of conflicting approaches to women's education in Japan, see Sharon L. Sievers, *Flowers in Salt: The Beginnings of Feminist Consciousness in*

Modern Japan (Stanford, Calif.: Stanford University Press, 1983), pp. 48–51, 115–37. Fukuda, whose school for working mothers was closed by the government in 1884, struggled throughout her career to broaden educational opportunities for all women. Shimoda focused her attention on the daughters of the elite.

8. On the Patriotic Girls' School, see Cai Yuanpei, "Wo zai jiaoyujie de jingyan" [My experiences in the world of education], in *Cai Yuanpei xuanji* [Selected works of Cai Yuanpei] (Hong Kong: Xianggang wenxue yanjiu-she, n.d.); Jiang Weiqiao, "Zhongguo jiaoyuhui zhi huiyi" [Memories of educational associations in China], in *Xinhai geming* [The 1911 Revolution], ed. Zhongguo shixuehui (Shanghai: Shanghai renmin chubanshe, 1956), vol. 1, pp. 485–96. Furthermore, in the transcription of lectures given at the Patriotic Girls' School, one finds such articles as Ye Haowu's "Zhongguo nüzi de renge yong zenyang de yangcheng fangfa cai shi wanshan de?" [What sort of educative methods can be used to perfect Chinese women's characters?], which was included in the newspaper *Jingzhong ribao*, Apr. 21, 1904.

9. Later, as Chancellor of Beijing University, Cai Yuanpei accepted women students into Beijing University, but his perspective on women was unique at the time. Cai had lost his first wife when he was director of the Zhong-Xi (Sino-Western) Academy. He announced five preconditions to his remarrying: (1) she would not have bound feet; (2) she would be literate; (3) he would take no concubines; (4) she could remarry after his death; and (5) if relations between husband and wife failed to be harmonious, they would divorce. He later wed Huang Shizhen. He is said to have convened a public meeting at his wedding ceremony. This occurred in 1898 or 1899, which makes him an extraordinarily progressive thinker for his time. His essays are collected in *Cai Yuanpei xuanji*. The most detailed study of Cai Yuanpei is Cai Shangzhi, *Cai Yuanpei xueshu sixiang zhuanji* [An intellectual biography of Cai Yuanpei] (Shanghai: Tangdi chubanshe, 1950). We still need a study that traces his views on women.

10. In 1904 Zhang Zhujun from Guangdong helped operate the Patriotic Girls' School. In line with her own views, a health training course was held, and a girls' manual training institute was established with it. (The rules for the health training course appear in *Jingzhong ribao*, May 24, 1904). It apparently became quite popular, and for that reason it became impossible to house all the students. Through her efforts, the Guangdong Yuxian (Nourish virtue) Women's Branch Factory was reestablished. (Zhang reportedly established the factory in opposition to the Patriotic Girls' School). In Shanghai as well, a number of women's training institutes were opened with the aim of gaining occupational independence for women. See the *Jingzhong ribao* for the details of these events.

11. There is a rather detailed introduction, upon which this discussion is largely based, to the *Nüjie zhong* in Chen Dongyuan, *Zhongguo funü shenghuo shi* [A history of the life of Chinese women] (Shanghai: Shangwu yinshuguan, 1927).

12. This article was published in the fifth issue of the journal *Zhejiang*. For a time *Zhejiang* had a column devoted to articles on women's education. It seems to have been more deeply interested in women's issues than other overseas student journals.

13. Qiu Jin's writings are collected in *Qiu Jin ji* [Writings of Qiu Jin] (Beijing: Zhonghua shuju, 1960). For memoirs about her and studies of her, see the following: Takeda Taijun, *Shūfū shūu hito o shūsatsu: Shū Kin joshi den* [Autumn rain, autumn wind, they make one die of sorrow: a biography of Qiu Jin] (Tokyo: Chikuma shobō, 1968), also in *Takeda Taijun zenshū* [Collected works of Takeda Taijun] (Tokyo: Chikuma shobō, 1972), vol. 9, pp. 176–295; Ōshima Toshikazu, "Shū Kin jokyō no shōgai" [The career of the female warrior, Qiu Jin], *Neiraku shien* 4 (July 1957), pp. 1–11; Hattori Shigeko, "Fujin kakumeika ō Shū Kin joshi no omoide (1)" [Memoirs of the venerable revolutionary, Ms. Qiu Jin], *Chūgokugo zasshi* 6: 1–3 (Mar. 1951); Nakayama Yoshihiro, "Kindai Chūgoku no joseizō: Shū Kin no sobyō" [The image of women in modern China, a portrait of Qiu Jin], *Ōshimo gakuen joshi tanki daigaku kenkyū shūhō* 3 (Dec. 1965), reprinted in his *Kindai Chūgoku ni okeru josei kaihō no shisō to kōdō* [Women's liberation thought and activities in modern China] (Kita Kyūshū: Kita Kyūshū Chūgoku shoten, 1983), pp. 115–38; Xu Shuangyun, "Ji Qiu Jin" [Remembering Qiu Jin], in *Xinhai geming huiyilu* [Memoirs of the 1911 Revolution] (Beijing: Zhonghua shuju, 1963), vol. 4, pp. 205–22; Wang Shize, "Yihui Qiu Jin" [Memories of Qiu Jin], in *Xinhai geming huiyilu*, vol. 4, pp. 223–32 (Japanese translation by Ōshima Toshikazu, "Omoide no naka no Shū Kin," *Neiraku shien* 13 [Feb. 1965], pp. 23–33); Fan Wenlan, "Nü gemingjia Qiu Jin" [Woman revolutionary Qiu Jin], *Zhongguo funü* (Aug. 1956), pp. 20–21; Qiu Zongzhang, "Qiu Jin nianpu" [Chronological biography of Qiu Jin], *Shixue yuekan* (July 1957), pp. 21–23. Photolithographs from manuscripts by Qiu Jin can be seen in *Qiu Jin shiji* [Historical relics of Qiu Jin] (Beijing: Zhonghua shuju, 1958).

Translator's note. In English, see Mary Backus Rankin, "The Emergence of Women at the End of the Ch'ing: The Case of Ch'iu Chin," in Margery Wolf and Roxane Witke, eds., *Women in Chinese Society* (Stanford, Calif.: Stanford University Press, 1975), pp. 39–66; and Jonathan D. Spence, *The Gate of Heavenly Peace: The Chinese and Their Revolution, 1895–1980* (New York: Viking, 1981), pp. 83–93.

14. The journal *Tianyi* began publication, as the organ of the Society for the Reinstatement of Women's Rights, in Tokyo under the editorship

of He Zhen in June 1907. It has been preserved by Takeuchi Zensaku, and issues 3, 5, 6, 8–10, 11–12, 15, 16–19 have been reproduced in *Chūgoku shiryō sōsho* [Collectanea of materials on China], vol. 6, document series 1 on early Chinese socialism, (Tokyo: Daiyasu, 1966). What readership or influence *Tianyi* had at the time of its publication is unclear. However, in August 1907, a bit later than the establishment of the Society for the Reinstatement of Women's Rights, a short lecture series on socialism given by Zhang Ji and Liu Shipei brought together overseas Chinese students who were dissatisfied with the principles of the Revolutionary Alliance. Clearly it was a theoretical journal of anarchism aimed at concerned young men and women. This contention is supported by some of the names that appear on the list of those who raised money for *Tianyi*: Fang Junying (a woman), who had received training at the Revolutionary Alliance's bomb-production factory; Tang Qunying, a later leader of the women's suffrage movement; and He Xiangning, wife of Liao Zhongkai. (We might note here, however, that Liu Shipei and his wife, He Zhen, eventually were bought off by the Manchu government, became spies, and betrayed the revolution.)

15. "Joshi fukken kai" [Society for the Reinstatement of Women's Rights], *Sekai fujin* 13 (July 1, 1907), p. 2.

16. No individual biographies of He Zhen exist. For brief mentions of her, we have only Liu Fuceng, "Wang zhi Shipei muzhi ming" [Epitaph of my departed nephew {Liu} Shipei], and Cai Yuanpei, "Liu jun Shenshu shilüe" [Brief account of Liu Shipei's life], both in *Liu Shenfu xiansheng ishu* [The remaining writings of Mr. Liu Shenfu {Shipei}], ed. Zheng Yufu (n.p., 1932–34).

17. Kōtoku Shūsui, "Fujin kaihō to shakaishugi" [Women's liberation and socialism], *Sekai fujin* 16 (Sept. 1, 1907), p. 1.

18. *Xin shiji*, a weekly magazine published by Chinese anarchists in Paris, first appeared on June 22, 1907. All issues through number 77 have been reproduced in *Chūgoku shiryō sōsho*, vol. 6, document series 1 on early Chinese socialism.

19. *North China Herald*, Sept. 23, 1911, p. 749.

Translator's note: The English text here is slightly longer than that in the Japanese edition.

20. On Xu Zonghan, see Feng Ziyou, "Xu Zonghan nüshi shilüe" [Brief account of the life of Ms. Xu Zonghan], in his *Geming yishi* [Unofficial history of the {1911} revolution] (Taibei reprint: Taiwan shangwu yinshuguan, 1965), vol. 3, pp. 334–37; and Xu Chongling, "Xu Zonghan," *Zhongguo funü* (Apr. 1958), pp. 18–20.

21. Du Wei, "Shanghai nüzi beifa gansidui" [The dare-to-die corps of Shanghai women in the northern expedition], in *Xinhai geming huiyilu*, vol. 4, pp. 59–62.

22. Zhao Liancheng, "Tongmenghui zai Xiang-Ao de huodong he Guangdong funüjie canjia geming de huiyi" [Memories of the activities of the Revolutionary Alliance in Hong Kong and Macao and the participation by women from Guangdong in the revolution], in *Xinhai geming huiyilu*, vol. 2, pp. 302–22. On the Women's Army, many related articles appeared at the time in the newspapers *Shibao* and *Minlibao*.

23. On Zhang Zhujun, see Feng Ziyou, "Nü yishi Zhang Zhujun" [Female doctor Zhang Zhujun], in his *Geming yishi*, vol. 2, pp. 41–45; T. Kobayashi, "Chang Chu-chün for Women's Rights," *Journal of the Oriental Society of Australia* 11 (1976), pp. 62–80.

24. On the sisters Yin Ruizhi and Yin Weijun, see Zhou Yawei, "Guangfuhui jianwen zayi" [Scattered memories of the Guangfuhui], in *Xinhai geming huiyilu*, vol. 1, pp. 624–36.

25. Tan Sheying, *Zhongguo funü yundong tongshi* [Comprehensive history of the women's movement in China] (Shanghai: Shangwu yinshuguan, 1936). On the history of prostitution in China, see Wang Shunu, *Zhongguo changji shi* [History of Chinese prostitution] (Shenghuo shudian, 1934; Taibei reprint: Dalin shudian, 2 vols., 1978). There is a fair amount of material on this subject as well in Guo Zhenyi, *Zhongguo funü wenti* [Chinese women's issues] (Shanghai: Shangwu yinshuguan, 1937).

26. The Chinese Socialist Party was a group deeply concerned with women's issues. At its second general meeting in 1912, slogans of gender equality were raised, such as regular elections (including women), equality in education for men and women, abolition of concubinage, and restrictions on prostitution. In his relations with women, however, Jiang Kanghu's behavior was said to have made proper young people hide their eyes. See Kojima Yoshio, "Shingai kakumei ki no rōnō undō to Chūgoku shakaitō" [The labor and peasant movements at the time of the 1911 Revolution and the Chinese Socialist Party], *Rekishigaku kenkyū* (Oct. 1971), separate issue entitled *Sekai shi ninshiki to jinmin tōsō shi no kadai* [Understanding world history and lessons in the history of popular struggles], pp. 106–15; Gu Jiegang, Cao Suizhi, and Cao Jiayin, "Zhongguo Shehuidang he Chen Yilong de si" [The Chinese Socialist Party and the death of Chen Yilong], in *Xinhai geming huiyilu*, vol. 6, pp. 495–506.

27. On Sun Yat-sen and women's liberation, see Liang Rui, "Sun Zhongshan xiansheng duiyu woguo funü yundong de gongxian" [Dr. Sun Yat-sen's contributions to the Chinese women's movement], *Zhongguo funü* (Dec. 1956), p. 1; Liu Qingyang, "Sun Zhongshan xiansheng gei wo de guwu" [Dr. Sun Yat-sen's inspiration for me], *Zhongguo funü* (Dec. 1956), p. 2; Zhongguo quanguo minzhu funü lianhehui (All-China Democratic Women's League), "Sun Zhongshan xiansheng he funü yundong, jinian Zhongshan xiansheng danchen jiushi zhounian xiang funü xuanchuan de tigang" [Sun Yat-sen and the women's movement, remembering the nine-

tieth anniversary of the birth of Dr. Sun Yat-sen with a proposal for women's propaganda], *Guangming ribao*, Nov. 12, 1956.

28. Although Lin Zongsu apparently expected opposition would result from her explicitly publishing these confirmed items, the right-wing element among the revolutionaries did not immediately issue a rejoinder. The Chinese National Federation was an organization formed by Zhang Binglin and others who, once the revolution had attained success, left the Revolutionary Alliance. They had grave doubts about whether women's suffrage conformed to the proper order and virtuous practices of society. They opposed as deplorable Sun Yat-sen's statement in recognition of women's suffrage. Sun himself offered several "clarifications," and Lin Zongsu fervently protested by publishing "Nüzi canzheng Tongmenghui Lin Zongsu xuanyan" [Lin Zongsu's declaration on women's participation in the Revolutionary Alliance].

29. On the mass actions with respect to the Nanjing parliament, there are detailed account in the newspapers of the time: *Shibao, Beijing ribao*, and *Minlibao*.

30. See Hannah Gavron, *The Captive Wife: Conflicts of Household Mothers* (London: Routledge & Kegan Paul, 1966); Japanese translation by Ogami Kyōko, *Tsuma wa torawarete iru ka* [Are women kept captive?] (Tokyo: Iwanami shinsho, 1970). Also Emmeline Pankhurst, *My Own Story* (London: Eveleigh Nash, 1914); Japanese translation by Hiroi Eiko, *Watakushi no kiroku, fujin sanseiken undō no tōshi Pankāsuto fujin jiden* [My story: The autobiography of a warrior in the women's suffrage movement, Mrs. Pankhurst] (Tokyo: Gendai shi shuppan kai, 1975).

31. Translator's note. I was unable to locate the original English text, so this is a retranslation from the Japanese.

32. Pankhurst, p. 238. On women's suffrage in Guangdong Province, see, in addition to the press of the time, documents of the Japanese Foreign Ministry; Wang Hongjin, "Qingmo Minchu de Guangdong yihui zhengzhi" [Guangdong parliamentary politics at the end of the Qing and beginning of the Republic], in *Guangdong Xinhai geming ziliao* [Materials on Guangdong in the 1911 Revolution] (Guangdong: Guangdong renmin chubanshe, 1981), pp. 426–36.

33. According to Yang Yuru, *Xinhai geming xianzhuji* [Earlier writing from the 1911 Revolution] (Beijing: Kexue chubanshe, 1958), the facts are that his wife was worried that the ammunition would be seized in a search by the military police, and thinking that her husband could not escape, she committed suicide.

CHAPTER FIVE

Translator's note. I would like to thank Yoshiko Miyake for assistance. Christina Gilmartin graciously reviewed the drafts and corrected errors, adding information (based on her own research) to the notes.

1. See Ono Kazuko, "Shinmatsu no fujin kaihō shisō" [Women's liberation thought at the end of the Qing dynasty], *Shisō* 525 (Mar. 1968), pp. 86–99.

2. Editor's note. Taken from Chen Duxiu, "Call to Youth," trans. in Ssu-yu Teng and John K. Fairbank, *China's Response to the West: A Documentary Survey, 1839–1923* (New York: Atheneum, 1970), pp. 240–46. On the way issues of concern to women were handled by *Xin qingnian*, see Francesca Cini, "Le 'problème des femmes' dans *La nouvelle jeunesse*, 1915–1922," *Etudes chinoises* 5: 1–2 (Spring–Autumn 1986), pp. 133–56.

3. Wu Yu, "Jiating zhidu wei zhuanzhizhuyi zhi genjudi" [The family system is the foundation of authoritarianism], *Xin qingnian* 2: 6 (Feb. 1, 1916), separately paginated pp. 1–4, (Tokyo reprint: Daiyasu, 1962, pp. 491–94). A Japanese translation of this essay, with interlinear commentary, appears in Miyazaki Ichisada, comp., *Seiji ronshū* [Essays on politics], vol. 11 of *Chūgoku bunmei sen* [Selections from Chinese civilization] (Tokyo: Asahi shimbunsha, 1971), pp. 52–81.

Translator's note. Wu Yu studied law and political science in Japan during the Russo-Japanese War and read widely in Western as well as Japanese sources on theories of jurisprudence and civil society. His radical critique of Confucian values, however, was grounded in his studies of the non-Confucian Chinese traditions, especially Taoism, as well as the thought of Mo Zi and the Legalist Han Fei Zi. In 1893 he married the writer Zhao Lan (1876–1917), who shared his philosophical, political, and literary interests. One of her essays, "Nüquan pingyi" [On women's rights] was published in *New Youth* in the year of her death. She also published essays in *Funü zazhi* [Ladies' journal] and other literary magazines of the May Fourth era. See Howard L. Boorman and Richard C. Howard, *Biographical Dictionary of Republican China* (New York: Columbia University Press, 1968), vol. 3, pp. 462–65.

4. For Lu Xun's views on women, see Shimada Yukiko, "'Ro Jin to josei kaihō' ni tsuite" [On Lu Xun and women's liberation], *Shūkan Tōyōgaku* 19 (June 1973), pp. 194–204; Nakayama Yoshihiro, "Ro Jin no fujinkan" [Lu Xun's view of women], *Ōshimo gakuen joshi tanki daigaku kenkyū shūhō* 9 (Feb. 1972), pp. 61–79; Xu Guangping, *Lu Xun huiyilu* [Lu Xun: A memoir] (Beijing: Zuojia chubanshe, 1961), and the Japanese translation by Matsui Hiromi, *Ro Jin kaisōroku* [A memoir of Lu Xun] (Tokyo: Chikuma shobō, 1968); Zhu Tong, "'Zhu Fu' fanying le laodong funü de beiju"

["The New Year's Sacrifice" reflected the tragic fate of a working woman], in his *Lu Xun zuopin de fenxi* [An analysis of the works of Lu Xun] (Shanghai: Dongfang shudian, 1953), vol. 1, pp. 123–41; and Hua Gang, "Lu Xun lun funü wenti" [Lu Xun on the woman question], in his *Lu Xun sixiang luoji fazhan* [The logical development of Lu Xun's thought] (Shanghai: Xin wenyi chubanshe, 1953), pp. 195–208. Lu's essay "My Views on Chastity" appears in Japanese translation in *Ro Jin senshū* [Selected works of Lu Xun] (Tokyo: Iwanami shoten, 1955), vol. 5, pp. 95–109.

Translator's note. For translations of "The New Year's Sacrifice," see Lu Hsun, *The Selected Stories of Lu Hsun* (Peking: Foreign Languages Press, 1954), pp. 158–79; C. C. Wang, trans., *Ah Q and Others: Selected Stories of Lusin* (New York: Columbia University Press, 1941), pp. 184–204 (here titled "The Widow"); and Lu Hsun, *Selected Works of Lu Hsun*, trans. Yang Hsien-i and Gladys Yang (Peking: Foreign Languages Press, 1957–59), vol. 1, pp. 150–73. The other essays by Lu Xun cited here appear as follows: "My Views on Chastity," in *Selected Works of Lu Hsun*, vol. 2, pp. 11–24, citations adapted from pp. 13, 18–19; "On the Emancipation of Women," in *Selected Works of Lu Hsun*, vol. 3, pp. 339–41, and in *Chinese Literature* 9 (Sept. 1973), pp. 30–32; and "What Happens to Nora After She Leaves Home?" in *Silent China: Selected Writings of Lu Hsun*, trans. Gladys Yang (London: Oxford University Press, 1973), pp. 148–54, and in *Chinese Literature* 9 (Sept. 1973), pp. 23–29. Lu Xun's story "Regret for the Past" appears in *Selected Works of Lu Hsun*, vol. 1, pp. 238–61. Hu Shi's essay on Ibsenism, "Yibushengzhuyi," was first published in *Xin qingnian* 4: 6 (1918), pp. 489–507; see Jerome Grieder, *Hu Shih and the Chinese Renaissance* (Cambridge, Mass.: Harvard University Press, 1970), esp. pp. 90–93.

5. Translator's/editor's note. In this connection, see Sharon Nolte, *Liberalism in Modern Japan: Ishibashi Tanzan and His Teachers, 1905–1960* (Berkeley, Calif.: University of California Press, 1987), pp. 72–73, 177–78. See also Brian Powell, "Matsui Sumako: Actress and Woman," in W. G. Beasley, ed., *Modern Japan* (London: Allen and Unwin, 1975), pp. 135–46.

6. For Mao Zedong's critical essays on the suicide of the young bride Zhao Wuzhen, see "Wusi shiqi Hunan xin wenhua yundong bufen ziliao" [Classified materials on the New Culture Movement in Hunan during the May Fourth era], in *Hunan lishi ziliao* [Materials on the history of Hunan province] 4 (1959).

Translator's/editor's note. On Mao's reactions to Miss Zhao's suicide, see Roxane Heater Witke, "Mao Tse-tung, Women, and Suicide in the May Fourth Era," *China Quarterly* 31 (July–Sept. 1967), pp. 128–47; and Nakayama Yoshihiro, "Mō Takutō no joseikan" [Mao Tse-tung's views on women], in his *Kindai Chūgoku ni okeru josei kaihō no shisō to kōdō* [Women's liberation thought and activities in modern China] (Kita Kyūshū: Kita

Kyūshū Chūgoku shoten, 1983), pp. 359–387, esp. pp. 372–78 subtitled: "Hanayome jisatsu jiken ni tsuite no ronpyō" [{Mao's} Critical essays on the suicide of a bride], which discusses each of the articles by Mao. As Witke notes, Mao in fact wrote nine pieces for the Changsha newspaper *Dagongbao* on this incident; Witke translates excerpts from several of them. The original texts (published Nov. 16–28, 1919) can be found in *Mao Zedong ji, bujuan* [The collected works of Mao Zedong, supplementary volumes], ed. Takeuchi Minoru (Tokyo: Sōsōsha, 1983), vol. 1, pp. 143–72. Six of the essays are listed in Jerome Chen, *Mao Papers: Anthology and Bibliography* (New York: Oxford University Press, 1970), pp. 164, 198. See also Stuart Schram, "Mao Tse-tung's Thought to 1949," in *The Cambridge History of China, Volume 13: Republican China 1912–1949, Part 2*, ed. John K. Fairbank and Albert Feuerwerker (Cambridge, Eng.: Cambridge University Press, 1986), p. 803. Lu Xun's story "A Madman's Diary" appears in *Selected Works of Lu Hsun*, vol. 1, pp. 8–21.

7. Li Dazhao, "Funü jiefang yu Democracy" [Women's liberation and democracy], *Shaonian Zhongguo* 1: 4 (1919), pp. 27–28.

Translator's note. Li Dazhao, soon to become a founder of the Chinese Communist Party, was at this time a member of the editorial board of *New Youth*. As chief librarian of Beijing University from February 1918, Li became a mentor and ally of radical students, who often held their meetings in his office. See Boorman and Howard, vol. 2, pp. 329–33; and Maurice Meisner, *Li Ta-chao and the Origins of Chinese Marxism* (Cambridge, Mass.: Harvard University Press, 1967).

8. *Funü pinglun* [Women's critic] was first published in Shanghai on Aug. 3, 1921, as a supplement to the *Minguo ribao* [Republican daily]; it ceased publication on May 25, 1923, after 104 issues. Chen Wangdao was the main editor; Mao Dun was one of its main contributors, along with Shao Lizi and others. As a journal it advocated women's economic independence, suffrage, and freedom of marriage; but it did not stop at bourgeois suffragism, as it came more and more to adopt socialist positions. The only known complete run of this journal is held in the library of the Research Institute for Humanistic Sciences at Kyoto University. Other women's journals of the period include *Xin funü* [New women], published semi-monthly in Shanghai, beginning on Jan. 1, 1920; another serial with the same name as the Shanghai journal, *Funü pinglun* [Women's critic], published semi-monthly and later monthly in Suzhou, beginning May 1, 1920; *Jiefang huabao* [Liberation illustrated news], a monthly publication, beginning on May 4, 1920, which carried popular articles devoted to women's issues; *Funü sheng* [Women's voice], published by the Chinese Women's World Alliance of Shanghai, beginning on Dec. 13, 1921, under the direction of the Chinese Communist Party; and *Funü zhoubao* [Women's

weekly], beginning Aug. 22, 1923, a supplement to *Shanghai Minguo ribao* [Shanghai republican daily]. All of these are briefly mentioned and their contents indexed in *Wusi shiqi qikan jieshao* [An introduction to periodicals from the May Fourth Period] (Beijing: Renmin chubanshe, 1959), vol. 2. In addition, *Funü zazhi* [Ladies' journal], which was published from Jan. 1915 until Dec. 1931, is held in the collection of the Center for Modern Chinese Research at the Tōyō bunko in Tokyo. This journal was originally founded as a ladies' magazine, and during the May Fourth period it began to publish articles of rather high quality. Since in China the class of bourgeois housewives who might have read women's magazines was relatively small, "ladies' magazines" grew only with great difficulty.

Translator's note. Mao Dun was the pen name after 1930 of Shen Yanping (*b.* 1896), who later became the foremost realist novelist of the Republican era. At the time of the May Fourth Movement, he was just beginning his career as a writer, while working first as a proofreader for the Commercial Press in Shanghai, later as editor and translator. His literary career took him back and forth across political lines; first associated with the left-wing Guomindang, he was later celebrated as a socialist realist writer by the Communists. After 1949 he stopped writing and took office as Minister of Culture, a post he lost under criticism in 1964. See Boorman and Howard, vol. 3, pp. 110–15. Chen Wangdao, one of the founders of the Chinese Communist Party in Shanghai in 1921, was an early member of the Shanghai Society for the Study of Socialism and was also involved in the publication of a Guomindang newspaper, the *Republican Daily*, which championed the cause of the New Culture Movement. In his editorials, he was an ardent critic of the traditional family system. He produced the first complete translation into Chinese of *The Communist Manifesto*, which the Society published in April 1920. (See Chow Tse-tsung, *The May Fourth Movement: Intellectual Revolution in Modern China* [Stanford, Calif.: Stanford University Press, 1960], pp. 246–99). Chen Wangdao's works have been reprinted in three volumes, the first containing his articles attacking the traditional family system: *Chen Wangdao wenji* (Shanghai: Shanghai renmin chubanshe, 1979). The involvement of Chen Wangdao and Mao Dun in women's issues was reflected in their presence in 1921 on the faculty of the Shanghai Girls' School for Commoners. Earlier, Chen also taught at the Zhejiang Provincial First Normal School in Hangzhou, where faculty and students were strongly influenced by anarchism. This school, like its counterpart in Changsha, was a center of the New Culture discourse attacking Confucian values. On journals of the period, see Chow Tse-tsung, *Research Guide to the May Fourth Movement* (Cambridge, Mass.: Harvard University Press, 1963); and Chow, *The May Fourth Movement*, pp. 178–81. On the *Ladies' Journal*, see Jacqueline Nivard, "Women and the Women's

Press: The Case of *The Ladies' Journal* (*Funü zazhi*), 1915–1931," *Republican China* 10: 1b (Nov. 1984), pp. 37–55.

Editor's note. The best piece in any language on the development of a women's press in China is Jacqueline Nivard, "L'Evolution de la presse féminine chinoise de 1898 à 1949," *Études chinoises* 5: 1–2 (Spring–Autumn 1986), pp. 157–84, which is followed (pp. 185–236) by an indispensable "Bibliographie de la presse féminine chinoise," compiled by Nivard.

9. The essays referred to below by Gao Xian, Shi Cuntong, Yun Daiying, and Li Hanjun are all reprinted from contemporary journals in the collection edited by Mei Sheng, *Zhongguo funü wenti taolunji* [A collection of essays concerning women's issues in China], 6 vols., (Shanghai: Xin wenhua chubanshe, 1934). The article by Gao appears in vol. 4, pp. 56–73; Shi's in vol. 4, pp. 195–99; Yun's in vol. 6, pp. 13–20; and Li's in vol. 1, pp. 88–90.

Translator's note. Gao Xian, a graduate of Tokyo Imperial University, was a chemical engineer by training. His contacts with May Fourth writers must have been formed while he served as an editor at the Commercial Press in Shanghai. Otherwise, little has been written about his political and literary career. See Yang Jialuo, *Minguo mingren tujian* [Famous people in the Republican Period, with pictures] (Nanjing: Cidianguan, 1937), vol. 1, p. 79. Shi Cuntong was influenced by anarchist thought while enrolled in the Zhejiang Provincial First Normal School, and later became one of the founders of the CCP. His essay "Oppose Filial Piety" became the center of a storm of controversy in the pages of *Republican Daily*, following its publication in a student newspaper in Nov. 1918; see Chow, *The May Fourth Movement*, p. 306. Biographies of Yun Daiying and Li Hanjun appear in Boorman and Howard, vol. 4, pp. 92–95, and vol. 1, pp. 198–99, respectively.

Editor's note. On Yun, see also the article by Ono Shinji, "Goshi jiki no risōshugi: En Daiei no baai" [Idealism in the May Fourth period: The case of Yun Daiying], *Tōyōshi kenkyū* 38: 2 (Sept. 1979), pp. 1–38.

10. For example, Mao Zedong as well, in a famous 1919 article, wrote: "We [women] are even more deeply immersed in an ocean of suffering! We are also human beings, so why won't they let us take part in politics? We are also human beings, so why won't they let us take part in social intercourse? . . . The shameless men, the villainous men, make us into their playthings, and force us to prostitute ourselves to them indefinitely. The devils, who destroy the freedom to love! . . . They keep us surrounded all day long, but so-called 'chastity' is confined to us women! The 'temples to virtuous women' are scattered all over the place, but where are the 'pagodas to chaste men'? Among us there are some who gathered together in schools for women, but those who teach us there are also a bunch of

shameless and villainous men. All day long they talk about something called being 'a worthy mother and a good wife.' What is this but teaching us to prostitute ourselves indefinitely to the same man?" See "Minzhong de da lianhe" [The great union of the popular masses], *Xiangjiang pinglun* 2–4 (July 21, July 28, and Aug. 4, 1919), in *Mao Zedong ji* [The collected works of Mao Zedong], ed. Takeuchi Minoru (Tokyo: Hokubōsha, 1970–72), vol. 1, pp. 57–69. Liu Dannong (Liu Fu), in an article entitled "Nangui zahua" [Random jottings on returning from the south], *Xin qingnian* 5: 2 (Aug. 15, 1918), pp. 117–30, wrote that: "the four virtues," "wisdom and intelligence," and "good wives and wise mothers" are all "nothing more than instructions for training women to be permanent prostitutes."

Translator's/editor's note. The excerpt from Mao's article comes from the complete translation (with commentary) by Stuart Schram, "From the 'Great Union of the Popular Masses' to the 'Great Alliance,'" *China Quarterly* 49 (Jan.–Mar. 1972), pp. 76–105, citation from p. 81 (more is included here than in the Japanese edition). Schram considers this essay to be Mao's "most influential" article of the May Fourth era; see also Stuart Schram, *Mao Tse-tung* (Baltimore, Md.: Penguin Books, 1967), p. 53, and "Mao Tse-tung's Thought to 1949," esp. pp. 796–99.

11. Editor's note. Not exactly correct. The famous mention of "glad agreement" (*xinran tongyi*) appears in Zhang Zongxiang's exchange of notes with the Japanese over the establishment of a joint Sino-Japanese rail line in Shandong, to be guarded by Japanese troops. Zhang's note admitted Japan's right to certain former German privileges in the region. See Chow, *The May Fourth Movement*, p. 87.

12. Memoirs by women activists of the May Fourth era include the following, all of which appear in *Wusi yundong huiyilu* [Memoirs of the May Fourth Movement], comp. Third Bureau of the Historical Research Section of the Chinese Academy of Social Sciences (Beijing: Zhonghua shuju, 1959): Deng Yingchao, "Wusi yundong de huiyi" [Memoirs of the May Fourth Movement], pp. 85–93 (English translation in *Chinese Studies in History* 14 [Fall 1980], pp. 93–103), and "Manhua Wusi dangnian" [Recollections of that year of May Fourth], pp. 97–101; Liu Qingyang, "Wusi huiyi" [Memoirs of May Fourth], pp. 94–96, "Wo dui Wusi qianhou Tianjin xuesheng yundong de jidian huiyi" [Some recollections of the student movement in Tianjin around May Fourth], pp. 102–11, and "Wusi qijian de Guo Longzhen tongzhi" [Comrade Guo Longzhen in the May Fourth period], pp. 248–49; Huang Xiuzhen, "Wusi shiqi Shandong gejie de aiguo yundong" [Patriotic movements in various quarters in Shandong Province during the May Fourth era], pp. 122–25; Xia Zhixu, "Wusi de langhua" [The crest of the wave of May Fourth], pp. 148–55; Wang Yizhi, "Hunan Taoyuan nüzi ershi zai Wusi shi de aiguo huodong" [The patriotic deeds

of the Peach Blossom woman general in Hunan during the May Fourth Movement], pp. 156–58; Chen Su, "Wusi yu funü jiefang yundong" [May Fourth and the women's liberation movement], pp. 263–66. See also Liu Qingyang, "Juexing le de Tianjin renmin" [The people of Tianjin awakened], and Wang Yizhi, "Zouxiang geming—Wusi huiyi" [Toward revolution, memoirs of May Fourth], in *Guanghui de Wusi* [Glorious May Fourth], comp. China Youth Publishing Company (Beijing: Zhongguo qingnian chubanshe, 1959), pp. 107–40 and 177–85, respectively. Also Mao Huiqing, "Wusi yundong zai Tianjin" [The May Fourth Movement in Tianjin], and Liu Qingyang, "Guo Longzhen lieshi zhuan" [Biography of the martyr Guo Longzhen], *Jindai shi ziliao* 19 (1958), pp. 79–111 and 124–29, respectively; and Yang Zilie, *Zhang Guotao furen huiyilu* [Memoirs of the wife of Zhang Guotao] (Hong Kong: Zilian chubanshe, 1970).

Translator's note. Wang Yizhi was a Hunan activist during the May Fourth Movement. She moved to Shanghai, where she attended the Communist-run Shanghai Common Girls' School and joined the Party in 1922. She lived with Shi Cuntong and later with Zhang Tailei, who was killed in the Canton Commune Uprising. Her work for the Party continued through the 1940's. After 1949, she became principal of 101 Middle School in Beijing, a school for top-ranking cadres. See Christina Gilmartin, "Mobilizing Women: The Early Experiences of the Chinese Communist Party, 1920–1927," Ph.D. diss., University of Pennsylvania, 1986, pp. 59, 61, 71–72. Gilmartin interviewed Wang Yizhi for a total of thirty hours between 1979 and 1983. Her dissertation is the best available account in English of women in the early Communist movement.

13. No research has as yet been done on workers' strikes during the May Fourth period, particularly on strikes by women workers. However, an abundance of relevant materials from contemporary newspapers has been collected and reprinted in *Wusi yundong zai Shanghai shiliao xuanji* [Selected materials on the May Fourth Movement in Shanghai], comp. History Section of the Shanghai Academy of Social Sciences (Shanghai: Shanghai renmin chubanshe, 1960).

Translator's note. On activism among Shanghai's cotton mill workers, see Emily Honig, *Sisters and Strangers: Women in the Shanghai Cotton Mills* (Stanford, Calif.: Stanford University Press, 1986).

14. Editor's note. Liu Qingyang's activities in the May Fourth era are briefly mentioned in Chow, *The May Fourth Movement*, pp. 129–30; and in Peng Ming, *Wusi yundong shi* [A history of the May Fourth Movement] (Beijing: Renmin chubanshe, 1984), pp. 374–76.

15. From Sui Lingbi et al., "Wusi shiqi Jinan nüshi xuesheng yundong pianduan" (Notes on the women's student movement in Jinan during the May Fourth period), in *Wusi yundong huiyilu* [Memoirs of the May Fourth

Movement] (Beijing: Zhongguo shehui kexue chubanshe, 1979), pp. 684–92.

16. Articles on the controversy surrounding women's haircuts appear in *Zhongguo funü wenti taolunji*, vol. 6, pp. 127–41. At the time, it was not easy to have short hair, as we see in the following excerpt from the memoirs of Yang Zilie (cited in n. 12 to this chapter). She recalls the time she cut her hair while she was a student at the Provincial Girls' Normal School in Wuchang: "One day, after study period was over, six of us went to the lavatory. It was pitch black inside; all the electric lights had been put out after the evening meal. Out in the corridor a dim lamp was burning; it cast the barest flicker of light through a window. We groped in the dark for the drawer with the combs in it, opened it, took out a pair of shears, and one by one cut each other's hair. Each of us picked up the scissors, said 'One, two, three . . . ,' and sent cascades of long, soft hair tumbling to the floor. . . . The proctor Zhou summoned the six of us to her office, and when she saw our hair, she looked as if she were seeing ghosts. But she only winced, shook her head in silence, and sighed. The next day, at morning ceremonies, our school principal, Wang Shiyu, made a calm announcement: 'Last night, certain pupils, without consulting me, cut off their hair. This is not permissible. It is a very risky thing to do. If it should become known to the governmental authorities, it will be very bad for our school. And it will surely cause inquiries from your fathers! On the other hand, the ordinary conduct of the students in question has borne no resemblance to their recent actions. You have always been correct in your personal conduct, and your academic standing is high. Since this is your first offence, therefore, the school will not punish you. But, you must make a bun out of the hair you have cut off and arrange your hair so that it looks like it did before it was cut. . . .' And so when we went to class, we all meekly wore a hairpiece shaped like a dunghill on top of our heads. Over it all we wrapped a net like a spider's web, but even then we couldn't bend our heads respectfully while listening to the teachers' lectures."

17. There are a number of questions about the admission of female students to Beijing University classrooms. It seems that the decision was made at the end of 1919, and in fact women were admitted to classes early in 1920. See Cheng Zhefan, *Zhongguo xiandai nüzi jiaoyu shi* [A history of contemporary women's education in China] (Shanghai: Zhonghua shuju, 1936), p. 106; "Nanjing gaoshi jianshou nüsheng" [Nanjing Normal College opens admission to female students], *Shibao* (Dec. 31, 1919); and "Beida nannü tongxiao zhi xiankuang" [The current state of coeducation at Beijing University], *Shibao* (Mar. 3, 1920).

18. Among the works that treat this question, see Li Guangye, "Jin hou de nüzi jiaoyu" [The future of women's education], and Tang Gongxian,

"Woguo nüzi de wuxue yu qi jiuji" [The lack of education among the women of our country, and how to remedy it], both reprinted in *Zhongguo funü wenti taolunji*, vol. 1, pp. 170–74 and 174–79, respectively. Countless other studies take up the problem of women's education in China. Without exception, all are critical of both all-male and children's education. All insist that since women are individuals, the same as men and children, they require an education through which they can create their own ideals and which will awaken them to their full potentials and worth. They stand in sharp contrast to the 1898 reformers' calls for women's education that were justified on the grounds that it would educate good mothers. This kind of criticism of the idea of "good wives, wise mothers" retains its freshness even today.

19. See Tan Sheying, *Zhongguo funü yundong shi* [Comprehensive history of the women's movement in China] (Shanghai: Shangwu yinshuguan, 1936), p. 107. According to Tan, Wang Changguo and two other women were elected to the Hunan provincial assembly, but only Wang's name appears on the list of assembly members printed in *Hunan sheng zhi* [Provincial gazetteer of Hunan] (Changsha: Hunan renmin chubanshe, 1959), *juan* 1. In addition, according to Yang Zhihua, *Furen yundong yu guomin geming* [The women's movement and the national revolution] (Shanghai: Dong-Ya tushuguan, 1938), women won the right to vote in both Zhejiang and Sichuan provinces; Shimizu Yasuzō, in his *Shina shinjin to reimei undō* [China's new people and the Awakening Movement] (Tokyo: Ōsaka yagō shoten, 1924), says that women were even elected to the provincial assembly in Guangdong. However, there is no detailed evidence for the Guangdong, Zhejiang, and Sichuan cases. In this book, I have not touched on the suffrage movement of the 1920's. For information on the movement and its organization, see Tan Sheying's study; Guo Zhenyi, *Zhongguo funü wenti* [Chinese Women's Issues] (Shanghai: Shangwu yinshuguan, 1937); and Gao Shan, "Zhongguo de nüqian yundong" [The women's rights movement in China], *Dongfang zazhi* 19: 18 (Sept. 25, 1922), pp. 86–88.

Translator's note. See the comprehensive review of histories of the Chinese women's movement in Gilmartin, pp. 273–77.

CHAPTER SIX

Translator's note. I would like to thank Andrew Gordon for assistance with some of the technical and historical matters relating to labor in prewar Japan.

1. Translator's note. For a fuller treatment of the material presented in the first half of this chapter, see Ono Kazuko, "Kyū Chūgoku ni okeru Jokō aishi" [*The Sad History of Women Workers* in old China], *Tōhō gakuhō* 50 (Feb. 1978), pp. 253–312.

2. The connection between China's industrial development and the prohibition of night-shift labor in Japan is outlined in Nakamura Ryūei, "Go sanjū jiken to zai-Ka bō" [The May Thirtieth Incident and the Japanese textile industry in China], *Kindai Chūgoku kenkyū* 6 (May 1964), pp. 99–169.

3. *Diyici Zhongguo laodong nianjian* [The first Chinese labor annual] (Beiping: Beiping heji yinshuguan, 1928), p. 176.

4. Translator's note. In another northern city, Tianjin, women in 1929 accounted for 9.1 percent of cotton mill workers; women and female children together, 13.2 percent. See Gail Hershatter, *The Workers of Tianjin, 1900–1949* (Stanford, Calif.: Stanford University Press, 1986), p. 56.

5. Statistics concerning the number of women workers in most provinces between 1912 and 1920 may be found in the government publication *Nongshang tongji biao* [Statistics on agriculture and commerce] (Beijing, 1914–24), vols. 1–9. My estimate of the number of women in the textile industry has been derived by multiplying the number of workers, as recorded in *Gongren xunbao* [Workers' magazine] on the basis of reports submitted by the unions (these figures are given in *Diyici Zhongguo laodong nianjian*, p. 15), by the male-female percentages given in *Nongshang tongji biao*, vol. 8 (1923), p. 277. But these figures are very rough, and we still need considerable research to be more precise about them.

Translator's note. More precise figures for Shanghai are given in Emily Honig, *Sisters and Strangers: Women in the Shanghai Cotton Mills, 1919–1949* (Stanford, Calif.: Stanford University Press, 1986), p. 24.

6. This passage comes from one of the three reminiscences collected and edited by the Shanghai People's Press under the title *Baoshengong de xueleichou* [The blood, tears, and grief of contract workers] (Shanghai: Renmin chubanshe, 1966).

7. Concerning contract labor, see three articles by Okabe Toshiyoshi, "Shina bōsekigyō ni okeru rōdō ukeoi seido, sono josetsu teki kadai to shite" [The contract-labor system in China's cotton-spinning industry, preliminary themes], *Tō-A keizai ronshū* 1: 1 (Feb. 1941), pp. 216–30; "Shina bōseki rōdō ukeoi seido no yōshiki, hon seido no naiyō o nasu gutai teki shokankei" [Forms of the contract-labor system in China's cotton-spinning industry, various specific relations that form the system], *Tō-A keizai ronshū* 1: 2 (May 1941), pp. 136–56; and "Shina bōseki rōdō ukeoi seido no hattatsu, sono sonritsu no kiso narabi ni fukyū no teido ni tsuite" [The development of the contract-labor system in China's cotton-spinning industry, the basis of its existence and the extent of its spread], two parts, *Tō-A keizai ronshū* 1: 3 (Sept. 1941), pp. 221–34; and 1: 4 (Dec. 1941), pp. 198–207. See also the reportage pieces by Xia Yan, *Baoshengong* [Contract

labor], in *Xia Yan xuanji* [Selected works of Xia Yan] (Beijing: Renmin chubanshe, 1980).

8. Translator's note. This view of the contract-labor system as a product of the foreign presence in industrial Shanghai has been questioned by Emily Honig in *Sisters and Strangers*, chap. 5. She sees contract labor as beginning only in 1928 through the growing influence of the Green Gang as a result of its role in the suppression of the workers' uprisings of 1925–27. Honig (chap. 8) also challenges the assumption that women mill workers in Shanghai were developing class solidarity and a revolutionary consciousness.

9. Translator's note. Where possible, the names of Japanese textile companies operating in China are given as they appear in *The Chinese Year Book, 1923* (Tianjin: The Tientsin Press, 1923), pp. 469–71. Modern pinyin romanizations follow in parentheses.

10. Editor's note. Hosoi Wakizō, *Jokō aishi* (Tokyo: Kaizōsha, 1948).

11. Translator's note. Xia Yan (Shen Duanxian) was a founding member of the League of Left-Wing Writers. He wrote *Baoshengong* in 1936; in addition to its inclusion in *Xia Yan xuanji*, it has also been reprinted separately in several editions (including Beijing: Tongsu duwu chubanshe, 1955; and Beijing: Gongren chubanshe, 1959).

12. As translated into Japanese in Udaka Yasushi, *Shina rōdō mondai* [Labor problems in China] (Shanghai: Kokusai bunka kenkyūkai, 1925).

Translator's note. The strike against this Japanese-owned factory occurred in mid-July in the wake of the May Thirtieth Incident and involved some 3,000 workers; it was unsuccessful.

13. Although work songs are extremely valuable material for learning about the thoughts and feelings of women workers of this period, songs about working in factories are few, for whatever reason. Some were collected after 1949 and have appeared in such journals as *Wenyi yuebao* and *Minjian wenxue*.

14. Material concerning spinsters' homes can be found in Ma Jingyun, "Guangdong Shunde nüzi zhi shenghuo xisu" [Customs among the women of Shunde country, Guangdong], *Shenbao yuekan* 4: 7 (Sept. 1935), pp. 222–24. On lesbianism and marriage resistance, see Laohan Laigao (pseud.), "Yuezhong nüzi zhi bujiazhe" [Guangdong women who do not marry], *Xin shiji* 60 (Aug. 15, 1908), pp. 9–11; "Panyu nüzi zhi bu luojia" [Women of Panyu county who "do not go down to the family"], "Shunde nüzi zhi jinlanqi" ["Golden orchid matches" between women in Shunde county], and "Shunde nüzi zhi bu luojia" [Women of Shunde county who "do not go down to the family"], in Hu Puan, *Zhonghua quanguo fengsu zhi* [National gazetteer of Chinese customs] (Taibei reprint of 1933 original: Oriental

Culture Service, n.d.), vol. 4 (Guangdong); Jin Sheng, "Yue Gui de 'zishu nü' he 'bu luojia'" [Women who "dress their own hair" and "do not go down to the family" in Guangdong and Guangxi], *Dongfang zazhi* 32: 8 (Apr. 16, 1935), pp. 89–90.

Translator's/editor's note. For a pioneering study in English, see Marjorie Topley, "Marriage Resistance in Rural Kwangtung," in *Women in Chinese Society*, ed. Margery Wolf and Roxane Witke (Stanford, Calif.: Stanford University Press, 1975), pp. 67–88. A recent study of this phenomenon is Janice Stockard, *Daughters of the Canton Delta: Marriage Patterns and Economic Strategies in South China, 1860–1930* (Stanford, Calif.: Stanford University Press, 1989).

15. Concerning the strike against the Sino-Japanese Cotton Manufacturing Company, see Udaka Yasushi, *Shina rōdō mondai*; Zhu Zhenxin, "Yijiuerer nian de Zhongguo funü laodong yundong" [The Chinese women's labor movement in 1922], *Funü pinglun* (May 1, 1923), pp. 1–4.

16. On strikes in silk-reeling mills, see Zhu Zhenxin; also Shao Lizi, "Shanghai xichang nügong ji" [Record of women workers in Shanghai silk-reeling factories], *Funü pinglun* 53 (Aug. 9, 1922), pp. 2–4; 54 (Aug. 16, 1922), p. 3.

17. Translator's note. Jean Chesneaux characterizes Mu as a moderate labor leader; she tried to avert a later strike in 1924 and opposed the Shanghai General Labor Union's reorganization of silk workers in 1926. See Chesneaux, *The Chinese Labor Movement, 1919–1927* (Stanford, Calif.: Stanford University Press, 1968), pp. 224, 282, 339, 487 n.211.

18. He Xiangning (1877–1972) has been called "the mother of the Chinese revolution." She was born in Nanhai county, Guangdong, and was raised in a middle-class family in Hong Kong. She married Liao Zhongkai, who would later become a leading revolutionary member of the GMD, in 1897 and then sold her bridal trousseau in order to accompany him to Japan, where she enrolled in the Tokyo Women's Art School. There she joined Sun Yat-sen's Revolutionary Alliance and worked hard to promote his movement. After the failure of the 1911 Revolution, He and Liao were forced to flee back to Japan, where they joined the Chinese Revolutionary Party and continued to support Sun Yat-sen. Liao was assassinated in 1925 by reactionary elements in the GMD. After 1949, He served in a number of official posts, including honorary chair of the All-China Women's Federation. She died in 1972 at the age of 95. She is buried with her husband in Nanjing. See Takenouchi Yasumi, "Son Bun kakumei no tenkai to Ka Kōnei" [He Xiangning and the unfolding of Sun Yat-sen's revolution], three parts, *Kagoshima keidai ronshū* 9: 3–4 (1969), pp. 299–322; 10: 1 (1969), pp. 19–45; 10: 2 (1969), pp. 289–316; He Xiangning, "Wo de huiyi" [My reminiscences], in *Xinhai geming huiyilu* [Reminiscences of the 1911

Revolution] (Beijing: Zhonghua shuju, 1961), vol. 1, pp. 12–59; and Liao Mengxiang, *Wo de muqin He Xiangning* [My mother, He Xiangning] (Hong Kong: Chaoyang chubanshe, 1973).

19. Translator's note. For an extended study of the CCP in the early women's labor movement, see Christina Gilmartin, "Mobilizing Women: The Early Experiences of the Chinese Communist Party, 1920–1927," Ph.D. diss., University of Pennsylvania, 1986.

20. Translator's note. The men went on strike to oppose the company's decision to substitute women workers for men; see Honig, p. 205.

21. Udaka Yasushi provides a detailed account of the February Strike. In addition to a collection of numerous leaflets issued by the unions, with Japanese translation, there is a host of other relevant material in *Taishō jūyo nen Shanhai hompō bōseki kaisha hikō keika hōkokusho* [Report on the course of the strike against Japanese textile companies in Shanghai in 1925], comp. Japanese Consulate in Shanghai for the Ministry of Foreign Affairs, unpublished.

22. Translator's note. The term translated here as "Asians," *Dongyang ren*, meaning Orientals, was taken from a Japanese expression (*Tōyōjin*) used by many Japanese to give themselves a pan-Asian rather than narrowly nationalistic identity. Although it remains the main Japanese term for East Asians, it became for Chinese a term of derogation for Japanese.

23. Deng Zhongxia, *Zhongguo zhigong yundong jianshe (1919–1926)* [Concise history of the workers' movement in China, 1919–1926] (Shanghai: Xinhua shudian, 1949), pp. 172–204.

24. Translator's note. The Mixed Court was a joint Chinese-foreign tribunal charged with handling legal cases involving Chinese residents of the International Settlement.

25. Shi Xiaomei, *Muzi nao geming* [A mother and son make revolution] (Shanghai: Shaonian ertong chubanshe, 1961). Shi's memories of the events of the 1922 strike vary somewhat from what I have given above.

26. Translator's note. Soviet trade unions affiliated with the Amsterdam International Federation of Trade Unions sent 40,000 rubles in support of the May Thirtieth strikes. See Chesneaux, p. 266.

27. Concerning Xiang Jingyu, see *Lieshi Xiang Jingyu* [Xiang Jingyu, martyr] (Beijing: Zhongguo funü zazhishe, 1958); *Jinian Xiang Jingyu tongzhi jiuyi wushi zhounian* [In memory of comrade Xiang Jingyu on the fiftieth anniversary of her death] (Beijing: Zhongguo funü zazhishe, 1978). These books include roughly a dozen of her essays.

Translator's/editor's note. For Xiang's biography in English, see Donald Klein and Anne Clark, eds., *Biographical Dictionary of Chinese Communism* (Cambridge, Mass.: Harvard University Press, 1971), pp. 317–19. Recently, a more substantial article on Xiang appeared: Catherine Gipoulon,

"Xiang Jingyu, ou les ambiguïtés d'une carrière entre communisme and féminisme," *Etudes chinoises* 5: 1–2 (Spring–Autumn 1986), pp. 101–31. See also Gilmartin.

28. Translator's note. Cai Chang's biography appears in Klein and Clark, pp. 847–51. See also Chapter 7, pp. 158, 167.

29. Helen Foster Snow, *Women in Modern China* (The Hague: Mouton, 1967), p. 245.

30. Concerning the work-study movement in France, see He Changgong, *Qingong jianxue shenghuo huiyi* [Reminiscences of my life in the work-study movement] (Beijing: Gongren chubanshe, 1958); Japanese translation by Kawata Teiichi and Mori Tokihiko, *Furansu kinkō kengaku no kaisō: Chūgoku Kyōsantō no ichi genryū* [Memoirs of the work-study program in France: One origin of the Chinese Communist Party] (Tokyo: Iwanami shoten, 1976). See also Mori Tokihiko, "Furansu kinkō kengaku undō shōshi" [A short history of the work-study movement in France], two parts, *Tōhō gakuhō* 50 (1978), pp. 191–252; 51 (1979), pp. 321–460.

31. Ge Jianhao was already over 50 at the time. Under the influence of the 1911 Revolution, she had decided to get an education and pawned her clothes in order to enroll in a primary school for children. After graduating, she founded her own school, where Cai Chang first studied.

32. Wang Duqing, *Wo zai Ouzhou de shenghuo* [My life in Europe] (Shanghai: Daguang shuju, 1936; Hong Kong reprint, 1976), p. 49.

33. Translator's note. While organizing factory workers in Shanghai, Xiang found herself in conflict over political goals with the silk worker Mu Zhiying. See Chesneaux, p. 496 n.125.

34. Snow, p. 248.

CHAPTER SEVEN

1. Almost all village surveys and population analyses around the year 1930 discussed sex ratios (see Supplementary References, 7 g–i). Table 6 is based on *Zhongguo jingji niankan* [China economic yearbook, 1924] which summarized village surveys. Also concerning sex ratios, see Li Changnian, "Nüying shahai yu Zhongguo liangxing bujun wenti" [Female infanticide and the problem of China's sex imbalance], *Dongfang zazhi* 32: 11 (June 1, 1935), pp. 97–101.

2. Editor's note. On this practice, see Arthur P. Wolf and Chieh-shan Huang, *Marriage and Adoption in China, 1845–1945* (Stanford, Calif.: Stanford University Press, 1980), pp. 230–41.

3. See Chapter 1, n.1.

4. On the issue of renting wives (*dianqi* or *zuqi*), see Amano Motonosuke, *Shina nōson zakki* [Notes on Chinese villages] (Tokyo: Seikatsusha, 1942), p. 174. The practice of renting wives is the theme of Rou Shi's

novel, *Wei nuli de muqin* [Mothers who have become slaves], in *Rou Shi xiaoshuo xuanji* [Selections from the fiction of Rou Shi] (Beijing: Renmin chubanshe, 1954), pp. 1–26; also in *Rou Shi xuanji* [Selected works of Rou Shi] (Beijing: Renmin chubanshe, 1959), pp. 194–217; and in a bilingual edition, *Wei nuli de muqin, Slave Mothers,* trans. Shi Nuo (Guilin: Yuanfang shudian, 1943). Japanese translation by Matsui Hiromi, *Dorei ni natta hahaoya* [Mothers who have become slaves], in *Chūgoku kakumei to bungaku* [The Chinese revolution and Chinese literature], vol. 5: "Kōsenki bungaku 1" [Literature in the period of the War of Resistance, vol. 1] (Tokyo: Heibonsha, 1972), pp. 3–22.

5. In some areas a widow's remarriage was not necessarily a problem. It seems as though there were major regional differences, and in many instances, among poor peasants a widow's remarrying to stay alive was accepted.

6. Qi Yuan, ed., "Benbu yinian lai gongzuo baogao gaiyao" [Summary of the last year's work report at headquarters], *Zhongguo nongmin* 2 (1926), pp. 147–207.

7. On the struggles of women in the Guangdong peasant movement, see *Diyici guonei geming zhanzheng shiqi de nongmin yundong* [The peasant movement during the period of the First Revolutionary Civil War] (Beijing: Renmin chubanshe, 1953). Within this volume can be found the especially important work by Peng Pai, *Haifeng nongmin yundong* [The peasant movement in Haifeng], pp. 40–138 (originally published in 1926 by Guoguang shudian).

Editor's note. Peng's work has been translated by Donald Holoch as *Seeds of Rebellion: Report on the Haifeng Peasant Movement by P'eng P'ai* (Ithaca, N.Y.: Cornell University China-Japan Program, 1973).

8. Although Mao Zedong noted that the weak point of another of his reports, "Investigation of Xingguo County," was its lack of any attention to the situation of women and children, references to women's issues can in fact be found here and there in it. He clearly was aware of the problems facing women. In his "Changgang xiang de diaocha" [Investigation of Changgang township] of 1933, Mao devoted an entire section to changes for women after the establishment of the Soviet Republic.

9. Editor's note. The rest of this section is little more than a paraphrase of the relevant section of Mao's "Report on an Investigation of the Peasant Movement in Hunan"; see *Selected Works of Mao Tse-tung* (Beijing: Foreign Languages Press, 1967), vol. 1, pp. 42–47. It should be noted that the "facts" as depicted by Mao here have been called into serious question by a number of scholars, notably Roy Hofheinz and Lucien Bianco. See Roy Hofheinz, Jr., *The Broken Wave: The Chinese Communist Peasant Movement, 1922–1928* (Cambridge, Mass.: Harvard University Press, 1977),

p. 35; and Lucien Bianco, "Peasant Movements," in *The Cambridge History of China, Volume 13: Republican China 1912–1949, Part 2,* ed. John K. Fairbank and Albert Feuerwerker (Cambridge, Eng.: Cambridge University Press, 1986), esp. pp. 305–6.

10. Editor's note. See Chapter 5, pp. 98–99.

11. Editor's note. *Selected Works of Mao Tse-tung,* vol. 1, p. 46.

12. Translator's note. See Chapter 5, pp. 100–101.

13. Concerning women's activities in the Chinese Soviet Republic and during the Long March, see Tang Tiehai, *Zhongyang genjudi fangwen ji* [Record of a trip to the central base area] (n.p.: Huadong renmin chubanshe, 1953); Wang Boyan, *Dierci guonei geming zhanzheng shiqi de nongcun geming genjudi* [Rural revolutionary base areas during the Second Revolutionary Civil War] (Shanghai: Shanghai xinzhishi chubanshe, 1956); and the special columns entitled "Zhongguo funü [Chinese women] in *Jiefang ribao,* 1941–47.

14. For research on marriage laws in the Chinese Soviet Republic and the base areas, see Fukushima Masao and Miyasaka Hiroshi, "Chūka Sobieto oyobi henku jiki no kon'inpō no tokushitsu" [Special features of marriage laws in the period of the Chinese Soviet Republic and the border regions], in *Gendai Ajia no kakumei to hō* [Revolution and law in contemporary Asia] (Tokyo: Keisō shobō, 1966), vol. 2, pp. 321–38; and Ubukata Naokichi, "Chūgoku: Kon'in shisō no tenkai no shakai kiso, kon'in kaikaku to tochi kaikaku no fukabunsei" [China: The social basis for the development of ideas about marriage and the inseparability of marriage reform and land reform], in *Kōza: Kazoku* [Symposium: Family], vol. 3: *Kon'in no seiritsu* [The establishment of marriage], (Tokyo: Kōbundō, 1973), pp. 135–49.

15. Editor's note. The Marriage Regulations of 1931 are translated in M. J. Meijer, *Marriage Law and Policy in the Chinese People's Republic* (Hong Kong: Hong Kong University Press, 1971), pp. 281–82. See also Delia Davin, *Women-Work: Women and the Party in Revolutionary China* (Oxford: The Clarendon Press, 1976), pp. 28–30; and Kay Ann Johnson, *Women, the Family and Peasant Revolution in China* (Chicago: University of Chicago Press, 1983), pp. 51–62.

16. Translator's note. For an excellent account of the Marriage Law of the People's Republic of China, see Johnson, pp. 115–37.

17. This discussion of "Family Law" is based on Wang Ruqi, "Chedi suqing wei minfa 'Qinshu bian' de yingxiang baozheng xin Zhongguo funü hefa quanyi" [Eliminate thoroughly the influence of the "Family Law" in the bogus civil code and guarantee women's legal rights in the new China], *Renmin ribao,* Sept. 1, 1952; and Rui Mu, "Xin Zhongguo shinian lai hunyin jiating guanxi de fazhan" [Ten years of the development of

marital and family relations in the new China], *Zhengfa yanjiu* 5 (Oct. 1959), pp. 54–60. There seems to be no current research on this issue.

Editor's note. The "Family Law" of the GMD is summarized in Meijer, pp. 26–29.

18. Translator's note. The "four big families" were those of Chang Kai-shek (Jiang Jieshi), T. V. Soong (Song Zewen), H. H. Kung (Kong Xiangxi), and Chen Lifu. Three of these families were connected through the famous Soong (Song) sisters: Song Meiling, wife of Jiang Jieshi; Song Ailing, wife of H. H. Kung; and Song Qingling, wife of Sun Yat-sen. T. V. Soong was their brother. For a colorful depiction of this illustrious family, see Sterling Seagrave, *The Soong Dynasty* (New York: Harper and Row, 1985); for a more scholarly account, see Parks Coble, *The Shanghai Capitalists and the Nationalist Government, 1927–1937* (Cambridge, Mass.: Council on East Asian Studies, Harvard University, 1980).

19. Editor's note. These figures may be inflated. James Harrison gives 750,000 men and 150 planes. See his *The Long March to Power: A History of the Chinese Communist Party, 1921–72* (New York: Praeger Publishers, 1972), p. 239.

20. Deng Yingchao, "Mantan changzheng" [Informal talk about the Long March], *Xin Zhongguo funü* 13 (Aug. 1950), pp. 16–18. With certain material added here and there, the following description is based primarily on *Zhongguo gongnong hungjun diyi fangmianjun changzheng ji* [Record of the First Front Army of the Chinese Workers' and Peasants' Red Army during the Long March] (Beijing: Renmin chubanshe, 1958).

21. Editor's note. The following superhuman adventures are described (from essentially the same Chinese sources) in Dick Wilson, *The Long March 1935: The Epic of Chinese Communism's Survival* (New York: Avon Books, 1971), pp. 182–218, 240–58.

22. Nym Wales (Helen Foster Snow), "Women and Revolution," in *Inside Red China* (New York: Doubleday and Company, 1939), pp. 165–201. The names of the other 30 women who made the Long March with the First Front Army are not clear. Women also participated in the Second and Fourth Front Armies. For information about women in the Fourth Front Army, see the memoirs of Zhao Lan, "Funütuan shenghuo pianduan" [Episodes in the experiences of the Women's Corps], in *Xinghuo liaoyuan* [A single spark can light a prairie fire] (Beijing: Renmin wenxue chubanshe, 1979), vol. 3, pp. 374–80. A novel about a young heroine who joined the Second Front Army is Ma Yixiang, *Chaoyang hua* [Flower in the morning sun] (Beijing: Zhongguo qingnian chubanshe, 1961); Japanese translation by Shimada Masao and Itō Katsu, *Chōsei no musume* [Daughter of the Long March] (Tokyo: Seinen shuppansha, 1977).

23. Editor's note. See Wales, pp. 178–91. Ono's account includes more information than can be found in Wales's biographical sketches.

24. For further biographical information on Cai Chang, see "Zhong-guo jiefangqu funü lingxiu Cai Chang he Deng Yingchao" [Cai Chang and Deng Yingchao, women leaders in China's liberated areas], included in *Funü yundong wenxian* (see Supplementary References, 7 e). On Cai Chang and the Long March, see Zhao Chang, "Gensui Cai dajie de shihou" [When I accompanied Big Sister Cai], *Zhongguo funü* 131 (1959), pp. 14–15.

25. Editor's note. Wales, p. 188.

26. Huang Liangcheng, *Yi changzheng, geming douzheng huiyilu* [Re-membering the Long March, reminiscences of the revolutionary strug-gle] (Shenyang: Chunfeng wenyi chubanshe, 1959); Japanese translation by Matsui Hiromi, in *Chūgoku gendai bungaku senshū* [Selections from contem-porary Chinese literature] (Tokyo: Heibonsha, 1963), vol. 17, pp. 213–323.

27. Editor's note. This figure is probably high. Citing reliable firsthand witnesses, Lloyd Eastman offers a minimum figure of 42,000 murdered. See Eastman, "Facets of an Ambivalent Relationship: Smuggling, Puppets, and Atrocities During the War, 1937–1942," in Akira Iriye, ed., *The Chinese and the Japanese: Essays in Political and Cultural Interactions* (Princeton, N.J.: Princeton University Press, 1980), pp. 275–303, esp. pp. 292–97; the figure of 42,000 is on p. 295.

28. On the rape of Nanjing, see Hora Tomio, *Nankin jiken* [The Nan-jing Incident] (Tokyo: Jimbutsu ōraisha, 1972); and Nit-Chū sensō shiryō hensan iinkai (Editorial committee for materials on the Sino-Japanese War), ed., *Nit-Chū sensō shi shiryō* [Historical materials on the Sino-Japanese War], vols. 8 and 9 (Tokyo: Kawade shobō shinsha, 1973).

29. Hora Tomio, p. 126.

30. Song Qingling, "Zhongguo funü zhengqu ziyou de douzheng" [Chinese women's struggle for freedom, July 1942], in *Song Qingling xuanji* [Selected works of Song Qingling] (Kowloon: Zhongguo shudian, 1967), pp. 154–65. This essay concisely describes the history of modern Chinese women; it is a must. It is included in a Japanese translation of some of Song's writings by Niki Fumiko, *Josei wa sora no hambun o sasaeru: Sō Keirei senshū* [Women hold up half the sky: Selected works of Song Qingling] (Tokyo, Domesu shuppan, 1972). The description that follows of the anti-Japanese resistance is based mainly on this work by Song Qingling, but sources for the section concerning women's fighting during the war are the least complete. During that period few Chinese newspapers came to Japan, and no articles dealing with the anti-Japanese resistance arrived at all. Re-search into this issue will have to be accomplished through examination of Chinese sources and memoirs. I should point out that a number of arti-cles on women's resistance did appear in the serial *Dongfang zazhi* during

the period, such as Wang Ruqi, "Zenyang shi funü yundong yu kang-zhan lianjie qilai" [How the women's movement and the war of resistance against Japan linked up], *Dongfang zazhi* 35: 7 (Apr. 1, 1938), pp. 51–54; Bai Xiang, "Zenyang kaizhan Huanan gesheng de funü yundong" [How women's work in the provinces of South China developed], *Dongfang za-zhi* 35: 11 (June 1, 1938), pp. 71–74; and Li Zezhen, "Jianguo sanshi nian yu Zhongguo funü yundong" [Thirty years after the founding of the {Republican} state and the Chinese women's movement], *Dongfang zazhi* 38: 2 (Jan. 16, 1941), pp. 7–10. The Women's Steering Committee described in Song Qingling's work is also mentioned in the special section on women in *Jiefang ribao* (Oct. 26, 1941), among references to the history and organizations of the women's movement. Regarding the women's movement during the war against Japan and the civil war following it, see Supplementary References, 7 n, i–vii.

31. See *Zhongguo funü da fanshen* [The great transformation of Chinese women] (Hong Kong: Xin minzhu chubanshe, 1949), p. 2. This point is also made in Peng Dehuai, "Guanyu Huabei genjudi gongzuo de baogao, 1942 nian 12 yue 18 ri zai Taixingqu yingji ji xianji yishang ganbu huiyi shang de baogao" [Report on work in the North China base areas, report on a meeting of cadres above the battalion and county level in the Tai-xing region, Dec. 18, 1942], in *Gongfei huoguo shiliao huibian* [Collection of historical materials on the Communist bandits' destruction of the nation] (Taibei: n.p., n.d.), vol. 3, pp. 346–406; Japanese translation by Takeshima Kingo, "Kahoku konkyochi no kōsaku ni tsuite no hōkoku, Taikōku no ei ken kurasu ijō no kanbu no kaigi ni okeru hōkoku," in *Chūgoku Kyōsantō shi shiryō shū* [Collection of materials on the CCP] (Tokyo: Keisō shobō, 1975), vol. 11, pp. 224–87.

32. See Quanguo minzhu funü lianhehui choubei weiyuanhui (Pre-paratory Committee of the All-China Federation of Democratic Women), *Zhongguo jiefangqu funü yundong wenxian* [Documents of the women's move-ment in the liberated areas of China] (Shanghai: Xinhua shudian, 1949).

33. In a special edition on hygiene of *Jiefang ribao* (Mar. 31, 1942), birth control was discussed by Bao Jingheng, "Jieyu wenti" [Problems of birth control], based on an interview with Jin Maoyue.

34. Edgar Snow, "College of Amazons," in *The Battle for Asia* (Cleve-land, Ohio: World Publishing Company, 1942), pp. 273–78. Japanese trans-lation by Moriya Iwao, "Jōjōfu no daigaku," in *Ajia no sensō* (Tokyo: Misuzu shobō, 1956).

35. Ding Ling, "San ba jie yougan" [Thoughts on March 8], *Jiefang ribao*, Mar. 8, 1942. Japanese translation by Ōzaki Shōtarō, in *Chūgoku Kyōsantō shi shiryō shū*, vol. 11, pp. 75–79. After 1949, Ding Ling's essay was revived during the Anti-Rightist Campaign. For example, it was re-

published in *Wenyibao* 210 (Jan. 26, 1958), pp. 8–10; *Wenyi yuebao* 63 (Mar. 1958), pp. 83–84 carried Luo Hong, "Du 'San ba jie yougan'" [Reading "Thoughts on March 8"].

Editor's note. An English translation of "Thoughts on March 8" appears in Gregor Benton, "The Yenan 'Literary Opposition,'" *New Left Review* 92 (July–Aug. 1975), pp. 102–5.

36. Translator's note. Ono offers here the standard party-line interpretation of that time that Ding Ling's brand of feminism was out of kilter with the stage then reached in the revolutionary process. For other, more persuasive and sympathetic treatments of Ding Ling's dilemma at this juncture, see Johnson, pp. 72–75; Jonathan D. Spence, *The Gate of Heavenly Peace: The Chinese and Their Revolution, 1895–1980* (New York: Viking Press, 1981), pp. 328–30; and Yi-tsi Mei Feuerwerker, *Ding Ling's Fiction: Ideology and Narrative in Modern Chinese Literature* (Cambridge, Mass.: Harvard University Press, 1982), pp. 101–2.

37. The women's movement in areas under GMD control is described in detail in Li Dequan, "Guomindang tongzhiqu minzhu funü yundong baogao" [Report on the women's democratic movement in areas under GMD control], in *Zhongguo funü diyici quanguo daibiao dahui* [First All-China Congress of Women] (Hong Kong: Xin minzhu chubanshe, 1949).

38. "Fulian gongzuo de xin chengjiu" [New achievements in the work of the Women's Association], in Preparatory Committee of the All-China Federation of Democratic Women, *Zhongguo jiefangqu nongcun funü fanshen yundong sumiao* [Depictions of rural women in the liberated areas of China in the transformation movement] (Shanghai: Xinhua shudian, 1949). For more details on the process of land reform, see *Zhongguo jiefangqu funü yundong wenxian*. See also William Hinton, *Fanshen: A Documentary of Revolution in a Chinese Village* (New York: Monthly Review Press, 1967), parts 1 and 2; Japanese translation by Katō Yūzō et al., *Hanshin* (Tokyo: Heibonsha, 1972). Also Fukuchi Ima, *Watakushi wa Chūgoku no jinushi datta, tochi kaikaku no keiken* [I was a Chinese landlord, experiences under land reform] (Tokyo: Iwanami shinsho, 1954).

39. On women's participation in military activities during the second civil war, see Preparatory Committee of the All-China Federation of Democratic Women, *Zhongguo jiefangqu funü canzhan yundong* [Women's participation in the war in the liberated areas of China] (Shanghai: Xinhua shudian, 1949).

40. On women's participation in medical aid activities, see Preparatory Committee of the All-China Federation of Democratic Women, *Zhongguo jiefangqu de Nandinggeermen* [{Florence} Nightingales in the liberated areas of China] (Shanghai: Xinhua shudian, 1949).

41. Regarding Liu Hulan, see Shanxi Liu Hulan xiezuo zu (Writing

group on Liu Hulan of Shanxi), *Nü yingxiong Liu Hulan* [Heroine Liu Hulan] (Beijing: Renmin chubanshe, 1975). The heroic death of another unnamed woman cadre is described along with that of Liu Hulan in Jōno Hiroshi, *Sanshi dokuritsu sen ki* [Report on the war for the independence of Shanxi] (Tokyo: Sekkasha, 1967).

CHAPTER EIGHT

1. The documents of the First All-China Congress of Women have been collected in *Zhongguo funü diyici quanguo daibiao dahui* [First All-China Congress of Women] (Hong Kong: Xin minzhu chubanshe, 1949). Short biographies of the following important leaders of the All-China Women's Association are appended: Cai Chang, Deng Yingchao, Zhang Qinqiu, Li Dequan, Chen Shaomin, Kang Keqing, Ding Ling, and He Xiangning.

2. Editor's note. Following the translation in Albert P. Blaustein, ed., *Fundamental Legal Documents of Communist China* (South Hackensack, N.J., Rothman, 1962), pp. 36–37.

3. Relevant materials on the Marriage Law have been collected in the following: *Guanche hunyinfa xuexi wenjian* [Study documents on thoroughly implementing the Marriage Law] (Beijing: Zhonghua quanguo minzhu funü lianhehui [All-China Federation of Democratic Women], 1951); Zhongyang renmin zhengfu fazhi weiyuanhui (Legal Committee of the Central People's Government), ed., *Hunyin wenti cankao ziliao huibian* [Reference materials on marriage issues] (Beijing: Xinhua shudian, 1950); Zhongyang renmin zhengfu fazhi weiyuanhui, ed., *Hunyinfa ji qi youguan wenjian* [The Marriage Law and related documents] (Shanghai: Xinhua shudian, 1950); and *Hunyinfa xuexi shouce* [Study handbook on the Marriage Law] (Wengong: 1950). For scholarly analysis of these materials, see Niida Noboru, *Chūgoku no dentō to kakumei* [Tradition and revolution in China] (Tokyo: Heibonsha, 1974), vol. 1; Ōtsuka Katsumi, "Chūgoku kon'in kazoku hō no henkaku" [Changes in Chinese marriage and family law], in *Gendai Ajia no kakumei to hō* [Revolution and law in contemporary Asia] (Tokyo: Keisō shobō, 1966), vol. 1, pp. 411–34; Ono Kazuko, "Kon'inpō kantetsu undō o megutte" [On the movement for the thorough implementation of the Marriage Law], *Tōhō gakuhō* 49 (Feb. 1977), pp. 263–311; Li Zheng, "Zhonghua renmin gongheguo hunyinfa dui jianli gonggu jiating de zuoyong" [The function of the Marriage Law of the People's Republic of China in establishing a strong family], *Zhengfa yanjiu* 5 (1955), pp. 24–26; and M. J. Meijer, *Marriage Law and Policy in the Chinese People's Republic* (Hong Kong: Hong Kong University Press, 1971). For further materials on the Marriage Law, see Niida Noboru.

4. Editor's note. These and other quotations from the Marriage Law

follow the English text: *The Marriage Law of the People's Republic of China* (Beijing: Foreign Languages Press, 1950).

5. Edgar Snow, *Red Star over China* (New York: Grove Press, 1961), p. 242.

6. From *Renmin ribao*, Mar. 20, 1963.

7. To spread the Marriage Law, many novels sensitive to marriage-related issues were published or reissued at this time. For example: Ma Feng et al., *Jiehun* [Marriage] (Beijing: Renmin wenxue chubanshe, 1953); Zhao Shuli, *Xiao Erhei jiehun* [Little Erhei gets married] (Hong Kong: Xin minzhu chubanshe, 1947); and Zhao Shuli, *Dengji* [Registration] (Beijing: Xinhua shudian, 1950). This last work was translated into Japanese under the same title by Ono Shinobu (Tokyo: Iwanami shoten, 1953).

8. Editor's note. Shi Lang was Minister of Justice for roughly a decade following the founding of the PRC; she was also vice-chair of a special committee that oversaw "thorough implementation" of the Marriage Law. See Donald Klein and Anne Clark, eds., *Biographical Dictionary of Chinese Communism* (Cambridge, Mass.: Harvard University Press, 1971), pp. 764–66.

Supplementary References

What follows are Ono Kazuko's supplementary sources. References that appear in the Notes are not included here, except for general works (listed in the first section below), documentary collections, and works by Ono Kazuko.

GENERAL WORKS

a. Kishinabe Shigeo, ed., *Kakumei no naka no joseitachi* [Women in revolution] (Tokyo: Hyōronsha, 1976). Published as one volume in the series "Sekai no josei shi" [History of women in the world], this book deals with themes and individuals over the period from the Taiping Rebellion to the present and gives a lively portrait of women in modern China. The volume *Jukyō shakai no joseitachi* [Women in Confucian society], in the same series and by the same editor, is a good reference work for material on the history of Chinese women before the modern period.

b. Chen Dongyuan, *Zhongguo funü shenghuo shi* [A history of the life of Chinese women] (Shanghai: Shangwu yinshuguan, 1927). This volume covers the period from antiquity through the May Fourth era. It is the only comprehensive history of women in China. There are problems with this book as concerns the modern period; constricted by circumstances at the time of its writing, Chen completely overlooks the Taiping Rebellion.

c. Liuwang Liming, *Zhongguo funü yundong* [The Chinese women's movement] (Shanghai: Shangwu yinshuguan, 1934). This book generally describes women's issues in the 1930's and touches on the importance of the women's movement. There are a number of references as well to the earlier history of the women's movement.

d. Tan Sheying, *Zhongguo funü yundong tongshi* [Comprehensive history of the women's movement in China] (Shanghai: Shangwu yinshuguan,

1936). This compilation of materials on the bourgeois women's movement from the 1911 Revolution through the era of GMD rule includes a certain amount of explanatory text as well. It is particularly valuable for the many documents, such as manifestos of women's groups, which are unavailable in any original form today.

e. Guo Zhenyi, *Zhongguo funü wenti* [Chinese women's issues] (Shanghai: Shangwu yinshuguan, 1937). This book, published as a volume in the "Series on Contemporary Issues," deals with such questions as the general condition of women in the 1930's, rural women, women laborers, and the like. It also touches on the history of the Chinese women's movement and the emancipation of women as an issue under socialism.

f. Lu Fu, ed., *Funü wenti xinjiang* [New discussions of women's issues] (Hong Kong: Xin minzhu chubanshe, 1949). With the theme of women's issues generally, this book looks at women's history in the contemporary period.

g. *Funü yundong wenxian* [Documents on the women's movement] (Hong Kong: Xin minzhu chubanshe, 1949). This is a compilation of CCP resolutions and editorials concerning women's issues in the 1940's.

h. Zhang Yufa and Li Youning, ed., *Jindai Zhongguo nüquan yundong shiliao, 1842–1911* [Materials on the women's rights movement in modern China, 1842–1911], 2 vols. (Taibei: Zhuanji wenxueshe, 1975). This inclusive collection of materials dealing with women's rights brings together editorials, biographies, press articles, and the like concerning women's issues from the Taiping period through the 1911 Revolution.

i. Delia Davin, *Women-Work: Women and the Party in Revolutionary China* (Oxford: The Clarendon Press, 1976). This collection of essays deals with such topics as women's issues in the Jiangxi Soviet, women's organizations after 1949, and women's issues in cities and villages. It includes a detailed bibliography at the end.

I. THE TAIPINGS

a. Hatano Yoshihiro, "Taihei tengoku no josei" [Women in the Taiping Rebellion], *Gakkai* 4: 2 (Feb. 1947).

b. Hatano Yoshihiro, "Zoku Taihei tengoku no josei" [Women in the Taiping Rebellion, continued], *Gakugei* 33 (Oct. 1947).

c. Ono Kazuko, "Taihei tengoku to fujo kaihō" [The Taiping Rebellion and women's liberation], *Tōhō gakuhō* 43 (Mar. 1972), pp. 159–200.

d. Ōtsuka Katsumi, "Taihei tengoku to fujin kaihō: Gendai Chūgoku kakumei no genryū" [The Taiping Rebellion and women's liberation: Origins of the contemporary Chinese revolution], in *Kita Kyūshū daigaku kaigaku nijūgo shūnen kinen ronbunshū* [Essays in commemoration of the twenty-fifth year of classes at Kita Kyūshū University] (Kita Kyūshū: Kita Kyūshū

University Press, 1972), pp. 323–42. Ōtsuka has recently completed more comprehensive work on this issue of women's liberation in the Taiping Rebellion: "Taihei tengoku to fujin kaihō" [The Taiping Rebellion and women's liberation], four parts, *Kita Kyūshū daigaku shōkei ronsō* 7: 2 (Dec. 1971), pp. 111–42; 7: 3–4 (Mar. 1972), pp. 51–70; 8: 1–2 (Aug. 1972), pp. 39–59; 8: 3–4 (Mar. 1973), pp. 59–78.

e. Ichiko Chūzō, "Taihei tengoku jokan kō" [An investigation of the women's halls in the Taiping Rebellion], in *Chūgoku no seiji to keizai* [Politics and the economy in China] (Tokyo: Tōyō keizai shimpōsha, 1975).

f. Yu Yining, "Taiping tianguo de hunyin zhidu" [The marriage system under the Taipings], *Guangming ribao*, Feb. 3, 1955.

g. Zhang Yichun, "Taiping tianguo geming shiqi de funü" [Women during the period of the Taiping revolution], *Lishi jiaoxue* 52 (Apr. 1955), pp. 16–19.

h. Luo Ergang, "Taiping tianguo de funü" [Women under the Taipings], in *Taiping tianguo shishi kao* [Studies in the history of the Taiping Rebellion] (Beijing: Sanlian shudian, 1955), pp. 317–40.

i. For original documents concerning the Taipings, see: Xiang Da et al., eds., *Zhongguo jindai shi ziliao congkan, II: Taiping tianguo* [A Collection of Historical Materials on Modern Chinese History, Part II: The Taiping Rebellion], 8 vols. (Shanghai: Shenzhou guoguangshe, 1952); Zhang Xiumin, ed., *Taiping tianguo ziliao mulu* [Bibliography of materials on the Taipings] (Shanghai: Renmin chubanshe, 1957); Taiping tianguo lishi bowuguan, ed., *Taiping tianguo ziliao congbian jianji* [Compilation of materials on the Taiping Rebellion] (Beijing: Zhonghua shuju, 1961).

2. THE 1898 REFORM MOVEMENT

a. Ono Kazuko, "Shinmatsu no fujin kaihō shisō" [Women's liberation thought at the end of the Qing dynasty], *Shisō* 525 (Mar. 1968), pp. 86–99.

b. Yamazaki Jun'ichi, "Shinmatsu hempōron dankai no fujin dōtokuron to kyōikuron" [On women's morality and women's education at the stage of the 1898 Reform Movement late in the Qing], *Chūgoku koten kenkyū* 17 (1970), pp. 1–26.

c. Zhongguo shixuehui (Chinese historical association), ed., *Wuxu bianfa* [The 1898 Reform Movement], 4 vols. (Shanghai: Shenzhou guo-guangshe, 1953).

3. THE BOXER REBELLION

a. Zhongguo kexueyuan Shandong fenyuan lishi yanjiusuo (Institute of History, Shandong Branch of the Chinese Academy of Sciences), ed.,

"Yihetuan shi yi nongmin wei zhuti de fandi aiguo zuzhi" [The Boxers were an anti-imperialist, patriotic organization based in the peasantry], in *Yihetuan yundong liushi zhounian jinian lunwenji* [Essays commemorating the sixtieth anniversary of the Boxer Movement] (Beijing: Zhonghua shuju, 1961), pp. 256–74.

b. Jian Bozan et al., eds., *Yihetuan* [The Boxers], 4 vols. (Shanghai: Shenzhou guoguangshe, 1951).

4. THE 1911 REVOLUTION

a. Ono Kazuko, "Shinmatsu no fujin kaihō shisō" [Women's liberation thought at the end of the Qing dynasty], *Shisō* 525 (Mar. 1968), pp. 86–99.

b. Ono Kazuko, "Shingai kakumei jiki no fujin undō, joshigun to fujin sanseiken" [The women's movement in the period of the 1911 Revolution, the women's army and women's suffrage], in *Shingai kakumei no kenkyū* [Studies in the 1911 Revolution], ed. Shimada Kenji and Onogawa Hidemi (Tokyo: Chikuma shobō, 1978), pp. 283–316.

c. Suetsugu Reiko, "Shingai kakumei jiki no fujin kaihō undō to Puro-tesutanto joshi kyōiku" [The women's liberation movement and Protestant women's education in the period of the 1911 Revolution], *Rekishi hyōron* 280 (Sept. 1974), pp. 95–105; 281 (Oct. 1974), pp. 101–10.

d. Nakayama Yoshihiro, "Nijisseiki hajime no Chūgoku fujin zasshi to fujin kaihōron" [Chinese women's magazines and women's liberation ideas in the early 20th century], *Ōshimo gakuen joshi tanki daigaku kenkyū shūhō* 4 (Dec. 1966), pp. 51–71.

e. Chai Degeng, et al., eds., *Xinhai geming* [The 1911 Revolution], 8 vols. (Shanghai: Renmin chubanshe, 1957).

5. THE MAY FOURTH MOVEMENT

a. Ono Kazuko, "Goshi undō jiki no fujin kaihō shisō, kazoku seido ideorogii to no taiketsu" [Women's liberation thought in the May Fourth period, the confrontation with the ideology of the family system], *Shisō* 590 (Aug. 1973), pp. 103–20.

b. Ono Kazuko, "Ie to wa nani ka, goshi undō jiki ni okeru kekkon ron o chūshin ni" [What is the "family?"—views on marriage in the May Fourth period], *Tōyō shien* 11 (Dec. 1977), pp. 1–17.

c. Nakayama Yoshihiro, "Minkoku hajime ni okeru fujin kaihō ron" [On women's liberation in the early Republican period], *Ōshimo gakuen joshi tanki daigaku kenkyū shūhō* 8 (Feb. 1972), pp. 85–104.

d. Nakayama Yoshihiro, "Goshi jiki no fujin kaihō undō" [The women's liberation movement in the May Fourth period], in *Kōza Chūgoku kin-gendai shi* [Symposium: modern and contemporary Chinese history], vol. 4: *Goshi undō* [The May Fourth Movement], ed. Nozawa Yutaka and Tanaka Masatoshi (Tokyo: Tokyo University Press, 1978), pp. 181–209.

e. Pei Wei, "Shijie liang daxi de furen yundong yu Zhongguo de furen yundong" [Two great international women's movements and the Chinese women's movement], in *Furen yundong* [The women's movement] (Shanghai: Shangwu yinshuguan, Dongfang wenku series no. 27, 1923).

f. Mei Sheng, ed., *Zhongguo funü wenti taolunji* [A collection of essays concerning women's issues in China], 6 vols. (Shanghai: Xin wenhua chubanshe, 1934) originally published 1923.

g. Mei Sheng, ed., *Funü nianjian* [Women's annual], 4 vols. (Shanghai: Xin wenhua shushe, 1924).

h. Mei Sheng, ed., *Nüxing wenti yanjiuji* [A collection of studies on women's issues] (Shanghai: Xin wenhua shushe, 1928).

6. WOMEN WORKERS

a. Okabe Toshiyoshi, "Shina joshi bōseki rōdōsha sōshutsu katei no tokushitsu" [Characteristics of the emergence of women workers in spinning mills in China], 2 parts, *Tō-A keizai ronsō* 2: 2 (May 1942), pp. 139–64; 2: 3 (Sept. 1942), pp. 163–93.

b. Ono Kazuko, "Kyū Chūgoku ni okeru *Jokō aishi*" [*The Sad History of Women Workers* in old China], *Tōhō gakuhō* 50 (Feb. 1978), pp. 253–312.

c. Zhang Chonghou, "Ku'nan de suiyue, yige funü de xuelei kongsu" [Years of suffering, one woman's appeal with tears of blood], *Lishi yanjiu* 93 (Mar. 1965), pp. 37–52.

d. Shanghai Municipal Council, *1938 Annual Report*. Japanese translation by Yatsunami Ryūtarō, "Shanhai ni okeru kōgyō gaikan" [An overview of commerce in Shanghai], *Mantetsu chōsa geppō* 20: 3 (Mar. 1940), pp. 91–132.

e. "Da geming shiqi de Guangdong funü yundong" [The women's movement in Guangdong during the period of the great revolution], *Zhongguo funü* (Aug. 1957), p. 22.

Items f–k contain a considerable number of references to women laborers:

f. Nishikawa Ki'ichi, "Shanhai rōdōsha no genjō to rōdō undō" [The present state of workers in Shanghai and the labor movement], 2 parts, *Tō-A keizai kenkyū* 9: 1 (Jan. 1925), pp. 82–110; 9: 2 (Apr. 1925), pp. 75–115.

g. Takahisa Hajime, *Saikin Shanhai ni okeru rōdō undō fūchō* [Recent currents in the Shanghai labor movement] (Dairen: Mantetsu chōsaka, 1926).

h. Sanshigyō dōgyō kumiai chūōkai (Central Association of the Cooperative Association of the Silk Industry), comp., *Shina sanshigyō taikan*

[General survey of the silk industry in China] (Tokyo: Okada nichieidō, 1929).

i. Sugihayashi Yōko, "Chūgoku ni okeru bōseki kōgyō rōdōsha no jōtai" [Conditions of spinning mill workers in China], *Shigaku kenkyū* 112 (Aug. 1974), pp. 19–35.

j. Fang Xianting, *Zhongguo zhi mianfang zhiye* [The cotton spinning and weaving industry in China] (Shanghai: Shangwu yinshuguan, 1934).

k. *Zui e de jiu shehui, jiu Zhongguo jingji zatan* [The criminal old society, discussions concerning the economy in old China], 3 vols. (Shanghai: Shanghai renmin chubanshe, 1965).

7. RURAL WOMEN

a. Suetsugu Reiko, "Chūgoku nōson ni okeru fujin no jōtai" [The conditions of women in Chinese villages], in *Kōza Chūgoku kin-gendai shi* [Symposium: modern and contemporary Chinese history], vol. 4: *Goshi undō* (The May Fourth Movement), ed. Nozawa Yutaka and Tanaka Masatoshi (Tokyo: Tokyo University Press, 1978), pp. 211–44.

b. Suetsugu Reiko, "Chūgoku nōson ni okeru fujin kaihō undō no genten" [The origins of the women's liberation movement in Chinese villages], *Rekishi hyōron* 333 (Jan. 1978), pp. 85–89.

c. In roughly every other issue of the journal *Dongfang zazhi*, from number 29: 4 (1934) through number 36: 15 (1939), a special section entitled "Funü yu jiating" [Women and the family] was included. With each such issue three or four articles on women were appended. Also, articles describing "rural realities" in *Dongfang zazhi* often made reference to the conditions of women in Chinese villages. For example: Chen Biyun, "Nongcun pochan yu nongcun funü" [Rural destitution and rural women], 32: 5; Luo Qiong, "Jiangsu Jiangyin nongcun zhong de laodong funü" [Working women in villages in Jiangyin county, Jiangsu province], 32: 8; and Zhao Chun, "Henan nongcun funü de shehui shenghuo" [The social life of women in the rural villages of Henan], 33: 10.

d. Jiangsu sheng funü lianhehui (Women's federation of Jiangsu province), ed., *Jiangsu funü geming douzheng gushi* [Stories of the revolutionary struggles of women in Jiangsu province] (Beijing: Zhongguo funü zazhi, 1963).

e. Zhonggong Tianjin shi weihui funü gongzuo weiyuanhui (The women's labor committee of the municipal committee of the CCP in Tianjin), ed., *Funü yundong wenxian* [Documents on the women's movement] (Tianjin: Zhonggong Tianjin shi weihui funü gongzuo weiyuanhui, 1949).

f. Jack Belden, *China Shakes the World* (New York: Monthly Review

Press, 1970). Japanese translation by Andō Jirō and Kugai Saburō, *Chūgoku wa sekai o yurugasu* (Tokyo: Aoki shoten, 1965).

References to women in rural China can be found in items g–m:

g. Yan Xinzhe, *Nongcun jiating diaocha* [An investigation of rural families] (Shanghai: Shangwu yinshuguan, 1925).

h. Li Jinghan, *Beijing jiaowai zhi nongcun diaocha* [An investigation of villages on the outskirts of Beijing] (Shanghai: Shangwu yinshuguan, 1929).

i. Li Jinghan, *Dingxian shehui gaikuang diaocha* [An investigation of the social conditions in Ding county] (Beijing: Zhonghua pingmin jiaoyu cujinhui, 1933).

j. Fukutake Tadashi, *Chūgoku nōson shakai no kaizō* [The structure of rural Chinese society] (Tokyo: Yūhikaku, 1951); later included in vol. 9 of *Fukutake Tadashi chosakushū* [The writings of Fukutake Tadashi] (Tokyo: Tokyo University Press, 1976).

k. Chūgoku nōson kankō chōsa kankōkai (Publication Association for the Investigation of Rural Chinese Customs), ed., *Chūgoku nōson kankō chōsa* [Investigation of rural Chinese customs], 6 vols. (Tokyo: Iwanami shoten, 1953–58).

l. John Lossing Buck, *Chinese Farm Economy: A Study of 2,866 Farms in Seventeen Localities and Seven Provinces in China* (Chicago: University of Chicago, 1930). Japanese translation by Tō-A keizai chōsakyoku, *Shina nōka keizai chōsa* [Investigation of China's farming economy] (Tokyo: Tō-A keizai chōsakyoku, 1936).

m. Peng Hui, *Minzu kangzhan yu funü de renwu* [The national war of resistance against Japan and women's responsibilities] (Hankou: Hankou dazhong chubanshe, 1938).

n. A number of volumes have been published by the Preparatory Committee of the All-China Federation of Democratic Women (Quanguo minzhu funü lianhehui choubei weiyuanhui). The seven listed here were published as the *Fuyun congshu* [Series on the women's movement] at the time of the meeting of the First All-China Women's Representative Assembly. (I have not as yet seen iv through vi). Two other volumes were also published in 1949: *Zhongguo jiefangqu de ertong* [Children in liberated areas of China] and *Guoji minzhu funü yundong wenxian* [Documents on the international democratic women's movement].

i. *Zhongguo jiefangqu nongcun funü fanshen yundong sumiao* [Depictions of rural women in the liberated areas of China in the transformation movement] (Shanghai: Xinhua shudian, 1949).

ii. *Zhongguo jiefangqu funü yundong wenxian* [Documents of the women's movement in liberated areas of China] (Shanghai: Xinhua shudian, 1949).

iii. *Zhongguo jiefangqu funü canzhan yundong* [Women's participation in the war in liberated areas of China] (Shanghai: Xinhua shudian, 1949).

iv. *Zhongguo jiefangqu nongcun shengchan yundong* [The village production movement in liberated areas of China] (Shanghai: Xinhua shudian, 1949).

v. *Xin shehui de xin nügong* [The new woman worker in the new society] (Shanghai: Xinhua shudian, 1949).

vi. *Guomindang tongzhi diqu minzhu funü yundong wenxian* [Documents on the democratic women's movement in the areas {formerly} under GMD control] (Shanghai: Xinhua shudian, 1949).

vii. *Zhongguo jiefangqu de Nandinggeermen* [{Florence} Nightingales in the liberated areas of China] (Shanghai: Xinhua shudian, 1949).

8. THE MARRIAGE LAW OF 1950

a. Ono Kazuko, "Shakaishugi Chūgoku no fujin kaihōron" [Ideas concerning women's liberation in Chinese socialism], in *Nyūmon josei kaihōron* [Introduction to ideas concerning women's liberation] (Tokyo: Aki shobō, 1975).

b. Ono Kazuko, "Kon'inpō kantetsu undō o megutte" [On the movement for the thorough implementation of the Marriage Law], *Tōhō gakuhō* 49 (Feb. 1977), pp. 263–311.

c. Zhonghua quanguo minzhu funü lianhehui xuanchuan jiaoyubu (Propaganda and Education Department of the All-China Federation of Democratic Women), ed., *Zhongguo funü yundong de zhongyao wenjian* [Important documents on the Chinese women's movement] (Beijing: Renmin chubanshe, 1953).

d. *Nongye hezuohua daolushang de funü* [Women on the road to agricultural collectivization] (Shanghai: Zhongguo funü zazhishe, 1956).

e. Claudie Broyelle, *La moitié du ciel* (Paris: Denöel, 1973). Japanese translation by Amaki Shiomi and Takei Asako, *Sora no hambun, Chūgoku no onnatachi* [Half the sky, Chinese women] (Tokyo: Shinsensha, 1976). English translation by Michèle Cohen and Gary Herman, *Women's Liberation in China* (Atlantic Highlands, N.J.: Humanities Press, 1977). This extremely interesting volume is not simply reportage, but deals with theoretical issues as it links women's liberation with the structure of the Chinese socialist revolution.

f. Kojima Kotoko, "Chūgoku nōson ni okeru denka to fujin rōdō" [Electrification in Chinese villages and women workers], *Chūgoku kenkyū geppō* 365 (July 1978), pp. 2–18.

g. In addition, basic sources for this period would include such serials as *Renmin ribao* [People's daily], the official organ of the Chinese Communist Party, which began publication in 1948; *Xinhua yuebao* [New China monthly], which began publication in 1949 and changed its name to *Xinhua banyuebao* [New China semi-monthly] in 1956; and *Xin Zhongguo funü* [New Chinese women], which began publication in 1949 and changed its name to *Zhongguo funü* [Chinese women] in 1956. *Zhongguo funü* not only deals with concrete issues of concern to women in different periods, but also includes memoirs and histories of women revolutionaries; it is indispensable for research on Chinese women's history.

Index

Library of Congress Cataloging-in-Publication Data

Ono, Kazuko, 1932–
    Chinese women in a century of revolution, 1850–1950.

    Translation of: Chūgoku joseishi.
    1. Women—China—Social conditions. 2. China—
Politics and government—19th century. 3. China—
Politics and government—20th century. I. Fogel,
Joshua A., 1950–   . II. Title.
HQ 1767.05613 1989   305.4'2'0951   88-8630
ISBN 0-8047-1496-7
ISBN 0-8047-1497-5 (pbk.)